£3

BE A BETTER HORSEMAN

THE AUTHOR AND HIS PHOTOGRAPHER

Be a Better Horseman

AN ILLUSTRATED GUIDE
TO THE ENJOYMENT OF MODERN RIDING

By

Captain
Vladimir S. Littauer

With two hundred and eighteen
photographs by
BERT CLARK THAYER

Publishers

since 1812

HURST & BLACKETT LTD

London   New York   Toronto   Melbourne   Sydney   Cape Town

First Published 1953

Made and Printed in Great Britain by
GREYCAINES
(Taylor Garnett Evans & Co. Ltd.)
Watford, Herts.

ACKNOWLEDGMENTS

THIS book would, of course, have been impossible without the gracious help and co-operation of the persons listed below, to whom we wish to express our warm gratitude.

First of all to MISS NANCY MARTIN who so patiently played the part of our heroine throughout the book, then:

CHAPTER I

To MR. JOHN LOSTY .... For playing the part of the Riding Instructor—"Mr. Brown".

To MR. & MRS. CHARLES V. HICKOX For lending their horse "Silver Plate" and for the permission to take photographs on their estate—Boxwood Farm, Glen Head, Long Island.

CHAPTER II

To DR. WALTER T. KEES .... For playing the part of "Mr. Strong".

To MISS PEGGY CARPENTER ...... For playing the part of "Miss Peggy Merritt", on her own horse "Little Flight".

To MASTER ARCHIE DEAN .... For playing the part of "Master Archie Cole", on his own horse— "Salmo".

To MRS. ELIZABETH CORRELL ..... For lending her horses "Back Porch" and "Slieve Bloom".

To MR. GORDON WRIGHT .... For permission to use the facilities of his jumping field at the Secor Farms Riding Club, White Plains, N. Y., and in appreciation of the finished riding of his pupils Miss Peggy Carpenter and Master Archie Dean.

CHAPTER III

To DR. LAWRENCE T. WAITZ ..... For playing the part of "Dr. Scott" and for the valuable help in writing this chapter.

To Mr. George Hoblin .... For playing the part of "Mr. Brooks".
To Mrs. Elizabeth Correll ..... For lending her horse "Dalchoolin".
To Captain Prince Gregory
    Gagarin .... For permission to use the facilities of
                                 his Horse Shoe Stables, Westbury,
                                 Long Island.

CHAPTER IV

Was illustrated by the author on his own horse "Arnoldean".

CHAPTER V

To Mrs. F. Linsley Roessler .... For playing the part of "Mrs. White".
To Mr. Homer B. Gray, M.F.H. of
    Rombout Hounds .... For permission to take pictures.
To Mr. William Schemerhorn,
    Huntsman .... For his most helpful co-operation.
To Mr. Charles Peckham .... For lending his horse to Miss Nancy
                                 Martin.

CHAPTER VI

To Miss Anne Martin .... For playing the part of "Jane Merrill".
To the Piping Rock Stables, Locust
    Valley, Long Island .... For lending their horse "Ballycanew"
                                 and their pony "Gold Tee", both the
                                 property of Mr. Edward J. Maloney.
To Mrs. Edward C. Lynch ...... For the permission to use the jumping
                                 ring on her estate in Locust Valley,
                                 Long Island.

                            V. S. Littauer
                            Bert Clark Thayer

CONTENTS

PREFACE

THE term "riding" may have many implications. It may mean anything from a primitive form of transportation to a sophisticated art. While the former does not require anything more than a certain knack, the latter demands extensive studies. In any simple form of riding the expression "natural rider" makes sense; while this same "natural rider" is nothing more than a person with potential abilities if his goal in riding is high. This complicated art cannot be mastered by mere years in the saddle, just as a man who has eaten all his life is not necessarily a gourmet.

The art of riding requires study; a part of this study consists in reading. It is obvious that it is impossible to learn how to ride from books, but it is impossible to become a horseman without reading them. The experiences and opinions of other riders are valuable to one who has the ability to sift them through his own critical observations based on logic and knowledge.

There is a special reason for writing this book at this particular time, for cross-country riding and jumping today are in a period of transition; the old ideas are being gradually replaced by new ones. As always happens in such cases, a certain confusion has resulted and I believe that although many books have been written on Modern Riding a few more will be necessary to help a modern rider understand where and why he is different from his forefathers and what makes him better. My experience tells me that the greatest misunderstanding of our times is the belief that the recent reform in riding has consisted solely in introducing the Forward Seat. Of course the Forward Seat is a novelty, but it is merely a part of a new method of schooling and controlling a hack, hunter, or jumper.

In any type of riding we adopt a certain method of sitting and controlling the horse, depending on the aims, and consequently the schooling. Take, for instance, Dressage: in this type of Equitation most of the movements are executed at highly collected gaits; the horse progresses comparatively little, and acts, with his legs, upward a lot. The general reaction of the horse's movements received by the rider is vertical. Consequently, to be one with the horse, the rider must sit in the saddle, having the stirrups rather long and the torso vertical. So, as you see, in this instance, the position is the result of the way the horse was schooled to move, and is afterwards made to move by a specific method of control.

Modern field riding demands that the movements of a cross-country horse or of a jumper should be efficient; consequently, horses are schooled to move forward with strides close to the ground, so that every bit of the energy produced goes towards the covering of the ground. Having this as a goal, Modern Riding has created a certain system of schooling a horse and controlling him. In riding such a horse the rider does not experience vertical reactions, but rather horizontal ones. Hence the old method of being vertical in the saddle disconnects the rider from the horse and the Forward Seat becomes a necessity. There are much closer ties between the method of schooling, method of controlling, and method of sitting than is generally appreciated; the unity of these three parts of riding is the main theme of this book.

Now a few words about its form. I have recently come to the conclusion that most books on riding have the same weak point: written in the ordinary form of text books, they are nothing more than a series of statements, and many of these are not properly understood by the readers. It is different during the actual lesson, because then a pupil can always interrupt his teacher with a question. That is why I have chosen to write this book in a conversational form, since then all the common questions an instructor hears during his lessons may be heard and answered.

There is another great difference between normal books and normal lessons. As a rule, a book is systematically constructed. Only after one subject has been completely exhausted is the discussion of the next one begun. This results in a certain dryness and monotony common to all text books. During the actual lesson the instructor has no chance of being rigid, no matter how hard he tries to be pedantic. The pupil's abilities or disabilities, his questions and the resistances of the horse will often take him far away from the main theme of the lesson. Consequently, lessons are more lively and the pupil more easily assimilates the theory of riding. This is why it seemed better to talk about different points of riding as they usually come up in actual practice, rather than in their chronological sequence. An index is available for reference concerning specific details.

Once it was decided to construct the book in this way, it seemed logical that the order of chapters should represent a normal case of the development in this sport of one who, due to his abilities and efforts, would be certain to reach the top.

The illustrations give a pictorial lesson. Very few of them reveal the position of the rider, his aids, or the movements of the horse in their perfection; as few show obvious, elementary defects. Not many of us are faultless; and normally both we and our horses are constantly making all sorts of little mistakes which it would be desirable to avoid.

Those photographs which aim to illustrate good points show normal good riding and the little faults of the rider or of the horse which one will find are discussed in the text. Thus the illustrations are so closely connected with the story that captions would be superfluous; and in a sense the whole text is but a minute description of the pictures.

Of course all these pictures had to be posed in order to present important points, and I wish to express my appreciation of the abilities of Mr. Bert Clark Thayer who has succeeded in making them so natural, artistically combining the presentation of riding technicalities with the beauties of this sport.

Publisher's Note

With reference to Chapter II, the regulations and rules of the *Fédération Equestre Internationale* govern all international jumping competitions. The horses are judged solely on their performance over the jumps, and although the element of time enters into the judging, the style of the horse and rider is not considered. Other jumping competitions in England are judged according to the B.S.J.A. Rules.

CHAPTER I

HACKING

ANNE: Are you Mr. Brown? How do you do? I am Anne Randall and I wonder if you would give me some riding lessons.

INSTRUCTOR: Are you a beginner?

ANNE: Not exactly. I have ridden since I was six, not very consistently, but I feel at home in the saddle. Lately I've noticed that many good riders sit differently from the way I do, and everyone talks and argues now about the Forward Seat and the modern way of riding a field horse. I should like to get an idea of what it is all about.

INSTRUCTOR: Very well; our ring will be free in an hour and we can start the lesson.

ANNE: Oh, I hate to ride round and round a ring. Can't you teach me in the fields?

INSTRUCTOR: Of course, but not as well as in the ring. Our work will not be as efficient.

ANNE: Even though it is not as efficient, I would appreciate your doing it for me. I also want to ask you many questions about field riding. Have you time to go for a really long hack?

INSTRUCTOR: Yes, indeed.

ANNE: I would like you to tell me in the course of this ride not only

15

how I should sit but also how I should control the horse, and what I should know about taking the horse across country. Please remember that I know very little, so don't hesitate to talk to me even about elementary things.

INSTRUCTOR: Good! I'll get the horses ready right away.

A FEW MINUTES LATER

INSTRUCTOR: We could begin the lesson, Miss Randall, right away. You see we are mounting in different ways. Are you interested in knowing anything about mounting?

ANNE: Yes, indeed.

INSTRUCTOR: I think your method and mine are both correct, but there are people who go in so much for form that they will tell you there's only one way to mount a horse, and of course, it's always the way that this particular person himself mounts.

I look at it differently. To me the most important thing is to mount and dismount in such a way that the horse is not in the least disturbed by it. Consequently I never jump suddenly on or off the horse's back but always gradually. I am also careful not to touch the horse's croup with my right leg when it swings over. I am in the habit of mounting from the shoulder, facing the rear. This initial position helps me when the horse moves round, for I'm in the centre of his pivot. It's also the right place to be if the horse tries to move ahead. But if I wanted to mount a horse that had a tendency to back, then I would place myself as you did.

Anyhow, I don't think it's very important. Of course, you probably know that when going up you should pull the toe of your left foot way down so that it goes under the body of the horse. Some horses will get fidgety if your toe presses in their side. These horses stand well while being mounted. I'm always very careful in teaching a horse this; it annoys me when a horse begins to move the moment I put my foot in the stirrup. You probably know that if we were to mount poorly disciplined horses we wouldn't be able to do it on practically loose reins as we do now; we'd have to have our reins tight throughout mounting so as to control our horses.

ANNE: I remember one horse I rode which always tried to bite me while I was mounting. That's probably why I got into the habit of mounting from the rear.

INSTRUCTOR: This is one way of coping with the situation, and the other is to shorten the right rein and pull on it so as to turn the horse's head to the right. But I have also known horses which cow-kicked. To avoid this the rider has to place himself at the shoulder.

ANNE: When mounting, should the rider hold the saddle or the mane with his left hand?

INSTRUCTOR: It really doesn't matter except in one case. A saddle with a loose girth may easily slip if you grab it with both the left and right hands. Then, of course, you don't have to grab the mane and make an enemy of the groom who takes care of it. If you are fairly agile you need only put your hand on the neck as you would in the case of a horse without a mane.

ANNE: Tell me, Mr. Brown, are my stirrups the correct length?

INSTRUCTOR: Is that the length you are used to?

ANNE: Yes.

INSTRUCTOR: Then I prefer to tell you later how to adjust your stirrups. First, I should like to see how you normally ride and I should like you to be as comfortable as you can; so, for a while, let's leave the stirrups as they are. Does the saddle fit you?

ANNE: Yes, it's very comfortable, only I have never ridden in a saddle with knee-rolls, like this one.

INSTRUCTOR: That will be all right. They will not bother you, and if you succeed in changing your position to a forward one then you will find out that it will be a great help. This is a Forward Seat saddle. Is this how you always sit?—with your legs stuck forward, or haven't you taken your position yet?

ANNE: No, this is the way I sit at all gaits.

INSTRUCTOR: Don't you change even when galloping fast?

B

ANNE: I don't think so, except for one thing: I lean forward with my body.

INSTRUCTOR: You mean that you get out of the saddle and incline with the body?

ANNE: No, I sit in it, as I'm doing now, only I lean forward.

INSTRUCTOR: Well, from my point of view, or rather from the point of view of modern field riding, your position is all wrong. During our ride today I will explain little by little what I consider a good position. But first let's get in the field.

INSTRUCTOR: This horse of mine blows up a lot when he is saddled and won't relax till he starts walking, so I always have to adjust my girth later, a hundred feet or so away from the stable. *You* don't have to do it, because I'm certain your girth is all right; but it's always better to check up on the groom. They make mistakes—like anyone else.

ANNE: I've never tightened the girth from the saddle. How do you do it?

INSTRUCTOR: It's very simple. If you wish to adjust the girth on the left side, you move your left leg forward and up, ahead of the saddle so that you can lift the skirt. You take the reins in the right hand, with the left you raise the skirt, grab the girth leather and pull it up, first one then the other. You may tuck the end of the saddle skirt under your left thigh to give your hand more freedom, and see what you are doing.

ANNE: I've found out that when the horse is very big, it's simply impossible for me to tighten the girth from the ground, and I always had to ask someone else to do it for me. Couldn't I do it from the saddle?

INSTRUCTOR: Certainly.

ANNE: Well, I hope today I will learn a perfect method of riding so that I will never have a mishap.

INSTRUCTOR: I am sorry to say that a method which works one

hundred per cent with all horses does not exist. The best that I can promise you is that it will work in most cases. A poor system works in a few cases only. I think you will find out that what I shall tell you today will be effective with seventy-five horses out of a hundred. The other twenty-five will be so different physically and mentally from the average that when applied to them this method will have to be changed here and there. There is no use in talking about these variations; there might be too many of them. You learn them through experience. And in general, rules prescribed by Equitation will work only if the rider feels, and has the common sense to know when to apply this or that one. My experience tells me that an average beginner thinks there are only a couple of dozen such rules, and that if he learns them by heart he will be the master of his horse in any situation. It is very hard to make it clear that there are hundreds of them and that it takes many years' experience to learn when to use which. If riding were as simple as many beginners hope it is, there would be more good riders.

ANNE: I am in the habit of beginning my rides with a five- or ten-minute walk to limber my horse.

INSTRUCTOR: That's good. The first walk is most important; and besides the limbering, it gives you an opportunity to establish the mental co-operation of your horse and to impress upon him the necessity for obedience. This might prove highly important later on during a fast gallop.

There are some people who start a gallop the moment they are out of the stable yard. They are not horsemen; they just don't know how the horse's mind works. They fail to understand that the rider should not make the horse believe that as soon as he is mounted something violent will happen, and then when they have an excitable ride of course they blame the horse and everyone else but themselves.

ANNE: My experience is that some horses walk well for me, fast and

quietly, some "jig", and others seem to fall asleep walking very slowly. How do you regulate the speed of the walk?

INSTRUCTOR: The speed at all gaits is regulated by the co-operation of legs and hands. If you want to go faster, increase the leg action and decrease the pressure on the reins. If you want to go slower, stop the action of the legs completely and increase the pull on the reins. We will talk later about the way the hands and legs should act.

First, I want to change your position, but I may as well tell you now about horses that "jig". There might be several reasons for the horse "jigging". Some do it because their walk is very short and they cannot keep up with other horses; schooling will improve this. Others do it because irritated by the action of the rider's legs; again, schooling will have to remedy it by teaching the horse obedience to the rider's legs and spurs. The most common cause is plain nervousness. In the great majority of cases this nervousness has been developed by bad riders and can be corrected only by the very patient work of a good one. Comparatively few horses are nervous by nature. Many of them become so after a few months of bad riding.

When riding next to you I cannot see your position well enough to determine what its faults are nor what is the easiest way to correct them. This is why I suggested at first a lesson in the ring. There, when I stand in the middle of it and you move round me, nothing can escape my eye. Now, although we are in the fields, I would like to suggest that we imitate ring work for a few minutes. This is a good place; I shall stay where I am. Please trot round me on a very large circle.

I am certain now your position is very bad.

ANNE: I don't see why; I have ridden for years and I can't even remember my last fall.

INSTRUCTOR: Evidently you are secure in the saddle; but this is not

enough to make your seat good. You see, the seat, to be really good, as well as secure, should be undisturbing to the horse and should enable the rider to execute a quick and precise control over his mount. Now, the way you sit, far back in the saddle, certainly does not make the horse's work easy. First, because the rear part of the horse's back is not as fitted to carry weight as the front part—having lighter bones; and second, because the horse moves forward mostly by the action of the hindquarters, and the rear part of the back is very closely connected with them in their efforts to push the body forward. And how can you use your legs well for control when they are stuck forward, so far away from the sides of the horse to which you will have to apply them when giving orders?

I want to add a few words about the security of the position. Your position is incorrect, but you told me yourself that you fall very rarely —evidently it is secure. This is a very common case. The security of the rider in the saddle only depends somewhat on the correctness of his position; it is mostly the result of his particular physique. An athletic person with good balance, strong muscles and perfect control over his body will be securer in any funny position than a clumsy, soft person, no matter how correctly the latter may sit. This is why so many people can go on hunting and jumping for years without any idea of how to sit in the saddle, but rarely, if ever, meeting with an accident. Let's stop a minute and I will show you what the position should be and explain why.

INSTRUCTOR: Before beginning the explanation of the position I want to ask you whether you wish me to give you the detailed reasons

for different points, or whether at first I should merely give you a general idea?

ANNE: I imagine if we begin to discuss the position thoroughly a day would be too short, and I want to ask you so many questions about the control of the horse that I would prefer having it short and simple this time. I'll learn more about it later.

INSTRUCTOR: Very well. This is what your position should be at a walk, trot and canter (slow gallop). I shall tell you later how it will have to be changed for a fast gallop and jumping. Please note that my body is alert, that I cannot be compared with a tired man resting in an armchair. In this position I am prepared to follow any unexpected movement of my horse and consequently can always be one with him.

My weight is distributed between my stirrups and the contact of my legs with the saddle; very little weight is carried by the fleshy parts of the seat. This position enables the rider to interfere the least with the work of the horse's hind legs, and makes it easy for the horse to carry him. It is also very secure. And my lower legs are right where they should be to control the horse.

ANNE: I notice that you yourself don't ride a Forward Seat saddle.

INSTRUCTOR: I always do, but today you came unexpectedly during our busy hour and all our Forward Seat saddles were in use. I gave you the last one, so I have to suffer on this. Now I have adjusted my stirrups as for field riding, and because the skirts of the saddle are cut straight down, my knees are ahead of the saddle. In order to fit the saddle I would have to have my stirrups so long that it would be impossible for me to show how to sit correctly.

ANNE: Do you mean that a certain position of the rider necessitates a certain saddle?

INSTRUCTOR: Absolutely. The American cowboy can't use what we call an "English" saddle for his work, nor can a "High-School" rider use a stock saddle. A Forward Seat requires a forward saddle.

ANNE: What are the main characteristics of it?

INSTRUCTOR: There are three: first, the skirts are cut forward; second, the point of adjustment of stirrup leathers is very near the front edge of the skirt; third, the tree is made in such a way as to enable the rider to stay very near the pommel. In other words, the saddle is built to enable the rider to stay forward comfortably. You will notice throughout the ride that I will be able to stay forward even on this old-fashioned saddle, but only with a great deal of effort.

ANNE: Aren't these knee-rolls one of the characteristics also?

INSTRUCTOR: Only to the extent that all Forward Seat saddles have them. Some under the skirt, others both under and on top. But there is nothing new about a knee-roll. There is, however, another novelty which is included in all Italian Forward Seat saddles—a flexible tree, which gives more comfort to the rider than the old-fashioned stiff tree. Being flexible, of course it doesn't last as long as a solid one.

INSTRUCTOR: Now look only at the lower part of my body, and note the following:

(1) In order to put weight in the stirrups, my legs are bent back far enough to have the stirrups under the body. The point of the toe and the point of the knee are approximately on the same vertical line, and the stirrups hang straight down.

(2) My heels are well pulled down; this hardens the muscles of the legs and increases my adherence to the saddle. It is the key to a strong position.

(3) My toes are turned slightly out. This is to bring the calves closer to the horse's sides. The calves should gently rest at the horse's sides to control him, and also to grip when it is necessary.

(4) I hold my stirrups under the balls of the feet. It is easy to lose them when holding them under the toes (especially in jumping) and the elasticity in the ankle is lost to a large extent if the stirrups are held near the heels, but the latter way of holding the stirrups may be the best for many riders.

INSTRUCTOR: And now look at the upper part of my body. Do you see how erect and relaxed, in other words *alert*, I keep my torso? Notice how open and relaxed my shoulders are. Observe also that I am looking straight ahead where I am about to move, and my body is very slightly inclined forward, for I am ready to start moving.

My chest is open, and consequently my back is slightly caved in. It is a natural posture for us when we are on the alert, in readiness to spring, no matter whether we are in the saddle or on the ground. Many old-fashioned riders will tell you that this looks stiff. I don't care how it looks to them; I know—I can feel it—that I am relaxed. I have the greatest amount of relaxation possible for a body in action. These old-fashioned riders used to sit slouching in the saddle; they relaxed their bodies to the point where they became just a sack of meal. This kind of relaxation is all right for resting, but not for action. As a matter of fact, a whole generation of riders were brought up on the principle, "sit in the saddle relaxed, as you would sit in a chair". And I don't know why nobody thought then of the absurdity of this simile, for the chair stands still, and the saddle on the horse's back moves forward—and sometimes very fast.

INSTRUCTOR: Now, I shall imitate one of the bad points of your position: You keep your legs too much forward and consequently you cannot put your weight in the stirrups and are bound to sit on the rear part of the saddle.

ANNE: But I know that when holding the stirrups ahead of my body I can press against them very hard, if I wish to.

INSTRUCTOR: That is true—you can press against them, but you can't put any weight on them when they are ahead of your body. This pressure forward against the stirrups just pushes the seat of the rider

farther to the rear of the saddle. There are riders who do just the opposite; they keep their legs too far back and as a result collapse on the horse's neck. You see it so often in Horse Shows in the jumping classes. With the legs so much forward you will always be late controlling the horse, for it takes time to bring them back to the horse's sides. On the other hand, riders with the legs too far back usually annoy their horses with spurs or heels.

INSTRUCTOR: Another bad fault of yours is the position of your toes —they are kept in. If the toes are turned inward then the calves are kept away from the horse's sides and can neither grip well when it is necessary, nor control the horse quickly and smoothly.

There was a time in America when it was generally taught that the toes should be in. I have no idea how such an error could become a rule. You will see it used by the so-called "Saddle Horse" riders, and unfortunately many old Horse Show judges still look at it with pleasure, remembering their youth. I will show you what happens when one turns the toes in, and to make it clear I will exaggerate. Of course, when turning your toes slightly out, about 35°, you must make sure that your knees do

not leave the saddle and that you do not clutch the horse's sides with the lower legs; the latter makes some horses nervous and often causes a runaway.

Now I shall bring my legs again into a good position and you notice how my knees and thighs are lying flat against the saddle, and my upper calves are gently resting at the horse's sides (also on the saddle). When in motion these parts of my legs will cause friction with the saddle, and this will constitute the normal grip. A grip without any effort. I can add to it as much muscular effort as circumstances may require. The lower parts of my legs are not in contact with the horse's sides. The contact ends approximately at the lower point of the saddle skirt.

INSTRUCTOR: Now I shall move forward. You will notice that at the walk the position which I have described does not change in the least.

And, by the way, do you see how close to the pommel I sit, so that the crotch of my breeches touches it and there is a full hand's breadth between the rear of my seat and the cantle?

ANNE: How could you keep this position at the end of a long ride when you are really tired? Wouldn't it be better to take a rest, sitting in the saddle?

INSTRUCTOR: Of course it would, and I would sit in the saddle to get a rest. I might also drop my stirrups to stretch my legs. I may do all sorts of things to regain my strength, but then I will not be riding, I will just be taking a rest. I will not be concerned with how the horse moves under me, neither will I expect suddenly to start a faster gait in any direction. I will just be relaxing; I really could, circumstances permitting, just as well take my rest on the ground. Now I am walking, ready for action. Try to imitate me; change your position and let's walk. We shall talk more about it later.

ANNE: Oh, my horse stumbled! What shall I do if he does it again?

INSTRUCTOR: Once the horse has stumbled you really can't do much; the best you can do is to move your hands quickly forward, giving full freedom to the horse's neck and head, and this is why: If you were to walk a narrow plank you would balance yourself with your arms. The horse (when in motion) uses his neck and head as we use our arms—as a balancer. When he stumbles the gestures of his neck and head play an important part in restoring his balance. The first gesture will be down, and this is precisely the moment when most riders, urged by the instinct of self-preservation, hold back, and so interfere with the horse's efforts to recover.

You are also apt to feel as though you are giving the horse support by pulling on the reins, but this instinct is wrong, too. For, after all, the average horse is about eight or nine times heavier than you are, and also you are on his back, a part of him, so to say, so what can you do?

But if your horse has a tendency to stumble, and you know it, you can, in some cases, partly prevent it. There are four main causes of stumbling: (1) The horse being unsound. You can't do anything in this case; it is a veterinary job. (2) The horse stumbles because of poor balance; green horses will do it often; and this can be corrected through schooling. In some cases it may disappear of itself later, when experience has bettered his balance. (3) Stumbling may result because the horse is not alert, or because he has a "sleepy" character, or because he is tired; as when coming home from a strenuous hunt.

If your horse stumbles because he is of the sluggish type then by pushing him forward with your calves every stride, and at the same time holding him well in hand, you can better the situation somewhat. But I do think that the soundest way to awake him is again through schooling.

(4) Some horses stumble simply because they are not looking where they are going. If experience does not teach them anything, then the rider has to guide them, avoiding every stone and pitfall.

You are sitting much better now, at a walk at least. Your legs are back and some of your weight is forward in the stirrups, but still too much of it is carried by the seat.

INSTRUCTOR: Although you are sitting much better there are still many things which I should like to correct. For instance—you are not sitting squarely; your right shoulder is ahead of the left one, which means that you do not have as good balance as you should. You probably developed this from holding the reins in one hand. There are games, such as Polo for instance, where you have to hold the reins in one hand; but in hacking, hunting, or Horse Show riding you should hold your reins in both hands, which will increase the precision of your control. And once you do square your shoulders and sit straight, then look straight ahead between the horse's ears; this last is very important when trying to make a good performance. I do not mean to say that you should never take your eyes off the horse's neck—even when just leisurely walking and talking as we are doing now. But even in our case, although not looking at the horse's neck all the time, I am conscious of its position.

ANNE: Now that I looked at the neck of my horse I noticed that his mane is on the left side of it; while your horse has it on the right side. On which side do most of the horses have them?

INSTRUCTOR: I really cannot tell you how it works in nature, but the recognized form is that the mane should be on the right side and you can always train the mane to be on the side you desire. We bought this mare when she was already seven years old. Her mane had always been on the left side. It lies very well and is very beautiful, so we did not wish to change it.

ANNE: Why is your horse's mane braided?

INSTRUCTOR: He was kept in the rough on pasture for the past couple of months and his mane became very thick and long, and a lock or two went to the left side; so I had it shortened, thinned out and braided to train it to lie on the right side again.

ANNE: Why do you say that it's important to watch the horse's neck and head?

INSTRUCTOR: The position of the neck and head, and the changing of this position by the hands of the rider, plays a very important part where a really fine performace is required, as in the Horse Show. It's very easy, for example, in the jumping competition just to miss a ribbon because the horse's neck and head were wrongly placed before the decisive fence. It is a rather complicated matter, and I would prefer to explain it to you little by little when opportunities present themselves. Let's begin, however, with a simple case. Look at my horse;

he is walking straight and his body is also straight from nose to tail. He is comfortable and will probably work for me obediently and cheerfully. Now look at your horse; he is also walking straight while his neck and head are turned to the left; for either your right rein is shorter or you pull on it harder. He is bound to feel miserable. A docile animal will suffer quietly, a nervous horse will eventually become upset, and a horse with a will of his own may try to get rid of the rider. And the rider probably will not even know where the trouble is, and will look for all sorts of causes except the right one.

ANNE: What shall I do if, when riding on loose reins, the horse turns his head to the side by himself? Shall I leave him alone?

INSTRUCTOR: I would, if he is looking at some object that we are passing; I like the horse to know the country that we are riding through, but if I notice that he often carries his neck to one side and really is not looking at anything then I correct this before it becomes a habit.

INSTRUCTOR: We have walked enough; let's start trotting.

ANNE: Yes; and by the way, I want to ask you why some horses start very smoothly for me, and others rush forward almost with a plunge?

INSTRUCTOR: Tell me, do you squeeze or kick a horse when giving him the order to trot?

ANNE: I always kick.

INSTRUCTOR: That is the answer, then. Placid horses whose sides have become used to the abuse of the rider's legs are not surprised by your kicks; but nervous horses, or those that are used to finer riders, will be upset by such rough handling. To start a walk or trot you should just squeeze with your calves in their normal position, at the same time relaxing the tension on your reins. If this squeeze does not produce any effect you can animate it by giving a series of very small short pushes with the calves. If this fails, you can assist by clucking with your tongue, and finally, by closing in your spurs—not kicking with them, but just gradually driving them in. If this does not bring any response it means that the horse is simply stubborn and disobedient, and should be punished either by strong kicks with the calves or even with the spurs. This means that occasionally you will have to kick, but the better the rider and the better-schooled his horse, the less cause there is for kicking. Most of the time you should control your horse by variations of pressures, and now that your legs are back, gently resting at the horse's sides, it will be possible to do. Your legs should rest at the horses's sides gently but steadily; involuntarily swinging legs disturb and confuse the horse.

ANNE: Should you always press your legs when giving orders, at the same place where I do it now—slightly behind the girth?

INSTRUCTOR: No, not always. Let us stop again and I will show you different uses of the legs. There are three that you should remember.

(1) To move the horse straight forward, squeeze the horse on both sides evenly, just slightly behind the girth.

(2) To bend the horse in one side, use one leg only, pressing with it again just slightly behind the girth. If, for instance, your horse instead of walking straight, by the side of mine, should suddenly begin to move sideways to the right away from me, you would have to use the right leg alone slightly behind the girth. This action should bring him back to me or at least prevent his going farther to the right.

(3) If for one reason or another you wish to swing the horse's hind-quarters to one side, then you should use the opposite leg away behind the girth. For instance, if you are walking on a road and an automobile is passing you, and your horse begins to swing his quarters straight in the path of the car, that is the time for you to use one of the legs away behind the girth.

ANNE: Didn't you tell me a while ago that I should hold my stirrups under the ball of my feet and not under the toes?

INSTRUCTOR: Yes, I did.

ANNE: But look, you yourself are holding them under the toes.

INSTRUCTOR: You caught me in one of my worst habits. This is not the only one. When you know more about riding you'll be able to catch me in many others. The fact that I do it incorrectly doesn't mean that I teach it this way, nor should you blindly copy me!

INSTRUCTOR: Now let's trot; or, better still, you stand still a minute longer and let me trot round you and show you a correct position.

In order to remain with the horse, when moving faster than when walking, the rider puts a little more weight in the stirrups and inclines slightly more forward. The body should bend at the hips only, and at no point above them.

There are two ways of sitting to the trot—one is "sitting" it, the other, as you know, is called "posting", which consists in rising and sinking in the stirrups in rhythm with the horse's movements. A sitting trot is harder both for the rider and the horse and consequently is never used in the field riding. But it is very important in schooling, for it enables the rider to use his legs with more precision and quickness.

I will also show you how you should not sit at a trot, which is what you are doing now. Such a position is less secure, abuses the horse, and does not permit the rider to control him well. Forgive the exaggeration; I did it to make my point clearer.

Did you notice that when riding in a correct position I was one with the horse and we moved together; but when I imitated you we were two separate bodies and the horse dragged me along? That is because the line of the centre of gravity of the horse's body passes approximately through the girth. The stirrup leathers are attached on the line of the girth, and when I sit forward the line of the centre of gravity of my body passes through the stirrups. Thus the line of the centre of gravity of the horse's body and my body nearly coincide. We have the greatest possible physical unity; it's very apparent and you can see it; but if I sit the way you do then the line of the centre of gravity of my body is a foot or so behind the horse's.

ANNE: Would you ever sit back in the saddle at a trot?

INSTRUCTOR: Not on the rear part of the saddle, as you did; but I would sit back at a trot, or at any other gait when a horse pulled and tried to go faster than I wanted him to.

After all, if I sit forward to make the work easy for the horse, I will sit back every time I want to make it hard for him. You know, your question is much more important than you probably realize; the position of a good rider is always flexible and he changes it, depending on the requirements. This is very often misunderstood by novice Forward Seat riders, who so often think that they should never change their position—no matter what happens. I have seen cases where the horse practically ran away and the rider was still out of the saddle in a galloping position. I will explain to you in a few minutes what I mean by a galloping position.

ANNE: When I was a child I competed several times in "Good Hands" classes, but I somehow never understood what good hands really were. Can you tell me?

INSTRUCTOR: Well, it is a very complicated matter. Many people think that as long as you don't "hang" on the horse's mouth, or abuse it in some other way, you have good hands. This is not so. Such a rider has just a passive, non-interfering hand, which of course is better than a pulling one. Almost every beginner, due to the insecurity of his position, helps to balance himself by hanging on the horse's mouth. once he has acquired security in the saddle he normally stops hanging; only then can he begin to work towards acquiring "good hands" in

c

the full sense of the word. "Good hands" are a series of actions which are able quickly, definitely and softly to obtain the best results from the horse. In simple riding, if the horse is placid, "good hands" have not much opportunity to show their work and I do not wonder that you never understood what they are, for probably in the so-called "Good Hands" classes you were asked just to walk, trot and canter. Now, fortunately, different movements besides plain gaits are often asked for in these classes. There is really one way of acquiring this finesse of riding—that is through different exercises of ring riding.

But of course before you begin to train your hands you should get into the habit of holding your arms and hands in such a position that

it will be possible eventually to turn them into "good hands". Their relaxation is all-important, and in order to be relaxed the arms should form an angle at the elbow. The soft control of the mouth will largely depend on the straight line of action from the elbow through the forearm and rein, to the horse's mouth. And, last of all, the hands should be kept ten to twelve inches apart. If you were to hold your arms almost straight and your hands too low, as I do now, then all your orders would be felt harshly in the horse's mouth.

ANNE: I understand; but why should I keep my hands almost a foot apart?

INSTRUCTOR: Some day you should visit a pasture and watch free horses moving; or, still better, I can show you a slow-motion picture of them. You will then see that at the gallop the horse's neck and head make gestures back and forth. The same is true on the jump, and approximately the same condition takes place at a walk. It is only at the trot that the neck and head remain almost stationary. Consequently, in order not to interfere with the natural movements of the horse, the rider has to ride on loose reins, or if he is riding on contact, must move his arms and hands forward and back, following the movements of the neck. If he keeps his hands well apart they can move forward freely on either side of the horse's neck.

If I were to keep my hands together, like this, I would not be able to move them forward sufficiently, for the horse's neck would be in my way.

The faster the walk or the gallop, the bigger the gestures of the neck. Some day watch riders who keep their hands close together and stationary, and you will notice how, at every stride of the gallop, they jerk their horses. The rider should avoid making the horse uncomfortable. The expression "hands" is in general misleading as applied to field riding. It really means the action of the fingers, hands and arms. This expression originated in the time of High-School riding. High-School riding consists mostly of highly collected gaits; when galloping very slowly, collected, the horse's neck remains stationary and the head alone makes extremely small gestures. In this type of riding the rider did not have to use his arms; he held them fixed, and simply by the rotation of the wrists he followed the little movements of the head. As you will realize in the course of our ride, this is not for us. You should begin to slow down your horse by fixing your hand, following this by pulling.

ANNE: Your hands looked more relaxed to me when you kept them together.

INSTRUCTOR: Perhaps they were. Perhaps when showing how the hands should be, I stiffened myself, posing for you. Try it both ways yourself and you will see that you may have your hands and arms either relaxed or stiff, both when they are apart or together. The softness does not so much depend on the position in which you hold your arms, as on the relaxation of the muscles.

INSTRUCTOR: Now that we are really off at a trot let's have an even pace and a rather slow one. You probably know that a fast trot is rather hard on the horse and frequent changes of speed will tend to excite him. We also should, as much as the ground permits us, keep this trot for about ten minutes, thus stabilizing the horse at his gait and speed.

ANNE: What do you mean by "stabilizing" the horse at a gait and speed?

INSTRUCTOR: It is said that the horse is stabilized at the gait when he keeps the same gait and an even speed almost entirely by himself; then the only thing the rider has to do is to give an order for a certain gait, and indicate the speed. Only a very well schooled horse will do it—otherwise the evenness of the gait has to be imposed by the rider through constant control. In these cases the rider himself must have the feeling of speed and push the horse forward with his legs the moment the horse starts to slow down, or check him with the reins when he attempts to increase it.

ANNE: And what do you mean about the ground permitting?

INSTRUCTOR: I mean to say that we will not slow down to a walk to make a turn or to cross a dirt road or for a slight up or down grade, but I don't think we should keep on trotting over a ploughed field, for instance, or if we should strike a very stony path. In other words, throughout our ride we shall always consider our horses. And it pays if you do it day in, day out, for they will work for you better, and last longer. The normal speed of the walk should be four miles an hour, the normal speed of the trot about eight miles an hour. The gallop depends on how fast you have to go. A normal hunting speed is eighteen miles an hour.

Of course you realize that what I suggest often cannot be applied —for instance when hunting. But long, even gaits should be maintained when hacking nervous or young horses, and always when schooling.

ANNE: This horse is so willing to go that I really didn't have to wear my spurs.

INSTRUCTOR: My horse is very willing also, but I wear spurs. I think they should always be worn. Not to be used constantly and unnecessarily, but just in order not to be sorry that you haven't got them when a sudden unexpected resistance takes place. The best-behaving horse misbehaves once in a while, and in these moments it's very important to show the horse that you have a strong weapon with which to combat him. Once he knows this, he will consider twice before resisting you again. Very probably I won't have to use my spurs at all today and will get what I want just through the pressure of my calves; but who knows?—perhaps for a few seconds I shall need my spurs. Of course I wouldn't put them on a beginner, for with his unsteady seat he will probably disturb the horse with them all the time.

ANNE: And, by the way, how should you adjust your spurs?

INSTRUCTOR: The proper place to wear them is on the line of the seam where the box of the heel ends and the soft boot begins. However, you can't follow this fashion always when working. It is obvious that a rider with short legs, on a big-barrelled horse, will have to adjust his spurs lower, otherwise he will be constantly irritating the horse with them. You have to adjust them in such a way that you can press the whole length of your calves without touching the horse with the spurs.

Your legs, Miss Randall, are still slightly forward and I think it would be well if you shortened your stirrups.

ANNE: Shall I make mine as short as you have yours?

INSTRUCTOR: Not necessarily; as a matter of fact, I have just pulled mine up one hole and they are too short now; I feel uncomfortable in this old-fashioned saddle and I am trying different lengths of the stirrups; a length just between yours and mine would be right. I also think that

your hands could be an inch higher. But in general you have made a big improvement.

Of course, now you sit more or less correctly because you are making a conscious effort. This effort makes you stiff; consequently, although your seat is almost correct, it is really not good. Later you will be able to have the same position, and even a better one, without giving a thought as to how you sit; then you will be relaxed and the correctness of your position will really have value.

INSTRUCTOR: Well, here we had to interrupt our trot. Although I could go on trotting in spite of the fact that my horse shied at this strange looking hay rake, I think it is wiser to stop and make him acquainted with the object which caused him to shy. In doing so I hope that once he is familiar with it he won't pay any attention to hay rakes and similar machines any more.

ANNE: Why don't you punish him for it?

INSTRUCTOR: I don't think this is a case for punishment, but rather for explaining to him that there is nothing to be afraid of. You can't make us human beings brave through spanking. Instead, I intend gradually to bring him so close to this rake that he will be able to inspect it and sniff it. I will talk to him soothingly and will pat him, simply trying to convince him that this is nothing to fear. If I should have difficulty in bringing him to it while mounted, I might get off and lead him to it. Once he is at it I will stay there for a while and might even recompense him with a piece of sugar.

Of course there might be a different case. Some horses, when fresh and full of play, will pretend to shy at something, just for an opportunity to prance about; then they should be punished. If you know your horse, it's always easy to distinguish which mood is which. You realize that some horses are so shy by nature that no trainer can make bold animals of them.

Very often the rider, anticipating shying, can prevent it by giving confidence to his horse. In order to do so he should sit tight, give the reins, firmly close-in the legs, pat the horse and talk to him.

THE VAN EYCKS
AND THEIR ART

BY W. H. JAMES WEALE

HUBERT AND JOHN VAN EYCK

THEIR LIFE AND WORK

With upwards of 60 Illustrations.
Quarto.

JODOC VYT   ELISABETH BORLUUT

BERLIN : ROYAL GALLERY

By permission of the Berlin Photographic Co.

THE
VAN EYCKS
AND THEIR ART
BY W. H. JAMES WEALE
· WITH THE CO-OPERATION OF ·
MAURICE W. BROCKWELL

LONDON :
JOHN LANE THE BODLEY HEAD LIMITED.

FIRST PUBLISHED IN 1912.
REPRINTED - - 1928.

PRINTED BY WILLIAM BROWN & CO. LTD.,
2, BURY COURT, ST. MARY AXE,
LONDON, E.C. 3.

TO

H. A. W.

AND

U. E. M. B.

FOREWORD

It was not until the publication, in 1849, of the first volume of Laborde's work, *Les Ducs de Bourgogne*, that the biography of the Van Eycks began to be elucidated. The documents printed in that work were collated with the originals by Pinchart, who gave more correct readings, and also published the entries of payments to John van Eyck in 1422–1425, which he discovered in the household accounts of John of Bavaria at the Hague. Since then the present writer has not only published some important documents (3, 18, 19, 23, 25, 26, 29, 31), but has, in the present work, brought together and printed in chronological order all those documents yet discovered.

Unfortunately many documents which would no doubt have given us valuable information are still missing. Of the accounts of the Receivers-general of the Duke of Burgundy's finances, those for the years 1427, 1429, 1430, and 1438 are wanting. Of the seventeen yearly accounts of the Receivers of Flanders, embracing the period during which John van Eyck was in the Duke's service, only four, those of the years 1425, 1427, 1432, and 1441, have come down to us. Of the detailed accounts and receipts in John's handwriting, not a single one has been preserved. The originals of the Duke's letters-patent of May, 1426, and of those raising John's salary, are also lost ; and the accounts of the sale of life annuities and of the yearly payments of these, which would have given us the family name and the date of decease of John's wife, are also wanting.

It is probable that some further items of information may yet be gleaned from the municipal accounts of towns in the Duke's dominions, and, perhaps, also from documents in the archives of Spain and Portugal. Manuscripts, such as the interesting description of the Ghent polyptych discovered by Dr. Voll, may yet come to light. One such, probably lying unrecognised in some library, the *Leecken Philosophie* of Mark van Vaernewyck, is known to contain, in the twentieth book, all that the author had been able to gather concerning the Van Eycks. A careful examination of printed books, especially of chronicles and books of travel, may also add to our knowledge.

In 1900, the writer began to collect materials for a chronological bibliography of printed books and pamphlets relating to the Van Eycks and other early Netherlandish painters, a tedious work, nearly completed when a great number of the collected titles were accidentally lost. The undertaking was then abandoned, and not resumed until 1905, when the present work was commenced.

Every document has been collated, and all the bibliographical references verified. The author has spared no pains in his endeavour to secure accuracy ; he has, however, not found it possible to again go through the catalogues of the British Museum and National Art Libraries, but he doubts the omission of any important work. Should any such omission be remarked, he will feel greatly obliged by his attention being called to it.

He particularly wishes those who may consult this work to remember that it has no pretensions to literary merit, the author's aim being simply to provide those who in the future may attempt to write the history of the school of painting that

flourished in the Low Countries in the fifteenth
century, with as complete a guide as possible to all
that has been published concerning its founders
up to the present date.

CLAPHAM,
23rd October 1907.

P.S.—I desire to express my thanks to those
who in the review of my volume have pointed out
the omissions and errors, especially to Mr. Eric
Maclagan, Mr. Maurice W. Brockwell, Mr. L. Binyon,
and the reviewer in the *Guardian*.

Mr. John Lane being desirous of issuing a second
edition in a revised and more condensed form, and
my failing health and eyesight making it impossible
for me to undertake the work, I decided on obtain-
ing assistance. I doubt if I could find a more
capable collaborator than Mr. Brockwell, the editor
of this volume.

W. H. J. W.

CLAPHAM,
August 1912.

PREFACE

It is no easy task for me to address to the general reader a few prefatory remarks on the monumental work which Mr. Weale published some four years ago through Mr. John Lane, and at the same time to summarise briefly the circumstances which have brought about the preparation of a revised edition by the present joint-authors.

The *magnum opus* of 1908 was a fully-detailed and exhaustive treatise on the two brothers by one who had known Bruges since 1849. Great critical insight was demanded of Mr. Weale for the responsible examination of the heterogeneous mass of written or printed material accumulated during past centuries. Some of it was originally circulated in the dark ages of unscientific criticism with the purpose of wilfully misleading the unsuspecting, while a great proportion of it proved, from one cause or another, unattractive alike to the scientific research-worker and to the less exacting enthusiast. The first-hand knowledge resulting from the enjoyment, in different parts of Europe, of the friendship or acquaintance of the majority of those who, during the greater part of the nineteenth century, owned, wrote upon, or dealt in the paintings of the best period of Early Netherlandish art, has proved exceedingly useful to my friend Mr. Weale. This knowledge will now be found to be of the greatest assistance to the student, who is too often beset by the ever-varying output of the less competent followers of the great masters, the soulless copyists, and the skilled *falsificateurs* of nearly five centuries.

Although it must be borne in mind that the book now brought to completion is almost entirely the outcome of Mr. Weale's lifelong activities among pictures, documents, and books, it may not be out of place for the present writer to indicate briefly how he came to bear a part in the work now in the hand of the student. The present writer's long and whole-hearted, even if uninspired and unexacting, study of the general achievement of the Van Eycks; the close scrutiny to which, as reviewer to *The Athenæum*, he came to subject so authoritative and scholarly a book; his suggestion on that occasion that, as time went on, certain constructive and detailed emendations might be effected, and a more popular edition prepared; as well as the mere chance of juniority—these are, doubtless, among the causes which led Mr. Weale and Mr. Lane to ask him to undertake the arduous task of getting ready this revised edition. The disadvantages of his inferior equipment, his exceedingly restricted acquaintance with the subject-matter, and an entire lack of knowledge in regard to many of the wide issues involved, have, it is to be hoped, been amply compensated for by the fact that Mr. Weale has, with scrupulous care and characteristic attention to detail, read through the various proofs and revises that such an undertaking entails.

This edition has, it will be readily admitted, been planned on somewhat different lines to the earlier one. Mr. Weale in his original plan divided his book into two parts. The one dealt with pictures fully authenticated by documents and no longer doubted by any one; the other with pictures that are authentic, though not documentarily authenticated, and with doubtful works. The drawback of that method, which was apt to prove too exacting to the critic, and yet not sufficiently clear to the student, was that there had to be included in the second part of the book a certain number of pictures which obviously had no right, although such acceptation seemed at first sight to be implied, to inclusion among Eyckian pictures.

An effort has been made to separate all the paintings into more clearly-defined groups. This enables us to see at a glance, and in more accurate perspective, the probabilities as to the authorship of Hubert or John in certain works, and at what date ; and to study the vexed question of their joint participation in others, and in what proportion. We now give a systematic classification of pictures of doubtful authenticity, and of copies, variants, derivatives, and imitations. Moreover, the critical remarks on lost paintings and on drawings of varying degrees of importance now cover a wider range than was, perhaps, possible in the earlier edition.

Although we now set out in detail only twenty-four authentic paintings, and have added brief notices of others, we have drawn up in a special appendix a list of four hundred pictures which have appeared at public auction between 1662 and 1912 with an attribution, however loose, to the Van Eycks. Among them, it will be noted, are a number of paintings assigned, on purely hypothetical grounds, to their putative sister Margaret, who, in point of fact, never had a corporeal existence. The original statements by the poet Luke De Heere, in 1565, and the chronicler Mark Vaernewyck, were in good time embellished by later writers. Highly pictorial accounts of her were given in the official catalogues of the National Gallery forty years ago ; by Charles Reade in his *Cloister and the Hearth*, and in the usual " authorities " of later dates. In quite recent times the political propaganda of one of the newly-formed Suffrage Societies has put forward the demonstrably inaccurate contention that she is, owing to her ability as a painter, entitled to a place among the illustrious women of past centuries!

A century ago practically all early pictures of the Netherlandish, German, French, and even Spanish, Portuguese, and English schools were, in default of their authorship having been correctly ascertained, assigned to " Van Eyck " or " Vanek," Stuerbout (or Dirk Bouts), or Hemling (as Hans Memlinc was then called). Even during the last half-century many of the pictures that, by a consensus of critical opinion, are now rightly attributed to such different technicians as Antonello da Messina, Robert Campin, James Daret, Roger De la Pasture (Van der Weyden), Peter Christus I and II, Albert von Ouwater, Gerard David, Adrian Isenbrant, Joachim Patenir, John Prévost, Jerome Bosch, and Quentin Metsys, were indiscriminately hailed as the work of " Van Eyck." However, some of these painters were not born until after John van Eyck's death ; the last named no less than twenty-five years after.

It seemed needless to reprint the whole of Mr. Weale's exemplary Bibliography, which extended over fifty-nine pages. But it has been thoroughly checked and verified, while it has also been amplified by the addition of matter that had been overlooked and by the inclusion of all new material of any importance. In spite of the amplification of certain parts of the original work, notably in regard to Lost Paintings, the Drawings, and the Observations, the pruning of portions of the Documents and Bibliography has enabled us to provide the student with a less bulky book. Moreover, a really ample Index has been compiled. In conclusion, we may express the hope that the complete achievement of our task will render *The Van Eycks and Their Art* a reliable

and handy book of reference for the next few
years.

It now remains for the joint-authors to express
their grateful thanks to all those who have aided
their endeavours to make this work as complete
and as accurate as possible ; first, to Sir Claude
Phillips, who has cleared up difficulties presented
by pictures in St. Petersburg and elsewhere ; to
M. Achille Bouis, Conservateur of the Musée Ingres
at Montauban, for details in regard to a picture
there ; to Mr. Albert Van de Put, of the National
Art Library, for much help ; to Mr. James Greig,
and to Mr. W. Roberts for access to certain
information ; to Messrs. P. & D. Colnaghi and
Obach, Mr. A. H. Buttery and M. Sedelmeyer
for information in regard to pictures formerly in
their possession ; and to Mr. Eric Maclagan for
facsimiles of inscriptions and notes of details in
paintings, and more especially for the use of his
notes made under difficulties in front of the " St.
George " in the collection of General Plaoutine at St.
Petersburg. The joint-authors beg to convey their
best thanks also to all those gentlemen who gave
valuable assistance to Mr. Weale in the preparation of his large book on *Hubert and Jŏhn van Eyck*,
published in 1908.
In conclusion I must thank M. Joseph Casier,
M. G. Hulin de Loo, and M. Paul Bergmans, for
details of the monument by the sculptor, M. Georges
Verbanck, which it is intended to inaugurate at
Ghent early in August of next year, " pour con-
sacrer à Gand la gloire des maîtres de l'*Adoration
de l'Agneau Mystique.*"

M. W. B.

CHELSEA, 18*th September* 1912.

CONTENTS

LIST OF PLATES

A

B

C

D

DRAWINGS

ILLUSTRATIONS IN THE TEXT

CHRONOLOGY

CHRONOLOGY

1404, April 27. Death of Philip II, Duke of Burgundy.

1417, May 31. Death of William of Bavaria, Count of Holland.

1419. John of Bavaria at The Hague.

1419, September 10. John the Fearless, Duke of Burgundy, assassinated ; he is succeeded by Philip III.

1422, July 8. Death, at Ghent, of Michael of France, first wife of Philip III, Duke of Burgundy.

1422, October 24,—1424, September 11. John van Eyck working for John of Bavaria, Count of Holland, in the palace at The Hague.

1424, November 30. Marriage of Philip III, Duke of Burgundy, and Bonne of Artois, daughter of Philip, Count of Eu and Nevers.

1425, January 5. Death of John of Bavaria.

  May 19. John van Eyck at Bruges. Duke Philip appoints him his painter, with a yearly salary of 100*l.* parisis, payable in two moieties, commencing from Midsummer.

  Before August 2. Moves to Lille, and takes up his residence there.

  Hubert van Eyck makes two sketches for a picture for the magistrates of Ghent.

  September 17. Death of Bonne of Artois, second wife of Duke Philip.

1426, March. Hubert engaged at Ghent, painting an altarpiece and polychroming a statue of Saint Anthony for Robert Poortier.

  Before July 14. John van Eyck goes on a pilgrimage for the Duke.

  August. John van Eyck is sent on a secret mission by the Duke.

  September 18. Hubert van Eyck dies at Ghent.

  October 27. John van Eyck, having returned from

his mission, is paid 360*l.* of 40 groats Flemish in settlement.

1427, October 18. John van Eyck at Tournay—second secret mission—is presented with the wine of honour. The Duke's ambassadors are presented with wine on the 20th.

1428, February. John complains to the Duke that his receiver at Lille had refused to pay him his salary.

October 19. Starts from Sluus on third mission, by sea to John I. of Portugal.

October 20. Puts in at Sandwich.

November 13. Sails from Sandwich.

November 25. Puts in at Falmouth.

December 2. Sails from Falmouth.

December 11. Puts in at Bayona.

December 14. Sails from Bayona.

December 16. Calls at Cascaës.

December 18. Arrives at Lisbon.

1429, January. Sojourn at Arrayollos.

January 12. Leaves Arrayollos and arrives at Aviz.

The ambassadors are received by the King of Portugal and the Royal Family on the morrow. John van Eyck paints the portrait of the Princess Isabella, and sends it to the Duke of Burgundy.

February. Goes on a pilgrimage to Saint James of Compostella in Galicia. Visits John II, King of Castile, the Duke of Arjona, Mahommed, King of Granada, &c.

May. Returns to Lisbon.

June 4. Journey to Cintra to see the King; sojourn in that town.

July 23. Contract of marriage of the Duke and Isabella signed at Lisbon.

July 24—October 8. Sojourn at Lisbon.

September 30. The King of Portugal conducts his daughter to her ship.

October 8. The Portuguese fleet sets sail.

October 13. Puts in at Cascaës.

November 29. Puts in at Plymouth.

December 25. Arrives at Sluus.

1430, January 7. Marriage of the Duke and Isabella at Sluus. John van Eyck goes to Hesdin and returns to Bruges.

1431, December.   Draws the portrait of B. Nicholas Albergati.

1432, January.   Paints the portrait of the same cardinal, now at Vienna (see p. 103).
Buys a house at Bruges.
May 6.   Polyptych of the Adoration of the Lamb terminated and placed in the church of Saint John— now Saint Bavo—at Ghent (see pp. 35–66).
Before August 13.   The burgomaster and some other members of the town-council of Bruges visit John van Eyck, to view paintings.
October 10.   Paints portrait of a man, "Léal Souvenir," now in the National Gallery (see p. 108).

1433, before February 19.   The Duke visits John's studio.
John paints Our Lady and Child, now at Ince Hall (see p. 109).
October 21.   Paints the portrait of a man with a red headkerchief, now in the National Gallery (see p. 112).

1434.   Birth of John's first child.   The Duke is godfather.
Paints the portrait of John Arnolfini and wife, now in the National Gallery (see p. 114).

1434–1435.   John's salary raised from 100*l.* parisis payable in two half-yearly moieties, to 360*l.* of 40 groats Flemish (4320*l.* parisis), payable quarterly.

1435, March 12.   The Duke reprimands the accountants at Lille for raising difficulties as to verification of his letters patent, and bids them execute his orders with despatch.
John van Eyck polychromes six statues in the front of the Town-House at Bruges.

1436.   Paints an altar-piece for George Van der Paele, Canon of Saint Donatian, at Bruges, now in the Town Gallery (see p. 120).
Paints the portrait of John De Leeuw, now in the Imperial Gallery, Vienna (see p. 127).
Goes on a secret mission by order of the Duke, for which he is paid 360*l.* gr.
October.   Jacqueline of Bavaria, Countess of Holland, dies at Teylingen.

1437.   John van Eyck paints the picture of Saint Barbara, now in the Museum at Antwerp (see p. 129).

1439.   Paints the picture of Our Lady and Child by a fountain, now in the Museum at Antwerp (see p. 131).

1439. June 17.   Paints the portrait of Margaret his wife,
   now in the Town Gallery, Bruges (see p. 133).

1441. Paints an altar-piece for the Provost of Saint Martin's
   at Ypres (see p. 135).
      July 9. Death of John van Eyck.

1450. Livina, daughter of John van Eyck, enters the convent of Saint Agnes at Maaseyck.

1456. John van Eyck's wife, Margaret, was still living at
   Bruges.

1466, November 11.   Death of Henry van Eyck.

DOCUMENTS IN CHRONOLOGICAL ORDER

DOCUMENTS[1]

1422–1425

1. PAYMENTS to master John van Eyck, painter in the service of John of Bavaria, Count of Holland, for work executed at the Palace of The Hague from October 24, 1422, to September 11, 1424. John was paid at the rate of 8 lions a day ; his apprentices received 2 lions a day.

The Hague : Royal Archives.

1425

2. Payment to master Hubert van Eyck ("meester Luberecht") for two sketches of a painting, made by order of the magistrates of Ghent.

Ghent : Town Archives.

1425, August 2

3. Payment of 20*l.* to John van Eyck ("Iohannes de Heecq, varlet de chambre et paintre de mon dict seigneur"), in consideration of the trouble and expense incurred by him in moving from Bruges to Lille by order of Philip, Duke of Burgundy, who,

---

[1] These documents are printed at full length in Weale, 1908, pp. XXXVII–LI. Some of them were published, but not always accurately, by Laborde in his *Ducs de Bourgogne*. Pinchart, with greater accuracy, reproduced some of them in his " Annotations."

xxxi

by letters patent dated May 19, 1425, had appointed
him his official painter.

Lille : Archives of the Department of the North, B 1931.

1425

4. Gratuity to the apprentices at master Hubert's.

Ghent : Town Archives.

1426, March 9

5. Robert Poortier and Avezoete his wife, by
their will dated March 9, 1425, give directions for
their burial in the church of Saint Saviour, Ghent,
in the tomb they had prepared in the chapel of Our
Lady ; for the completion of the altar founded by
them in that chapel ; and for setting up above it
the statue of Saint Anthony, which statue, together
with other work pertaining to the same altar, was at
that date in the hands of master Hubert the
painter (" meester Hubrechte ").

Ghent : Town Archives.

1426

6. Three payments of 50*l*. each to John van
Eyck (" Jehan de Heick, jadiz pointre et varlet de
chambre de feu monseigneur le duc Jehan de
Bayvière "), being the amount of his salary from
Midsummer, 1425, to Christmas, 1426.

Lille : Archives of the Department of the North.

1426, August 26

7. Payment to John van Eyck (" Iohannes de
Eick ") of 91*l*. 5*s*. of 40 groats Flemish to the pound,
for a certain pilgrimage which the Duke had ordered

him to perform in his name, and on account of a
secret journey which he had ordered him to make
to certain distant places of which no mention was to
be made.

Lille : Archives of the Department of the North, B 1933.

1426, after September 18

8. Receipt by the treasurers of the town of
Ghent of 6s. gr. from the heirs of Hubert van
Eyck ("Lubrecht van Heyke"), tax on the pro-
perty of the deceased.

Ghent : Town Archives.

1426, October 27

9. Payment to John van Eyck ("Iohannes de
Eick") of 360*l.* of 40 groats Flemish to the pound,
in settlement of amount due to him for certain
distant secret journeys made by order of the Duke.

Lille : Archives of the Department of the North, B 1935.

1427, July

10. Payment to John van Eyck ("Iohannes de
Heecht") of a gratuity of 20*l.*, in consideration of
services rendered by him to the Duke.

Courtrai : Town Library.

1427, August

11. Payment to John van Eyck ("Iehannes
Eyk") of a gratuity of 100*l.*, in recompense for
services rendered by him to the Duke.

Courtrai : Town Library.

c

1428, after March 3

12. Payment to John van Eyck (" Jehan de Heick ") of 100*l*. parisis, amount of his salary for one year to Christmas, 1427, by special order of the Duke, notwithstanding the general revocation of pensions and salaries of officers of his household.

Lille : Archives of the Department of the North.

1428

13. Payment to John van Eyck (" Iohannes de Eck ") of 160*l*. of 40 groats Flemish to the pound, in consideration of services rendered by him to the Duke, and also in recompense for certain secret voyages made by him, and for the voyage undertaken in the company of the lord of Roubaix.

Lille : Archives of the Department of the North, B 1938.

1428, November

14. Payment to Michael Ravary of 46*l*. 4*s*., being the rent of a house (at Lille) in which John van Eyck (" Iohannes de Eck, varlet de chambre et paintre de mon dit seigneur "), by order of the Duke, resided during two years to Midsummer, 1428.

Lille : Archives of the Department of the North, B 1938.

1431, March

15. Payment to Lambert van Eyck (" Lambert de Hech, frère de Iohannes de Hech "), of 7*l*. 9*s*., for having on several occasions waited on the Duke concerning certain affairs.

Lille : Archives of the Department of the North, B 1942.

1432

16. Payment to John van Eyck (" Jehan de Heick, peintre et varlet de chambre de mon seigneur le duc "), of 50*l.* parisis, being the amount of his salary for a half-year to Midsummer, 1432.

Lille : Archives of the Department of the North.

17. Payment to John van Eyck (" Iohannes d'Eick, paintre "), of 19*l.*, for having, by order of the Duke, come to him at Hesdin from Bruges, and for his journey back.

Lille : Archives of the Department of the North, B 1942.

18. Gratuity of 3*l.* parisis given to the apprentices of John van Eyck (" Iohannes van Heyck ") when the burgomasters of Bruges and some members of the council went to see certain works.

Bruges : Town Archives.

19. Payment of 30*s.* parisis by John van Eyck to the receivers of the office of the obedience of Saint Donatian at Bruges, being the amount of an annual charge on his house, due at Midsummer, 1432.

Bruges : Episcopal Archives.

A similar entry occurs in each of the following yearly accounts until that for 1441, after which the entry is " Relicta Iohannis de Eyke."

1433

20. Gratuity of 25*s.* g. given to the apprentices of John van Eyck (" Iohannes d'Eyk ") by the Duke, when he went to see certain work executed by the said John.

Lille : Archives of the Department of the North, B 1948.

1434

21. Payment of 76*l.* g. to John van Eyck ("Iohannes van Eyck"), which sum the Duke had agreed to give him for several days spent in attending to his and the Duchess's requirements and business.

Lille : Archives of the Department of the North, B 1951.

22. Payment to John Peutin, goldsmith, of Bruges, of 96*l.* 12*s.* of 40 groats Flemish to the pound, for six silver cups weighing 12 marks, presented by the Duke to John van Eyck at the baptism of his child, held at the font by Peter de Beaufremont, lord of Charny, in the name of the Duke.

Lille : Archives of the Department of the North, B 1951.

1434, September 12

23. Letter relative to the payment of John van Eyck's (Jehan de Heict") pension, charged partly on the receipt of the tax of 2 groats on each piece of cloth at Wervick, addressed by Tassart Brisse, Receiver-General of Flanders, to the officers of the Chamber of Accounts at Lille.

Lille : Archives of the Department of the North, B 1283.

1435, March 12

24. Letter addressed by Philip, Duke of Burgundy, to the officers of the Chamber of Accounts at Lille. He hears they have raised difficulties as to the verification and registration of his letters patent granting a life pension to his painter, John van Eyck ("notre bien amé varlet de chambre et paintre, Jehan van Eyck"), in consequence of which the said John is inclined to leave his service. This would very greatly displease him, as he is about to employ John on certain great works and could not find another painter equally to his taste nor of such excellence in his art and science. Therefore he bids them, on receipt of this, to register his letters granting the pension, without further argument, delay, alteration, variation, or difficulty whatever, under pain of incurring his displeasure and wrath.

Lille : Archives of the Department of the North, Parchment, B 1955.

1435

25. Payment of 30*l.* gr. to master John van Eyck (" meester Ianne van Eick "), for painting and gilding six statues and the tabernacles in which they stand, adorning the front of the Town-House, and of 3*l.* 12*s.* g. for overwork on the same.

Bruges : Town Archives.

1435, September 29

26. Payment of 67*l.* 15*s.* to John Peutin, goldsmith, for six silver cups weighing 9 marks 5 ounces, at 20*s.* g. the mark, equals 67*l.* 15*s.*

Lille : Archives of the Department of the North, B 1957.

1436

27. Payment of 360*l.* to John van Eyck (" Iohannes d'Eick "), for certain distant journeys to foreign parts on some secret business undertaken by order of the Duke.

Lille : Archives of the Department of the North, B 1957.

1439

28. Payment of 6*l.* 6*s.* 6*d.* to John van Eyck (" Iohannes van Eicke ") in reimbursement of a like amount paid by him to an illuminator of Bruges who had illuminated a book for the Duke, in which are 272 large letters in gold and 1200 small.

Lille: Archives of the Department of the North, B 1966.

1441, June 24

29. Payment of 180*l.* of 40 groats Flemish to the pound, to John van Eyck, being the amount of his salary for two quarters to Midsummer, 1441.

Lille : Archives of the Department of the North.

1441, July 9

30. Receipt of 13*l.* 4*s.* parisis by the treasurer of the fabric of Saint Donatian's church at Bruges, for the burial fees of John van Eyck.

"Receptum pro sepultura magistri Iohannis Eyck, pictoris, xij lb. par."

" Receptum ex campana magistri Iohannis Eyck, pictoris, xxiiij s. par."

Bruges : Episcopal Archives.

1441, July 22

31. Payment of 360*l.* to Margaret, widow of John van Eyck (damoiselle Marguerite, vefve du dit feu Jehan van Eyck, paintre de mon dit seigneur, que trespassa environ la fin du mois de Juing oudit an mil cccc quarante ung), being the amount of a gratuity granted to her by the Duke, in recognition of the good and agreeable service rendered to him by her deceased husband, and out of compassion for her and her children.

Lille : Archives of the Department of the North.

1442, March 21

32. The Chapter of Saint Donatian, Bruges, at the request of Lambert van Eyck, grants permission for the body of his brother John, buried in the precincts, to be, with the bishop's licence, translated into the church and buried near the font, on condition of the foundation of an anniversary and of compliance with the rights of the fabric.

Bruges : Episcopal Archives.

1442

33. Receipt of 12*l*. parisis by the treasurer of the fabric of Saint Donatian, for the burial of master John van Eyck, painter, officer of the Duke.

" Receptum pro sepultura magistri Iohannis Eyck, pictoris, officiarii domini ducis, xij l. par."

Bruges : Episcopal Archives.

34. Receipt of 48*l*. parisis by the treasurer of the fabric of Saint Donatian, bequeathed by John van Eyck for the foundation of his anniversary.

" Receptum ex testamento Iohannis Eyck, pictoris, xlviij l. par."

Bruges : Episcopal Archives.

35. Entry in the obituary of the church of Saint Donatian of John van Eyck's anniversary.

" 9 Iulii. Aeffrem abbatis. Obitus Iohannis Eyck, pictoris, qui dedit xlviij lb. par. ; inde ad pitancias xl s. quos solvit obedientia."

Bruges : Episcopal Archives.

1450

36. Payment of 24*l*. to Livina, daughter of the late John van Eyck, painter, my lord's servant

(" Lyevine Van der Eecke, fille de feu Jehan Van. der
Eecke, jadis painctre, varlet de chambre de mon dit
seigneur "), being a gift from him to enable her to
enter the monastery of Maaseyck (Mazeck), in the
land of Liége.

Lille : Archives of the Department of the North, B 2002.

c. 1480

37. Description of a vestment given by John
van Eyck to the convent of Saint Agnes, at Maaseyck.

Brussels : Royal Library.

1768, April 28

38. The Chapter of the cathedral of Saint
Donatian at Bruges, at the request of Mr. John
Garemijn, director of the Academy of Fine Arts,
grant permission to erect an epitaph and inscription
to the memory of John van Eyck in the church.

" Actum in capitulo ordinario feria quinta 28
Aprilis, 1768, reverendo domino decano praesidente.

" Ut possent expensis per ipsos procurandis in
hac ecclesia cathedrali collocare epitaphium cum
inscriptione congrua, iuxta schema ad mensam
capitularem exhibitum, in perennem memoriam
inclyti et variorum scriptorum elogiis celebrati viri
Ioannis van Eyck Brugensis, pictoris suo aevo
celeberrimi et circa annum 1440 defuncti."

Bruges : Episcopal Archives.

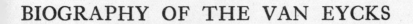

BIOGRAPHY OF THE VAN EYCKS

BIOGRAPHY OF THE VAN EYCKS

(The numbers in parentheses refer to the documents printed in chronological order in the preceding pages.)

AT a distance of some thirteen or fourteen miles from Maastricht, in a bend of the Maas, on the left bank of that river, lies the little town of Maaseyck, a veritable outpost of population, famous now for all time as the birthplace of the brothers Hubert and John van Eyck. Maaseyck was pillaged in 1395 and again in 1397. At the time of their coming the numerous monasteries and convents of the surrounding district were as so many nurseries of the arts and crafts, in which they had long been cultivated with considerable success. Maaseyck itself owed its origin to the convent of Eyck, or Aldeneyck, founded in the first half of the eighth century by two sisters of noble family, who had been educated in a Benedictine abbey at Valenciennes ; two illuminated manuscripts, and a chasuble and a couple of embroidered veils, the work of their hands, still preserved in the treasury of the parish church of Maaseyck, are evidence of their skill. At first the arts were confined to the monasteries, but in the thirteenth century sculptors and painters who were laymen were to be found in the principal towns, notably at Köln and Maastricht, where they had acquired celebrity by their skill.

It appears at least probable that Hubert and John received their early training in the latter town. The date of their birth and the names of their parents are alike unknown. The elder of the two, Hubert, is said to have been born about 1365, the younger, John, about 1385 ; [1] but these dates are purely speculative.

All we know for certain about Hubert's life is that he had settled in Ghent and acquired the freedom of that town before 1425, and, further, that he resided there until his death on the 18th of September 1426.

I

HUBERT VAN EYCK

As we have already intimated, absolutely nothing is known of Hubert's early years. Probability points to his having served his apprenticeship under some painter at Maastricht, to his having travelled at its close to Köln, Basel, and Italy, possibly returning to the Low Countries by France, Spain, and England. It is not known when he returned, nor where he at first settled, but it was most likely at Maastricht, Utrecht, Haarlem, or The Hague. There were certainly a number of painters and miniaturists in that part of the Low Countries who would seem to have come under his influence. Most remarkable among their works are certain miniatures executed for William IV of Bavaria, Count of Holland and Zeeland, or his daughter Jacqueline, between 1412 and 1418, in the splendid Book of Hours which perished in the lamentable fire at Turin in 1904, happily not before they had been photographed for Count Paul Durrieu, to whom we are indebted for their publication. [2] Some of these miniatures are

[1] He must have been born before 1392, as he was already a master painter in 1422.

[2] The fire took place on the night of January 25–26, 1904.

For an account of this " sventura mondiale," read Gorrini : L' Incendio della R. Biblioteca Nazionale di Torino, 1905.

For a description of the Book of Hours, read Durrieu: Heures de Turin, 1902.

thought to have been designed or painted by Hubert himself, owing to the many points of resemblance between them and portions of the Ghent polyptych. That great work, as suggested by Dr. Six, may indeed have been commenced to the order of William IV.

In any event, Hubert must have removed to Ghent at latest soon after William's death (May 31, 1417), about which time numbers of craftsmen migrated to the towns of Brabant and Flanders, where they could practise their art in greater security.

In 1425 Hubert made for the magistrates of Ghent either two sketches for a pair of panels or two alternative designs for a single panel ; he received for his pains six shillings (Doc. 2). As the sketches were paid for—an unusual occurrence— and as there is no record of any contract having been entered into, or of any further payment having been made to him, we may safely conclude that he was not commissioned to execute the work.

In 1425 he was engaged not only on the polyptych, but also on a painting for an altar erected by one Robert Poortier and his wife in the church of Saint Saviour,[1] and in polychroming a statue of Saint Anthony destined to be placed above it (Doc. 5). In the year 1425–1426 [2] the civic dignitaries paid him a visit, doubtless to view the works he had in hand, and marked the occasion by a gratuity of six groats to his apprentices (Doc. 4). On the 18th of September, 1426, the great master breathed his last, and was subsequently laid to rest in the crypt beneath the chapel for which he had painted the far-famed altar-piece. A brass plate bore this inscription—

---

[1] The dexter shutter of this triptych is now at Copenhagen ; see p. 67.
[2] The financial year at Ghent began on the 15th of August.

"Spieghelt u an my die op my treden :
Ick was als ghy, nu bem beneden
Begraven doot, alst is anschyne.
My ne halp raet, const, noch medicine.
Const, eer, wijsheyt, macht, rijcheyt groot
Is onghespaert, als comt die doot.

Hubrecht van Eyck was ick ghenant,
Nu spyse der wormen, voormaels bekant
In schilderye zeer hooghe gheeert :
Cort na was yet, in niente verkeert.

Int iaer des Heeren des sijt ghewes,
Duysent, vierhondert, twintich en zes,
In de maent September, achthien daghen viel,
Dat ick met pynen God gaf mijn ziel.
Bidt God voor my die Const minnen,
Dat ick zijn aensicht moet ghewinnen ;
En vliedt zonde, keert u ten besten
Want ghy my volghen moet ten lesten."

"Take warning by me, who o'er me tread :
I was as ye, now lie beneath,
Buried dead, as is apparent.
Availed me not counsel, art, nor medicine.
Art, honour, wisdom, strength, riches great,
Are all unspared when cometh Death.

Hubert van Eyck was I naméd,
Now food of worms, erstwhile well known,
In painting very highly honoured,
Yet shortly after changed to nought.

In the year of the Lord it is certain,
One thousand, four hundred, twenty and six,
In the month of September the eighteenth day, it befell
That I in suffering gave up my soul to God.
Pray God for me, ye who love art,
That I His vision may attain unto ;
And flee sin, turn ye to the best,
For ye must follow me at last."

The receipt by the treasurers of the town of six shillings (Doc. 8) tax on the property left by Hubert, paid by his heirs, is a proof that they were strangers.

In 1533 the chapel and the crypt beneath it were done away with to make room for a new aisle ; the remains of those who lay buried there were reinterred in the churchyard, with the exception of the bone of Hubert's right arm, which was enclosed in an iron case and suspended in the porch, while the brass plate was placed in the transept near the first pillar. There it remained until 1578, when, together with a number of other memorial brasses, it was stolen by the Calvinist iconoclasts. In 1585 the churchwardens, after calling on all relatives and descendants of persons buried in the church to repair the despoiled gravestones, removed those as to which no response was made. In 1892 a slab,

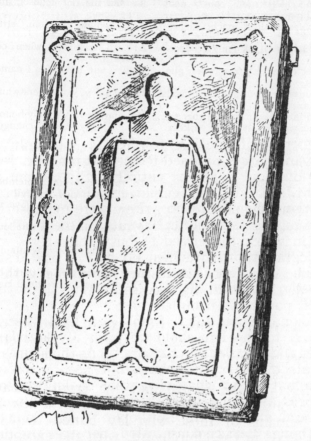

SEPULCHRAL SLAB, XVI CENTURY. GHENT: ARCHÆOLOGICAL MUSEUM.

From a sketch by A. Heins.

of which we reproduce a sketch above, was brought to light in the foundations of a side portal erected in 1769. This in 1895 was transported to the

Archæological Museum in the ruins of the abbey of Saint Bavo. The brass tablet commemorating Hubert may possibly have been let into this slab in 1533, but the slab itself is certainly not earlier than the sixteenth century. It was not shown to Münzer in 1495, and evidently De Heere had no knowledge of it in 1565.

II

JOHN VAN EYCK

AUTHENTIC information towards a biography of John van Eyck is confined to the last nineteen years of his life, and is almost entirely derived from the account-books of his employers. Contemporary Netherlandish and French writers were too absorbed in chronicling the political events of the troublous times in which they lived to busy themselves with the biography of craftsmen, no matter how distinguished. However, his history from the 24th of October, 1422, until his decease on the 9th of July, 1441, is now fairly complete.

In or before 1422 John van Eyck became attached to the household of John of Bavaria as painter and "varlet de chambre." As the household accounts of that prince have not been preserved, we do not know what were the emoluments and privileges attaching to the post. John of Bavaria had been elected prince-bishop of Liége in 1390, and, though neither consecrated, nor even ordained priest or deacon, he clung to the temporalities dependent on that dignity until 1418. His elder brother, William IV, Count of Holland and Zeeland, died on the 31st of May, 1417, leaving an only child, Jacqueline. John, determined to rob his niece of her rights, started from Liége in September of the following year on an expedition to Holland, and installed himself as count at Dordrecht; then, having seized Gorcum and other strongholds, he, towards the end of the year, journeyed into Luxemburg, and there married Elisabeth of Görlitz, Duchess of Luxemburg, and widow of Anthony of Burgundy, Duke of Brabant and Limburg. In the month of August, 1419, he removed to Holland, and settled at The Hague. There John van Eyck was employed in the decoration of the palace from the 24th of October, 1422, until the 11th of September, 1424; his pay was at the rate of eight lions a day, while his assistants received two lions a day each (Doc. 1).

John of Bavaria died at Delft on the 5th of January, 1425. The civil war, which broke out almost immediately, was no doubt the cause of John van Eyck's leaving Holland and repairing to Flanders, where, as we have already seen, his brother Hubert was settled.

Philip III, Duke of Burgundy, who not only had heard of John's talent as a painter from members of his court, but had himself, as he tells us, personal knowledge of his skill, took him into his service as painter and " varlet de chambre " on the 19th of May, conferring on him all the honours privileges, rights, profits, and emoluments attached to the office; and further, to ensure the prior command of his services as court painter, he granted him a yearly salary of 100*l.* parisis (equal to £5, 11s. 1⅓*d.* contemporary English currency), payable in two moieties at Christmas and Midsummer, commencing as from Midsummer, 1425 (Doc. 6). Shortly after his appointment, John removed to Lille by order of the Duke, who gave him 20*l.* to cover his expenses (Doc. 3). The yearly rent, 23*l.* 2s., of the house which he occupied from Midsummer, 1426, to Midsummer, 1428 (Doc. 14), was also paid by the Duke.

In 1426, at some date prior to the 14th of July, John made a pilgrimage on the Duke's behalf, and in the following month was sent by him on a distant secret mission. During this latter absence his brother Hubert breathed out his soul to God on the 18th of September. For the pilgrimage and the mission John was paid 91*l*. 5*s*. on account in August, 1426 (Doc. 7), and, in October, 360*l*. in settlement (Doc. 9). The Duke, to mark his appreciation of John's services as painter and in other ways, twice made him presents in 1427—once of 20*l*. (Doc. 10), and on another occasion of 100*l*. (Doc. 11).

John started in 1427, in the company of the Duke's ambassadors, Sir John de Lannoy, Sir Baldwin de Lannoy, Baldwin d'Ongnies, the Bastard of Bavaria, and other councillors, on a second secret mission, apparently to Alphonsus V of Aragon. The embassy arrived in July, 1427, at Barcelona, whence the King had, fleeing from the earthquakes in Catalonia, departed by sea some days previously. They reached Valencia early in August, but soon returned to the Low Countries. They halted at Tournai from the 18th to the 20th of October. This embassy had, doubtless, been sent to Alphonsus V to obtain the hand of Isabella, eldest daughter of James II, Count of Urgel, a match which would certainly have appealed to the ambitions of a prince such as Philip. If this was the object of the mission, it was not crowned with success, for the lady Isabella, in September, 1428, married Peter, Duke of Coimbra, third son of John I, King of Portugal.[1] Mean-

---

[1] John I, King of Portugal, bastard son of Peter I and Teresa Lourenço, born 1357, succeeded his legitimate brother Ferdinand in 1385. By his marriage in 1387 to Philippa, daughter of John of Gaunt (Ghent), Duke of Lancaster, he had eight children : Blanche, died 1388; Alphonsus, died 1400; Edward, born 1391, succeeded to the crown ; Peter, Duke of Coimbra, born 1392, married Isabella, daughter of James II, Count of Urgel ; Henry, Duke of Viseu, born 1394; John,

while, in February, 1428, John van Eyck had returned to Lille.

With a view to the reduction of his household expenditure, Philip, on the 14th of December, 1426, had issued an edict as to its future constitution, and as to the salaries and wages of all persons attached to his court. By virtue of this document, which is preserved in the State Archives at Brussels, several pensions were cancelled and a number of servants dismissed. No mention being made therein of John van Eyck, the Receiver of Flanders stopped payment of his salary. Complaints to the Duke no doubt followed, for Philip, on the 3rd of March, 1428, issued letters patent (Doc. 12) to the official in question, explaining that he never intended to include the pension granted to John van Eyck among those that were to determine, and directing the payment of all arrears due, and the continuation of the half-yearly pension.

Philip, anxious to secure an heir and successor, decided, in the autumn of 1428, to send an embassy to John I, King of Portugal, to ask for the hand of his daughter Isabella. At its head was Sir John de Lannoy, lord of Roubaix and Harzeele, councillor and first chamberlain of the Duke; with whom were sent Sir Baldwin de Lannoy,[1] lord of Molembaix and Governor of Lille; master Giles d'Escornaix, Doctor of Laws, provost of Harlebeke, and court referendary; Andrew de Thoulongeon, esquire, lord of Mornay, councillor and chamberlain; John van Eyck, master John Hibert, secretary, Peter de Vauldres, esquire, cupbearer, John de Baissi, esquire, Oudot Brain, esquire, Hector Sacquespée, Baldwin

Grand-Master of the Order of Saint James, born 1400; Ferdinand, Grand-Master of the Order of Aviz, born 1402; and Isabella, born February 21, 1397, married Philip III, Duke of Burgundy, January 7, 1430, died December 17, 1472.

[1] See biographical notice appended to the description of his portrait, p. 149.

d'Ongnies, esquire, steward ; a clerk of accounts, and two pursuivants, Renty and Portejoie.[1]

John van Eyck was absent from Flanders a little over fourteen months—from the 19th of October, 1428, until Christmas, 1429.[2] The ambassadors and their suite embarked in two Venetian galleys then lying in the harbour of Sluus,[3] whence they sailed on the 19th of October. On the morrow they reached Sandwich, where they landed and put up, while awaiting two other Venetian galleys then at London. These vessels arriving on the 13th of November, they again set sail, but were driven by contrary winds to seek shelter, first in the port of " La Chambre " (Shoreham), then in Plymouth harbour, and next, on the 25th, at Falmouth, where they remained until the 2nd of December. Reaching Bayona,[4] in Galicia, on the 11th, they again set sail on the 14th, and two days later landed at Cascaës, a small seaport town to the west of the Tagus estuary, about fifteen miles from Lisbon, where they arrived on the 18th.

Learning that the King was at Estremóz,[5] at a distance of three or four days' journey, the ambassadors sent a letter by the herald Flanders, informing him of their arrival and of the object of their mission. At his request they advanced to

[1] At the ambassadors' leave-taking prior to setting out on their mission, the Duke gave the lord of Roubaix 200l. ; Sir Baldwin de Lannoy, master Giles d'Escornaix, Andrew de Thoulongeon, and John van Eyck (Doc. 13), 160l. each ; the secretary received 80l. ; while smaller sums were given to the other members of the suite.

[2] For a lengthy and contemporary narrative—of about 1430—of the journey of this embassy sent by Philip, Duke of Burgundy, to John, King of Portugal, to which John van Eyck was attached as the Duke's painter, see Weale, 1908, pp. lv–lxxii.

[3] Sluus, a town ten miles north-east of Bruges, was at that time an important harbour at the mouth of the Zwijn, an arm of the sea which ran up to Damme, the port of Bruges, but has long been choked up with sand.

[4] Bayona, a town on the Atlantic coast of Galicia, between Vigo and the mouth of the Minho.

[5] Estremóz, a small town in the province of Alemtéjo.

Arrayollos, whence, on the 12th of January, they repaired to Aviz,[1] in the province of Alemtéjo, where the King was staying. On the morrow they were granted an audience, and presented Duke Philip's letters. On the 14th master Giles d'Escornaix made the Duke's proposals known to the court in a Latin oration, to which a doctor of the King's Council replied, likewise in Latin. The ensuing few days were spent by the ambassadors in discussing with the council the Duke's proposals. The time necessarily occupied in settling the details Van Eyck devoted to painting the Infanta's portrait. On its completion the ambassadors despatched messengers to the Duke, two by sea and two by land, with the portrait and a full account of all that had been done—there were evidently two portraits as well as two copies of the narrative.

While awaiting the Duke's reply, the ambassadors went northwards through Portugal on a pilgrimage to Saint James of Compostella,[2] and journeying thence through the province of Valladolid, visited John II,[3] King of Castile, the Duke of Arjona,[4] Mohammed,[5] King of the city of Grenada, and

[1] Aviz, from 1161 the seat of a military religious order which gave its name to the second royal house of Portugal, through the accession to the throne, in 1385, of its Grand-Master, John, bastard son of Peter I.

[2] Santiago de Compostella, in Galicia, on the Sar, was a celebrated place of pilgrimage throughout the Middle Ages, the tomb of Saint James the Greater, the patron of Spain, being contained in the cathedral.

[3] John II, eldest son of Henry III. of Castile and Katherine of Lancaster, daughter of John of Gaunt. He succeeded his father in 1407, and died in 1454.

[4] Frederic de Castro y Castilla, a prince of the royal blood of Castile. He was created Duke of Arjona in 1423, but being suspected of treachery by John II, was in the course of 1429 confined in the castle of Peñafiel, where he died in the following year. Arjona is an ancient city in Andalusia, situated south of the river Guadalquivir in the province of Jaen.

[5] Mohammed VII, surnamed Abu' Abdillah, who reigned from 1424 to 1445; or perhaps Mohammed VIII, surnamed As-saghir, who usurped the throne in 1428, and was slain in 1430.

several other lords, countries, and places, returning through Andalusia to Lisbon, where they arrived at the end of May.

At the King's request, they went on the 4th of the following month to visit him at Cintra. That same evening Peter de Vauldres, who had made the journey by sea, arrived with the Duke's reply, which was at once communicated to the King and the Infanta. The marriage contract, having been drawn up, was duly signed in the presence of a notary at Lisbon, on the 29th of July, and the espousals solemnised on the following day. While preparations were being made for the bride's journey to Flanders, brilliant festivities were held.

At length, on Saturday, the 8th of October, the party, numbering two thousand, set sail in fourteen large vessels. By the morrow they had reached Restel, where they stopped until the 13th, when they proceeded to Cascaës, and thence put out to sea. Contrary winds compelled them to return to Cascaës on the 15th, and abide there until the 17th, when a fresh start was made, but foul weather supervening dispersed the fleet. Four of the principal vessels, and among them those that bore the Infanta and the most distinguished of her escort, managed, on the 22nd, to make the harbour of Vivero,[1] where, after a delay of four or five days, they were joined by a fifth vessel. The voyage was resumed on Sunday, the 6th of November; three days later the five vessels put into the harbour of Ribadeu.[2] Here the lord of Roubaix, who had suffered severely from sea-sickness, landed from the Infanta's vessel, but after some days' rest he embarked with Baldwin d'Ongnies and a few others on board two Florentine galleys bound for Flanders, and on the 25th of November the seven vessels put

[1] Vivero, in Galicia, near the river Landoure.
[2] Ribadeu, in Galicia, at the mouth of the river Eo.

out to sea together. Owing to a mistake of the pilot, the Florentine galleys narrowly escaped being wrecked near the Land's End ; the other five vessels entered Plymouth harbour on the 29th. The Florentine galleys left Lizard Point [1] on the 1st of December, and reached Sluus on the 6th. My lord of Roubaix hastened to inform the Duke of the safe arrival of his bride at Plymouth, and in confirmation of the glad tidings the Infanta and her party sailed into the port of Sluus on Christmas Day. The event was the occasion of great popular rejoicing. The marriage was duly solemnised at Sluus on the 7th of January, and was followed by a succession of festivities which lasted several days.

Van Eyck no doubt remained in the company of the ambassadors until the close of their mission, but whether he reached Sluus on the 6th or on the 25th of December it is impossible to say. He appears then to have taken up his abode at Bruges, whence, not long after, he was summoned to Hesdin by the Duke to receive instructions regarding certain matters on which he wished to employ him. For his journey thither and back to Bruges he received 19l. (Doc. 17).

In 1431–32 he bought from John van Melanen a house with a stone-gabled front in the Sint Gillis Nieu Straet, now the Goude Handt Straet, opposite the Schottinne Poorte. There, on some day between the 17th of July and the 16th of August, 1432, he received a visit from the burgomasters, John Van der Buerse and Maurice van Versenare, who, with other members of the town council, came to view some of the master's works. The magistrates on this occasion gave his apprentices a

---

[1] Called in the narrative (which is given at length in Weale, 1908, pp. lv–lxxii) "le Camp de Caisart," which would seem to be a corruption of Cap Lézard, just as "La Chambre" certainly is of Shoreham, and "Pleume" and "Falemme" of Plymouth and Falmouth. There is no tradition of any Roman *castrum* having ever existed near the Land's End.

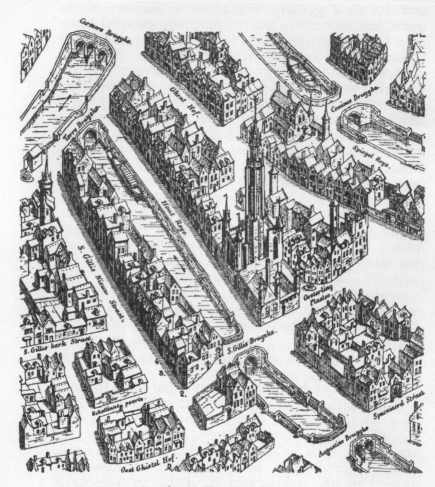

FROM THE BIRD'S-EYE VIEW OF BRUGES IN 1562, BY
MARK GHEERAERTS

1. House named Sint Gillis.
2.   „   „   Den Gentyl Pot.
3. John van Eyck's residence.
4. House built on the adjacent lane.
5. House named De Torre, renamed, in the sixteenth century, De
Goude Handt.

gratuity of 5s. g., duly entered in the accounts of the municipal treasurer (Doc. 18). Some months later, prior to the 19th of February, 1433, the Duke himself honoured his painter with a visit with the same motive, and gave his apprentices 25s. (Doc. 20). In April of the following year Van Eyck, having been occupied several days in attending to sundry affairs on behalf of the Duke and the Duchess, received 76l. in remuneration of his services (Doc. 21).

About this time he took to himself a wife. Her family name is not known. Some critics think she was a sister of Joan Cenani, the wife of John Arnolfini, an opinion founded on the apparent resemblance of their portraits, a resemblance no doubt accentuated by the similarity of their headdress ; the surmise, however, is strengthened by two details in the National Gallery picture—the peculiar wording of the inscription pointing to a connection between John van Eyck and Arnolfini, and the recently discovered fact that the Christian name of the painter's wife was Margaret (Doc. 31), of whose name-saint a carved figure surmounts the back of the chair at the side of the bride's bedstead, a present perhaps from her presumed sister. Against this, however, it may be urged that Saint Margaret was especially invoked by women in expectation of the birth of a child.[1]

The date of the marriage is not known, but by an order of the 30th of June, 1434, the Duke authorised the receiver-general of his finances to pay John Peutin, a goldsmith at Bruges, the sum of 96l. 12s. for six silver cups weighing 12 marks, presented in his name to Van Eyck at the baptism of his child, held at the font by Sir Peter de Beaufremont, lord of Charny, as the Duke's proxy (Doc. 22). This child would, in accordance with the custom of the

---

[1] See the remarks (p. 116) on the picture in the National Gallery, and on Arnolfini's portrait (p. 147) at Berlin.

time, have received the name of Philip or Philippina. Van Eyck had at least one other child, a daughter, Livina, who, in 1450, became a nun at Maaseyck.

About this time Philip granted Van Eyck, in lieu of the salary of 100*l*. parisis which had hitherto been paid in two half-yearly moieties, a life-pension of 360*l*. of 40 groats Flemish currency, equal to 4320*l*. parisis, without any reason being assigned for this enormous increase. Such increase may have been in part due to the fact that, after his marriage, the painter no longer took his meals with the Duke's household.

The accountants at Lille declined to register the letters patent granting this pension, and Van Eyck, justly annoyed, threatened, it appears, to throw up his appointment (Doc. 23), whereupon the Duke, who was about to employ him on certain great works and, as he says, could not find another painter equally to his taste nor of such excellence in his art and science, wrote on the 12th of March, 1435, bidding them register the patent and pay the pension without further argument or delay, under pain of incurring his extreme displeasure (Doc. 24).

In 1434 the municipality of Bruges had commissioned three of the principal sculptors of that town, James van Oost, Gerard Mettertee, and James van Cutseghem, to carve eight statues of Counts and Countesses of Flanders, which were to adorn the front of the newly erected Town-House. The sum of 5*l*. 10*s*. was paid for each statue, the stone included.

In 1435 these statues and the tabernacles in which they were placed were adorned with polychrome and gilding, six by John van Eyck, the other two by William van Tonghere [1] and John Van den Driessche. The painters received 5*l*. for the decoration of each statue, but to Van Eyck

---

[1] Was Dean of the gild of Saint Luke in 1441, and died in 1456.

the sum of 3*l.* 12*s.* was given in addition. He probably made the design of the eight statues for which the sum of 20*s.* g. was paid (Doc. 25). In the course of the same year the Duke made him a present of six silver cups purchased from John Peutin for 67*l.* 15*s.* (Doc. 26).

In 1436 John was once again sent on a secret mission to some distant place, for which he was paid 360*l.* (Doc. 27). In November of this year René, Duke of Anjou, who had fallen into Philip's power, was brought a prisoner to Lille, where he was detained until the 11th of February, 1437. It was probably during this period of his detention that he made Van Eyck's acquaintance.

In 1439 the receiver-general at Lille paid Van Eyck a sum of 6*l.* 6*s.* 6*d.* in reimbursement of moneys paid by him to an illuminator of Bruges who had adorned one of the Duke's books with 272 large and 1200 small capital letters (Doc. 28).

At Midsummer, 1441, John received 180*l.*, the amount of his pension for two quarters (Doc. 29). He had then in hand a large triptych for Nicholas van Maelbeke, provost of Saint Martin's, at Ypres, left unfinished at his death, which took place on the 9th of July of that year.[1] The great master, though not a parishioner, was, as a member of the Duke's household, buried within the precincts of the collegiate church of Saint Donatian (Doc. 30).

To the fabric of that church 12*l.* parisis were paid for his burial, and 24*s.* parisis for tolling the bell.

On the 21st of March, 1442, the Chapter, at the request of Lambert van Eyck, granted permission for the exhumation of his brother's corpse, and its reinterment in the church, near the font (Doc. 32); for this reinterment the sum of 12*l.* parisis was paid (Doc. 33); an anniversary Mass of requiem

[1] This picture is fully discussed at p. 135.

was also founded (Doc. 34), which continued to be
celebrated until the French invasion in 1792. The
following inscription was, probably in the sixteenth
century, engraved on a brass tablet, attached to
the last pillar on the south side of the nave, at the
foot of which was the great master's grave, covered
with a slab of white stone :—

> " Hic iacet eximia clarus virtute Ioannes,
>   In quo picturæ gratia mira fuit.
> Spirantes formas et humum florentibus herbis
> Pinxit, et ad vivum quodlibet egit opus.
> Quippe illi Phidias et cædere debet Apelles,
> Arte illi inferior ac Polycletus erat.
> Crudeles igitur, crudeles dicite Parcas,
> Quæ talem nobis eripuere virum.
> Actum sit lachrimis incommutabile fatum,
> Vivat [ut] in cœlis iam deprecare Deum."[1]

On the 22nd of July, 1441, the Duke granted
John's widow a gratuity of 360*l,* in consideration of
her husband's services, and in commiseration of the
loss she and her children had sustained (Doc. 31).
To one of these, Livina, he in 1450 made a present
of 24*l.* to enable her to enter the convent of Saint
Agnes at Maaseyck (Doc. 36), a convent to which
her father had presented some vestments (Doc. 37).

The brass tablet was stolen by the Calvinist
iconoclasts in 1578.

On the 28th of August, 1768, the Bruges Academy
of Fine Arts, being about to celebrate the fiftieth
anniversary of its foundation, petitioned the
Chapter for leave to erect a marble monument with
a medallion bust of John van Eyck and an inscription to his memory. This was granted, but the
Academy, finding the expense beyond its means,
had a medallion portrait painted by Paul De Cock
on a panel with a copy of the above inscription
beneath it, adding between the sixth and seventh

[1] MARK VAN VAERNEWYCK, Spieghel der Nederlandscher Audtheyt,
Lib. IV, cap. xlvii, fol. 117.

verses four lines composed by Father Fidelis of Courtray, a Capuchin friar :

"Ipse est qui primus docuit miscere colores,
 Hos oleo exprimere et reddere perpetuos.
 Pictores stupuere virum, stupuere repertum
 Quo perseverans est sine fine color ;"

and this chronostich at the end :

"hoC Ita restaVraVIt aCaDeMIæ zeLVs."

On the 23rd of May, 1782, the Academy removed this panel to their council-room, the Chapter having decided to whitewash the church and clear away all monuments and paintings attached to the pillars. Later on a painted wooden tablet, bearing this mendacious inscription, was affixed to the west wall :

D. O. M.

CI GIT	HIER RUST
LE CELEBRE	DEN ROEMWEERDIGEN
JEAN VAN EYCK	JAN VAN EYCK
QUI INVENTA	DIE UYTVOND
L'ART DE PEINDRE	D'OLIE SCHILDER
A L'HUILE	KONST
ET TREPASSA	HY STIERF
VERS L'AN	ONTRENT T JAER
M CCCC XL	M CCCC XL

R. I. P.

III

LAMBERT VAN EYCK

LAMBERT VAN EYCK, who is described in the documents as a brother of John, received in 1431 a monetary recompense (Doc. 15) for having on various occasions rendered a service to Duke Philip III. He survived John, and we hear of him as having applied for, and been granted, permission by the Chapter of Saint Donatian at Bruges to have the remains of John translated from the precincts (Doc. 32), and buried within the church near the font (*in ecclesia iuxta fontes*).

IV

MARGARET VAN EYCK

MARGARET, John van Eyck's widow, was left in reduced circumstances when her husband died, and Duke Philip, compassionating her misfortune, made her a present of 360*l*. g. (Doc. 31). She had, we know, an annuity of 2*l*. g. charged on the revenues of the town of Bruges. This she risked in the famous lottery drawn on February 24, 1446. Margaret had sold her house in the Sint Gillis Nieu Straat in 1444, when she went to dwell in the Oost Meersch, in a house named the Wild Sea, in the parish of Our Lady, where she was still living in 1456. We give particulars (p. 192) of a picture, now at Liége, that is traditionally assigned to her, and is held by some to bear her signature.

Whether John's putative sister Margaret ever really existed is a matter of much doubt. The lady—for whom a Christian name was not at first hazarded—is not mentioned in any document earlier than 1565, but by 1568 Vaernewyck, giving free rein to his imagination, alleged that her name was Margaret, adding that she remained a spinster, devoted herself to painting, lived in the same house as Hubert, and was buried by his side! We have little doubt that she was merely an airy conception of the over-fecund imagination of the poet-painter De Heere.[1]

[1] See *antea*, p. xiii, and p. 280; see also Brockwell in *The Athenæum*, April 18, 1908, p. 484.

V

LIVINA VAN EYCK

LIVINA VAN EYCK, the daughter of John and Margaret, took the veil in the convent of Saint Agnes at Maaseyck in 1450, being enabled to do so by the gift of 24*l*. (Doc. 36) from the Duke to her.

VI

HENRY VAN EYCK

HENRY would seem to have been a near relation, possibly a first cousin of Hubert, John, and Lambert. He was attached to the household of John of Bavaria at the time that John van Eyck was engaged in decorating the Count's palace. John IV, Duke of Brabant, the second husband of the unfortunate Jacqueline, on his arrival at The Hague, took him into his service at the request of members of the court. In consideration of the faithful service he had rendered his uncle, John IV appointed Henry van Eyck, on the 25th of February, 1425, to the post of master huntsman (" Jaghermeester "), with the same salary that previous holders of the office had enjoyed.

Henry, however, probably for the same reason as his kinsman, left Holland and entered the service of Duke Philip of Burgundy as falconer (" varlet des faulcons "). His name occurs in the list of the ducal household of the 24th of December, 1426. He is mentioned in the accounts of the receivers-general of the Duke's finances for the years 1433 and 1436, with the title of " garde de l'esprivier " and " espriveteur." In the latter year the Duke sent him on a secret mission, for which he was paid

14*l*. 2*s*., "pour aller en aucuns lieux secretz ou icellui seigneur l'envoya dont il ne veult aultre declaracion estre faicte." In 1444 he married Elisabeth, daughter of Louis Sallard, master-falconer of the Duke, who on that occasion made him a present of 100*l*. In 1452 he was living at Termonde, and in that year became a member of the confraternity of Our Lady established in the collegiate church of Saint Mary the Virgin ; in the register he is entitled "spoerwarier myns heeren." In 1461 he succeeded Sir William de Quienville as baillie of the town and territory of Termonde, which office he held until his death.

Dying on the 11th of November, 1466, he was buried in the church there, beneath a slab of blue stone adorned with an escucheon bearing Barry of eight *or* and *azure*, ensigned with a helmet ; crest, a falcon. In his epitaph he is styled "sparewannier, councillor and chamberlain of our gracious lord the Duke of Burgundy, Count of Flanders, and his high baillie of the town and territory of Termonde."

His widow died in 1505, and was buried in her husband's grave, as were also their son John, who died in 1523, and their daughter Katherine.

PLAN OF THE GHENT POLYPTYCH

INSIDE AND OUTSIDE

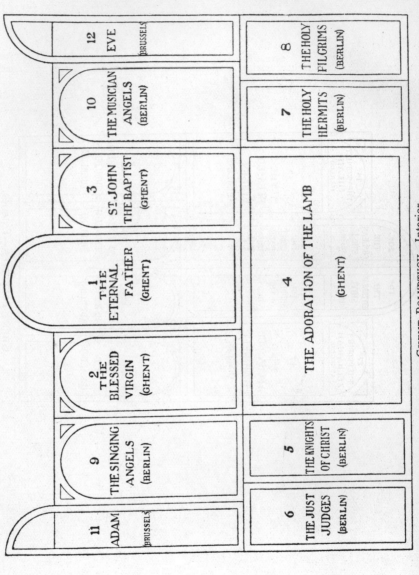

GHENT POLYPTYCH—Interior.

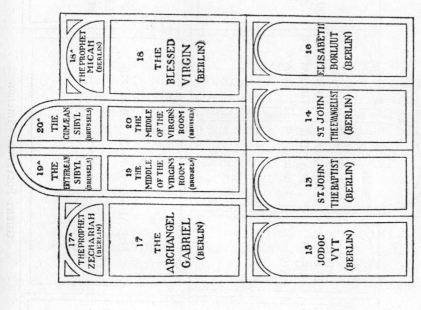

GHENT POLYPTYCH—Exterior.

EXPLANATORY REMARKS

THE terms *right* and *left* in the following pages denote the *dexter* and *sinister* sides of the picture—that is, the left and right of the spectator confronting the painting. Our descriptions, therefore, follow the rule of heraldry, where the escucheon is supposed to face the beholder.

The surface measurements of the pictures are given in feet and inches, as well as in metres. The abbreviations *h.* and *w.* indicate height and width.

Occasional reference in the following pages to "Weale, 1908" is intended to indicate Weale's book on "Hubert and John van Eyck: their Life and Work," published in 1908.

LIST OF PAINTINGS

A

By Hubert ; completed by John

B

By Hubert—but left uncompleted

29

C

By Hubert or John

D

By John or Hubert

E

By John—of which the Date is known

F

By John—of Uncertain Date

G

OF DOUBTFUL AUTHENTICITY

H

COPIES, VARIANTS, DERIVATIVES, AND IMITATIONS

CATALOGUE RAISONNÉ
OF THE PAINTINGS

CATALOGUE RAISONNÉ OF THE PAINTINGS

A

By HUBERT ; COMPLETED BY JOHN

I. THE ADORATION OF THE LAMB

THE GHENT POLYPTYCH

By HUBERT; completed by JOHN

THE INTERIOR

GHENT, CATHEDRAL—

The Four Central Panels

1. The Eternal Father. 6 ft. 11 in. × 2 ft. 8⅞ in. (2.10 × 0.835).
2. The Blessed Virgin. 5 ft. 6 in. × 2 ft. 5¾ in. (1.675 × 0.755).
3. Saint John the Baptist. 5 ft. 6 in. × 2 ft. 5¾ in. (1.675 × 0.755).
4. The Adoration of the Lamb. 4 ft. 5¾ in. × 7 ft. 11½ in. (1.365 × 2.42).

BERLIN, KAISER FRIEDRICH MUSEUM—

5. The Knights of Christ (No. 513). 4 ft. 10 in. × 1 ft. 8¼ in. (1.47 × 0.51).
6. The Just Judges (No. 512). 4 ft. 10 in. × 1 ft. 8½ in. (1.47 × 0.52).
7. The Holy Hermits (No. 516). 4 ft. 10 in. × 1 ft. 8¼ in. (1.47 × 0.51).
8. The Holy Pilgrims (No. 517). 4 ft. 10 in. × 1 ft. 8½ in. (1.47 × 0.52).

9. The Singing Angels (No. 514). 5 ft. 3½ in. × 2 ft. 3¾ in. (1.61 × 0.70).
10. The Angel Musicians (No. 515). 5 ft. 3½ in. × 2 ft. 3¾ in. (1.61 × 0.70).

BRUSSELS, ROYAL GALLERY—

11. Adam (No. 170). 7 ft. ½ in. × 1 ft. 3 in. (2.15 × 0.38). On the reverse of the panel, the Erythræan Sibyl.
12. Eve (No. 170). 7 ft. ½ in. × 1 ft. 3 in. (2.15 × 0.38). On the reverse of the panel, the Cumæan Sibyl.

THE EXTERIOR

BERLIN, KAISER FRIEDRICH MUSEUM—

13. St. John the Baptist (No. 518). 4 ft. 10 in. × 1 ft. 8½ in. (1.47 × 0.52).
14. St. John the Evangelist (No. 523). 4 ft. 10 in. × 1 ft. 8½ in. (1.47 × 0.52).
15. Jodoc Vyt (No. 519). 4 ft. 10 in. × 1 ft. 8¼ in. (1.47 × 0.51).
16. Elisabeth Borluut (No. 522). 4 ft. 10 in. × 1 ft. 8¼ in. (1.47 × 0.51).
17. The Archangel Gabriel (No. 520). 5 ft. 3½ in. × 2 ft. 3¾ in. (1.61 × 0.70). In the lunette is
17A. The Prophet Zechariah.
18. The Blessed Virgin (No. 521). 5 ft. 3½ in. × 2 ft. 3¾ in. (1.61 × 0.70). In the lunette is
18A. The Prophet Micah.

BRUSSELS, ROYAL GALLERY—

19. The Middle of the Virgin's Room. In the demi-lunette is
19A. The Erythræan Sibyl (on the reverse of the panel of Adam, No. 170). 7 ft. ½ in. × 1 ft. 3 in. (2.15 × 0.38).
20. The Middle of the Virgin's Room. In the demi-lunette is
20A. The Cumæan Sibyl (on the reverse of the panel of Eve, No. 170). 7 ft. ½ in. × 1 ft. 3 in. (2.15 × 0.38).

Marks says that the measurements of the panels, back and front, taken together as one picture, are—height, 23 ft. 9½ in. ; width, 42 ft. 5½ in.[1]

[1] Alfred Marks : *Hubert and John van Eyck*, 1903, p. 9.

POLYPTYCH, BY HUBERT AND JOHN VAN EYCK.   EXTERIOR

Plate IV

It has been calculated that the superficial measurement amounts to 12.3623 metres.

The seven panels of the upper zone of the interior contain twenty-three figures, and the five panels of the lower zone two hundred and nineteen figures, of which one hundred and seventy are to be counted in the panel of the " Adoration of the Lamb." There are ten figures on the exterior. In all an aggregate for the whole altar-piece of two hundred and fifty-two figures.

THE HISTORY OF THE ALTAR-PIECE

From 1432 until the Calvinist outbreak in 1566, the polyptych adorned the altar of the Vyts' chapel in the church of Saint John (now the cathedral of Saint Bavo) at Ghent. On August 19, 1566, two days before the iconoclasts broke into the church, it was taken up into the tower, and later on was removed for safety to the Town-House. While there it narrowly escaped being given to Queen Elizabeth, who had advanced money to the leaders of the Calvinist party ; this was due to the opposition of Jodoc Triest, lord of Lovendeghem, one of the collateral descendants of the donors. In 1584 it was brought back to the cathedral, and in September, 1587, replaced in the chapel. In deference, it is said, to an observation of Joseph II, when he visited the church in 1781, the panels representing Adam (11) and Eve (12) were removed from the church.[1]

The French agent did not care for the shutters, but in 1794 the four central panels (1, 2, 3, 4) were taken to Paris by the French Republicans, and there exhibited, on March 7, 1799, in the Central

[1] The numerals in brackets refer to the panels, the measurements of which are given on pp. 35–36.

Museum of Art, with other masterpieces acquired by
the French by conquest. The shutter-panels, after
being hidden for a while, were for safety stored in
the Town-House, and although claimed by Denon,
the Director of the Central Museum, who offered
in exchange some paintings by Rubens, were not
ceded, thanks to the firmness of the bishop, M. Fallot
de Beaumont.

After the battle of Waterloo, in spite of the violent
resistance offered by Denon, a considerable number
of the works of art carried off by the French were
brought back to Belgium, and on May 10, 1816,
the four central panels (1, 2, 3, 4) were replaced
over the altar ; but, owing to the general dislike
of shutters, the latter were not—a fatal mistake,
for, in the December following, during the absence
of the bishop, who had retired to France, the vicar-
general, M. Le Surre, a Frenchman, and the churchwardens, disposed of them for 3000 florins to the
dealer L. J. Nieuwenhuys, who sold them for 100,000
francs to M. Solly, by whom in turn they were sold
to the Prussian Government for 400,000 francs.
The panels representing Adam (11) and Eve (12)
were ceded to the Belgian Government in 1861, and
placed in the Brussels Gallery.

According to Mark van Vaernewyck, there was
also originally a predella representing Hell, painted
in distemper, which was effaced by a man who
cleaned the altar-piece, at some date before 1550.
If there be any truth in this statement, the subject
represented must have been Purgatory.

THE INTERIOR

The interior of the altar-piece is divided into
TWO ZONES. The Eternal Father (1) occupies the
centre of the UPPER ZONE, with the Blessed Virgin (2)
and Saint John the Baptist (3) at His either side ;

next, two groups of Angels, one group Singing (9), the other Playing Musical Instruments (10), and on the extreme right and left, respectively, Adam (11) and Eve (12) ; above the last two compartments, in demi-lunettes, the offerings of Cain and Abel, and the death of Abel at the hand of his brother. The panel beneath the three central compartments of the UPPER ZONE represents the Adoration of the Lamb (4) ; the remaining four lateral panels (5, 6, 7, 8) in the LOWER ZONE being filled by groups of saints advancing towards the centre.

The scheme of the picture, founded on the Vision of Saint John described in the fourth chapter of the Apocalypse, was no doubt more directly inspired by the liturgical Office for the feast of All Saints, and mediæval commentaries thereon.

A work constantly read at the time, the *Golden Legend* of the Dominican, Iacobus de Voragine, contains in the chapter on the feast of All Saints, an account of "a vision that happened in the second year after the feast was established by Pope Gregory. On a time when the sexton of Saint Peter had by devotion visited all the altars of the church, and had required suffrages of all the saints, at last he came again to the altar of Saint Peter, and there rested a little, and saw there a vision. For he saw the King of kings in an high throne sit, and all the angels about Him. And the Blessed Virgin of virgins came crowned with a right resplendishing crown, and there followed her a great multitude of virgins without number and continents also. And anon the King arose against her, and made her to sit on a seat by Him. And after came a man clad with the skin of a camel, and a great number of ancient and honourable fathers following him ; and after came a man in the habit of a bishop, and a great multitude in semblable habit following him ; and after came a multitude of knights without number, whom followed a great company of diverse people. Then came they all to fore the throne of the King, and adored Him upon their knees."

This work would certainly have been known to the theologian who drew up the scheme which Hubert carried out in such an admirable manner.

THE UPPER ZONE

The central panel of the upper zone out-tops the others. Here THE ETERNAL FATHER (I), solemn of mien, sits enthroned in majesty, crowned with a white tiara encircled with three bands of gold set with amethysts, diamonds, and a profusion of pearls ; its lappets adorned with crosses fall on each side of His face. Over a robe girt with a tasselled cord He wears a splendid red mantle fastened in front by a large circular jewelled morse, leaving visible one band of a precious stole crossed over His breast, showing the word "SABAωT" formed by pearls. The mantle has a jewelled border very deep at the foot and charged with the words "ANANX ANANXIN PEX PErῡ" (King of kings), partly in Greek characters. His right hand is raised in the act of blessing, while with the left He holds a sceptre of crystal with mountings and a finial of gold, of exquisite workmanship—this and a crown on the pavement at His feet, symbolising the kingdoms of the earth, are splendid specimens of the goldsmith's art. A brocaded cloth of honour stretched across the back of the throne shows, in gold on a dark-blue ground, a nest in which a pelican is billing its breast, the blood falling on its young and restoring them to life, this symbolical design being surrounded by vine-branches laden with grapes and a scroll inscribed "IHESVS XP̄S." The moldings of the high rounded back of the throne bear, in three concentric lines, the inscription :

✚ HIC Ē DEVS POTĒTISSIM' PP DIVINĀ MAIESTATĒ
✚ SV̄' OIM̄ OPTI' PP DVLCEDĪS BŌITATĒ
REMVNERATOR LIBERALISSIMVS PROPTER INME-
NSAM LARGITATEM.

(Hic est Deus potentissimus propter divinam maies-
tatem : summus omnium optimus propter dulcedinis boni-
tatem, remunerator liberalissimus propter immensam
largitatem.)

Along the front of the foot-pace is the legend :

VITA SINE MORTE IN CAPITE
IVVĒT SN̄ SENECTVTE I FRONTE
GAVDIV̄ SN̄ MERORE A DEXTRIS
SECVRITAS SN̄ TĪORE A SINIST'S.

(Vita sine morte in capite, iuventus sine senectute in
fronte, gaudium sine merore a dextris, securitas sine timore
a sinistris.)

The panel on the right is occupied by the BLESSED
VIRGIN (2) clothed in a blue dress with tight sleeves
buttoned at the wrist, and, over this, an ample
blue mantle, kept from slipping off the shoulders
by a tasselled cord attached to two jewels on its
border. A magnificent gold crown with symbolic
lilies and roses, above which float eight stars, binds
her long fair hair, which falls in wavy masses over
her shoulders. With both hands she holds an open
book, on a passage of which she is apparently
meditating. The neckband of her dress and her
mantle are bordered with precious stones between
two rows of pearls. The white damask cloth of
honour at her back has a diaper of gold flowers and
scrolls with Saracenic letters. The arched back of
her throne bears these words :

HEC Ē SPECIOSIOR SOLE ✚ SUP OĒM STELLARV̄
DISPOSICOĒ LVCI
CPATA ĪVEĪT PŌR CĀDOR Ē ĒIM LVCIS
ETERNE ✚ SPEC̄LM̄ SN̄ MAC̄LA DEI M.[1]

---

[1] The same inscription is found on the Dresden triptych (p. 85)
and on the altar-piece, with the portrait of Canon George Van der Paele,
in the Bruges Gallery (p. 123).

(Hec est speciosior sole super omnem stellarum disposicionem luci comparata invenitur prior, candor est enim lucis eternae : speculum sine macula Dei [maiestatis].)

On the panel to the left SAINT JOHN THE BAPTIST (3), an austere figure with long hair, thick beard, and bare feet, sits with hand upraised as though to emphasise the words of the Prophet Isaiah : *Consolamini, consolamini, popule meus*, in the book which lies open on his knees. Over a garment of brown camel's hair girt with a scarf, he wears an ample green mantle with an embroidered border studded with precious stones between two rows of pearls. A red cloth of honour suspended behind him has a floral pattern combined with an inscribed scroll. The legend on the back of his throne is :

+ HIC Ē BAPTISTA IOHĒS : MAIOR HOĪE :
PAR ANGLIS LEGIS
SV̄MA EWÄGELII SACIO APLOR VOX SILECIV
PPHETAR
LUCERNA MVN DMNI TESTIS

(Hic est Baptista Iohannes : maior homine : par angelis, legis summa, evangelii sanctio, apostolorum vox, silencium prophetarum, lucerna mundi, Domini testis.)

The pavement of these three panels (1, 2, 3) is composed of dull-red and dark-green tiles.

In the panel to the right of the Virgin (2) stands a choir of eight SINGING ANGELS [1] (9) in front of an oak lectern, on which an antiphoner lies open. Three other volumes lie on the stall from which the brass support of the lectern rises. The angels, one of whom, in front, is beating time with his

[1] "These angels," says Van Mander (fol. 200), amplifying the statement in strophe 5 of De Heere's ode, "are so skilfully painted that one can see the different key in which the voice of each is pitched." Two on the left are making an effort to sing high notes, but there is no further ground for his statement. (*See* A. W. AMBROS, *Geschichte der Musick*, vol. III, Introduction, "Die Zeit der Niederländer." Breslau, 1870.)

right hand, are vested in apparelled albs and copes —that worn by the foremost, over a dalmatic, is of crimson brocade, its orfreys embroidered with figures of saints in canopied compartments; the orfreys of another, with repeated representations of the Holy Face. Of the morses which fasten the copes of the two angels nearest the front, one, circular, shows a seated figure in high relief holding the tables of the Law, the other, quadrilobed, is set with precious stones. The end of the oak stall on the left is finely carved—the plinth, with an un- dulating stem of foliage and fruit, a lion sejant, and two apes; the panel above, with a fine figure of Saint Michael trampling on the dragon; the elbow-rests, with two seated figures of prophets.

On the frame at the foot of this panel of the Singing Angels is the legend :

MELOS DEO LAVS PHĒNIS GRĀR AC.IO

(Melos Deo, laus perhennis gratiarum actio).

In the panel to the left of the Baptist (3) are the MUSICIAN ANGELS (10). An angel,[1] in a mantle of black and gold brocade bordered with ermine, is seated on a metal faldstool, playing an organ.[2] The angel is accompanied by five others—one playing on a harp, another on a five-stringed viol of unusual form, having two semi-lunar sound-holes, but without cur- vatures. All the angels in these two panels have light wavy hair, kept in place by jewelled fillets, some of which are surmounted by crosses. The pavement in both panels is composed of tiles adorned with

[1] Van Mander calls this angel Saint Cecilia—an absurd mistake, into which he was led by De Heere's ode; repeated by Hotho, Waagen, Crowe, Kaemmerer, Champlin, and many others.

[2] This organ, a much enlarged regal, shows the original arrangement of the pipes, twenty-one in number, with a keyboard and a windchest. The Flemish organ in the triptych by Van der Goes, at Holyrood, has only fourteen pipes.

crosses, holy lambs, the ciphers of Jesus and Mary, ℧ and the mysterious " ΑΓΛΑ." [1]

On the frame at the foot of this panel of the MUSICIAN ANGELS (10) is the legend :

LAVDĀ[N]T EV̄[M] IN CORDIS ET ORGANO.

THE LOWER ZONE

The principal panel of the LOWER ZONE occupies the entire breadth of the three placed in the centre of the upper zone. It represents the *Adoration of the Lamb* (4) (Plate V). Upon an altar covered with a white cloth, in the middle of a flowery meadow gently sloping down to the front, stands the spotless Lamb, from whose breast a stream of blood flows into a chalice. The superfrontal of the altar bears in gold capitals the legend :

ECCE AGNVS DEI, QVI TOLLIT PEC[C]A[TA] MV̄[N]DI,

and the stole-ends,

IHES (Iesus), VIA, VĪTĀ (Veritas), VITA.

All around kneel purplish-winged angels, most of them clad in white girded albs shaded with blue or rose ; two at the farther corner on the right support the Cross with the title affixed, and the Lance ; the corresponding two on the left, the Pillar and the Reed with the sponge ; two others in front, swinging thuribles, are offering incense, symbolical of the prayers of the faithful ; eight others kneel at the sides in adoration.

In the centre of the foreground is a fountain, an

---

[1] " The awful AGLA, that most potent of all exorcisms," is composed of the initial letters of four Hebrew words : *Atha Gebir Leilam Adonai*, Thou art mighty for ever, O Lord. *See* GLASSIUS, Philologia Sacra, p. 438, and C. W. KING, in the *Archæological Journal*, XXVI, 229. See also *postea*, pp. 62 and 155.

THE ADORATION OF THE LAMB

GHENT: CATHEDRAL.

By permission of the Berlin Photographic Co.

Plate V

octagonal stone basin with a bronze annelated column rising in the middle ; on its summit stands an angel, from projecting gurgoyles beneath whose feet and from vases in whose hands, the water falls in tiny jets. Round the head of the basin is the legend :

HIC EST FONS AQVE VITE PROCEDENS DE SEDE DEI ET AGNI.[1]

To the right are grouped those who, under the Law or among the Gentiles, looked forward to the coming of the Redeemer : kneeling Prophets with upheld open books, Doctors, Philosophers, and Princes. All the figures in this group are deserving of close study on account of the variety of attitude and expression they display, three of the foremost standing, especially ; to wit, one—Vergil ?—draped in an ample white toga, holding an orange bough, and crowned with laurel ; the dark-bearded man on his right, in a red cap and dark-blue mantle, carrying a branch of myrtle, and the venerable-looking old man with a forked beard, draped in a red cloak.

Prominent in the corresponding group on the left are the Apostles, fourteen in number, including Saints Paul and Barnabas, barefooted, in light, greyish-violet robes, kneeling in adoration. Behind them stand three Popes, seven Bishops and Abbots, two Deacons—the one nearest the foreground, Saint Stephen, characterised by the stones he carries in his dalmatic ; the other, immediately behind him, Saint Livin, patron of Ghent, holding a crosier and the pincers with his tongue in them—and a number of monks and clerks.

Higher up the slope in the mid-distance are, on each side, flowering plants, shrubs, and trees, from between which two distinct groups are seen advanc-

[1] Apoc. XXII, I.

ing towards the centre. On the right, an army of Martyrs : Popes, Cardinals, Bishops, and other Saints, clad in blue vestments, with the exception of the pope in the front row, who wears a black dalmatic and cope embroidered with gold ; all carry palm-branches ; on the left, a multitude of Virgins, headed by Saints Dorothy, Katherine, Barbara, and Agnes, bearing their respective emblems and palms. Upon all fall illuminating rays from the Holy Dove poised high over the altar, and between the Eternal Father and the Lamb.

Through an opening between the wooded heights of the background, a river is seen winding towards the right from mountains in the far-off distance. To the right of the river rises the tower of Saint Martin's at Utrecht,[1] and on a height to the left, a city with numerous churches and towers, evidently inspired by, but not a faithful representation of, Köln ; farther to the left are numerous churches and towers, decidedly Rhenish in their architectural character ; these are balanced by trees and by a group of buildings on the extreme right, the most conspicuous of which, octagonal in shape, consist of three stories.

The background of the shutters of this lower portion of the altar-piece is formed by a landscape : that on the two dexter panels (5, 6) is wilder, more thickly wooded and rocky, with two church towers, a couple of castles, and, in the distance, snow-capped mountains,[2] whilst that of the other two panels (7, 8) with the exotic plants and deep-blue sky, wears a southern character.

To the right, on the sandy foreground strewn with fragments of rock crystal and coral, the KNIGHTS OF CHRIST (5)—C[H]RISTI MILITES—and the JUST

[1] Illustrated in Weale, 1908, p. 186.
[2] For the introduction of snow-capped mountains into pictures by the Van Eycks, see pp. 70, 78, 85, 89, 94, 159, 226.

THE JUST JUDGES   THE KNIGHTS OF CHRIST

Plate VI

JUDGES (6)—IVSTI IVDICES—are seen advancing towards the centre (Plate VI). Of the KNIGHTS OF
CHRIST, the foremost, Saint Martin, on a dapple-grey
steed, clad in armour over a gambeson with long
green sleeves, is crowned with a wreath of laurel,
and carries a banner charged with the arms of
Utrecht, *Gules*, a cross *argent*. On his left are two
others, also clad in armour, Saint George on a white,
and Saint Sebastian on a brown horse, the banner
of the former bearing, *Argent*, a cross *gules*, that
of the latter, *Gules*, a cross between four crosslets *or*.
Saint Sebastian carries a large silver buckler charged
with a red cross, bearing these words in gold capital
letters :

" D̄S FORTIS. ADONAY SABAOT VE
EMA[N]VEL I.H.S XPC AGLA."

Beyond and almost abreast of them are two more
figures : the farther on the line being an emperor,
Charles the Great (?), on a black charger ; on his
right a prince, in a fur cap, riding on a mule, doubtless Godfrey of Bouillon ; a third, in green, with a
small moustache, wears a fur hat with a crown
superposed ; whilst the one on the extreme right,
with a white beard, has a curious, helmet-shaped
head-dress, with a jewelled crown. Of the two
engaged in conversation in the background, the
younger wears a crown, the other a blue headkerchief, painted, as first observed by Dr. Six, over a
crown, the relief of which is clearly seen when the
panel is looked at in profile.

The immediate front of the outer panel of the
JUST JUDGES (6) is occupied by an elderly man
astride a white horse, with jewelled trappings and
green housings to his saddle. Of five others in
the front row, the third, wearing a black headkerchief and a dark-brown fur-trimmed dress, with a

red rosary round his neck, has his head turned towards those on his right;[1] all the others are looking towards the centre.

Upon the nearer of the two panels to the left (Plate VII) are the HOLY HERMITS (7)—HEREMITE S[AN]C̄[T]I —the foremost is Saint Paul, with at his left, leaning on a staff, Saint Anthony, and close to him another, bald-headed and bare-footed, these two telling their beads ; on their right, seven more ascetics, mostly dark-complexioned, with beards and tangled hair, are followed from behind some rocks by Saint Mary Magdalene, bearing her pot of ointment, and Saint Mary of Egypt.

On the outer panel are the HOLY PILGRIMS (8) —PE[RE]GRINI S[AN]C̄[T,]I—headed by Saint Christopher, a gigantic figure with a bushy beard, wearing a cap, and draped in a long red cloak ; he holds a pole in his right hand, and points to the centre, as if indicating the way to an old bare-headed man on his left, who is looking up to him ; they are followed by a dozen more of all ages, clad in a variety of garments. The background of these two panels, save on the extreme left, is a rocky bank, thickly covered with citron trees, above which rise a stone pine, some cypresses, and a couple of date-palms. Numerous birds are flying about above the figures in these two panels, among those high up above the hermits is a flock of cranes flying in V-like array.[2]

On the outermost panels of the UPPER ZONE, ADAM (11) and EVE (12) are represented (Plate VIII) by two nude figures painted with almost brutal exactitude direct from living models, just as they stood before the painter, who appears to have concentrated all his powers on the representation of these two

---

[1] For remarks on these two and other alleged portraits of the Van Eycks, see p. 229.

[2] For remarks on flocks of wild geese, see pp. 70, 78, 94, 130, 227.

THE HOLY HERMITS   THE HOLY PILGRIMS

BERLIN ROYAL GALLERY

By permission of the Berlin Photographic Co.

Plate VII

ADAM   EVE

BRUSSELS : ROYAL GALLERY

By permission of the Berlin Photographic Co.

figures. On the wall, above the round-headed niches in which they stand, their names are inscribed in capital letters, ADAM, EVA. In the demi-lunettes at the head of the panels are representations in high relief of the offerings of Cain and Abel, and the murder of the latter. On the frame at the foot of the panel :

ADAM NOS IN MORTE[M] PRECIPITĀT.
EVA OCCIDENDO OBFVIT.

THE EXTERIOR

The exterior is divided into three zones, each subdivided into four compartments. Those of the LOWER ZONE represent trefoliated round-headed niches : the two in the centre are occupied by full-length figures of SAINT JOHN THE BAPTIST (13) and SAINT JOHN THE EVANGELIST (14), in the form of statues on octagonal bases, which bear their names in incised capitals : S̄. IOH̄ES BAP^{TA}, and S̄. IOH̄ES EWAN^{TA}. The Baptist is pointing with his right hand to the lamb which he carries on his left arm, and the Evangelist is making the sign of the cross over the poisoned cup, from which three serpents are issuing. The heads of both saints are admirably modelled ; the dignified and earnest expression of the Baptist contrasting well with the delicate and youthful features of the beloved disciple. The drapery of both figures is rather heavy, with angular breaks in the folds. Both are painted in grisaille—the Baptist whiter and the Evangelist yellower—as if to imitate stone, but the folds of the draperies are in places so thin that they give the impression of having been drawn from carved box-wood or ivory models.

In the two outer niches the donors of the altarpiece (Frontispiece) are represented kneeling on a

D

pavement of square grey stones, their hands joined in prayer. On the right is JODOC VYT (15), bareheaded, in a simple robe of red cloth trimmed with brown fur, the sleeves of which, loose at the wrists, are of peculiar shape, pendent in bags from the elbows ; a large black purse hangs at his right side from the buckled belt which loosely encircles the body below the hips.

On the left is his wife, ELISABETH BORLUUT (16), dressed in a loose-sleeved gown of peach-coloured cloth with bright green lining, and a white linen collar turned down over it ; the hair is brushed back off her forehead into a net distinctly visible through the fine cambric veil lying flat over it and forming two folds above the temples, whence it hangs down over the ears and cheeks ; a white linen kerchief, spread over it, covers her head and shoulders.

These two figures, evidently faithful portraits, are inimitably lifelike. Jodoc's features, though not attractive, convey the impression of a capable and benevolent man. His forehead is low ; what little hair he has is cropped short ; his small grey eyes directed upwards, are without power ; his mouth is large, with a rather broad under-lip ; three warts, on the upper lip, nose, and forehead, are all faithfully set down. His wife is a really good-looking lady, with dignified matronly features full of expression.

A long room with a stone floor occupies the full breadth of the MIDDLE ZONE. Here the Annunciation is represented. On the extreme right, the ANGEL GABRIEL (17) in a white alb and voluminous mantle fastened over the breast by a circular morse, bends the right knee, and holding a lily-stem in his left hand, raises his right while greeting the Virgin. His wings are tinted of a soft hue. His light yellow hair, confined by a circlet with a jewel surmounted by a cross over the forehead, falls in wavy locks on to his shoulders.

At the opposite end of the room the BLESSED VIRGIN (18) is kneeling at a draped prayer-desk, from the open book on which she has half turned at the voice of the angel to express her humble submission to the Divine will and, with hands crossed on her bosom, is looking up with a mixed expression of timidity and wonder as the Holy Dove hovers over her head. She is enveloped in a gold-bordered white mantle, the ample folds of which cover the floor around ; it is fastened by a brooch set with pearls, and leaves her neck bare. Her light hair, confined by a cincture of pearls, falls behind her in undulating profusion. The clear evening light is streaming in through an arched window above the prayer-desk, and falls on both figures. In the background, beyond the prayer-desk, is a niche in which are a brass candlestick and a pewter ewer, and, on a shelf above these, a stoneware vessel and a couple of books. The angel's greeting : *Ave, gracia plena, Dñs tecum,* and the Virgin's reply : *Ecce ancilla Dñi* in calligraphic letters, are not inscribed on scrolls, but float in the air from the speaker, those of the reply from left to right, being inverted. At the rear of the lateral compartments is an ante-chamber with a couple of two-light round-headed windows with trefoliated tracery looking out on street views below ; on the sill of the window at the left end is a decanter of water, which catches a ray of light. This portion of the ante-chamber is seen through two arches supported by a Romanesque column resting on a low wall separating it from the inner chamber ; at the left end of the ante-chamber is a vaulted stone staircase with a two-light window, of which the upper part only is seen.

Strange to say, the background of the MIDDLE OF THE ROOM (19) (20) does not correspond with that of the extremities ; the portion of the ante-chamber connecting these being omitted, and the outer wall of the building being brought nearer to the foreground. The oak ceiling of the middle is at a higher level, and consequently the rafters do not unite; moreover, the street on to which the window of this middle portion looks is at a lower level than those seen from the ante-chamber, which discrepancies are a sufficient proof that these two and the adjoining compartments cannot have been painted by the same master. There is also a marked difference in the architectural character of the window of the central portion; on its left is a niche with a trefoliated *oculus* beneath which a brazen vessel is suspended over a basin, while a long towel hangs at the side.

Above the lateral compartments are two lunettes occupied by half-length figures of prophets. On the right, ZECHARIAH (17A) is seen in a loose-sleeved dress and ermine-lined mantle fastened over the right shoulder with a row of buttons. A large folio volume lies open before him, and he is pointing to a passage on one of the leaves which he holds up with his left hand. His complexion is brown and highly coloured, his beard crisp and vigorous; the features betoken a man of strong character; the ears are not seen, being covered by the lappet of his fur cap. A long scroll encircling this figure bears the prophecy :

Exulta satis filia Syō iubila, Ecce, rex tuus vēit, 9°.[1]

Inscribed on the frame beneath :

SACHARIAS PROPHETA.

In the lunette on the left MICAH (18A), bareheaded, wrapped in a mantle lined with vair, leans forward and looks down on the Virgin. A closed

[1] Zechariah IX, 9.

book lies at his side. Over his head is a scroll on which is inscribed the prophecy:

Ex te egredietur qui sit dominator in Israel, 5.[1]

Inscribed on the frame beneath:

MICHEAS PPHETA.

In the demi-lunettes above the middle portion of the Virgin's chamber are two kneeling figures: that to the right represents the ERYTHRÆAN SIBYL, (19A), clad in a loose white dress bordered with gold, a dark cape and a white turban striped with blue, placed on a kerchief which falls over her shoulders and down to below her waist. A pearl hangs from her right ear. The inscription on the frame below reads: *Sibylla Eritrea.* On a scroll above her head are the words:

Nil mortale sonā[n]s afflata es[t] numine celso,

slightly altered from a line of Vergil's *Æneid.*[2] The CUMÆAN SIBYL (20A), on the left, is more richly attired in a fur-trimmed robe open in front to the waist, displaying the gold-embroidered blue bodice of her under-dress. Her head-covering is a rich turban bordered with pearls, over which is thrown a veil. The inscription on the frame below reads: *Sibylla Cumana.* A scroll floating above her bears the words:

Rex advē[n]iet p[er] secla futur[us] sci[licet] i[n] carne,[3]

---

[1] Micah v, 2.
[2] Aeneid vi, 49 runs:

> Maiorque videri,
> Nec mortale sonans; afflata est numine quando
> Iam propiore dei.

[3] We know of only one other painting in which these prophetic words are attributed to the Cumæan Sibyl, a fresco of the sixteenth century in the Gonfalon oratory at Rome. See *Revue de l'Art chrétien,* XIII, 340. Arras, 1870.

taken, doubtless, from the acrostic prose sung in many churches on Christmas Eve:

> "Iudicii signum. Tellus sudore madescet
> E caelo Rex adveniet per saecla futurus
> Scilicet in carne presens ut iudicet orbem :
> Vnde Deum cernent incredulus atque fidelis
> Celsum cum sanctis aevi iam termino in ipso." [1]

THE INSCRIPTION

The names of the prophets and sibyls represented are inscribed on the portion of the frame separating the lunettes from the compartments of the middle zone ; those of the painters and the donor of the altar-piece, together with a chronogram recording the date of its completion, are on the foot :

> [Pictor] Hubertus eeyck · major quo nemo repertus
> Incepit · pondus · q[ue] Johannes arte secundus
> [Perf]ecit · Iudoci Vyd prece fretus.
> *Vers V seXta MaI · Vos CoLLoCat aCta tVerI.* [2]

In 1823 De Bast found in a manuscript collection of epitaphs and other inscriptions, compiled by Christopher van Huerne (died 1629), a copy of this inscription in which the first two words of the third line are given as *frater perfectus*. About the same time Waagen, who knew nothing of De Bast's discovery, had the green paint which covered the frame of the polyptych removed, thus revealing the inscription which he published, but, as was too customary at that time, with alterations of what he considered to be mistakes, substituting *ab Eyck* for *e Eyck*.

---

[1] A translation by Flaccianus from the Greek Sibylline Oracles given by him to Saint Augustine. See MIGNE, *Patrologiæ Cursus*, XLII, 579. He was given to understand that these verses were a translation from a Greek codex relating the poems of the Sibylline Oracle.

[2] If properly punctuated, the meaning is clearer :—Pictor Hubertus e Eyck, major quo nemo repertus, incepit ; pondusque Iohannes, arte secundus, perfecit, Iudoci Vyd prece fretus. Versu sexta Mai vos collocat acta tueri. The last verse contains the date of Sexta Mai, MCCCLLXVVVVII = 1432. For alternative readings, see p. 66.

The first two words of the third line were almost effaced,[1] and Waagen proposed *suscepit letus* as the probable correct reading; *suscepit* no doubt was suggested by *pondus*, which the author wrote instead of *opus*, probably because he could not think of a dissyllabic word that would rime with *opus*. The lines are Leonine hexameters with a double rime.

CRITICAL REMARKS

Probably no other picture has given rise to so much discussion as has this. Until recently every one accepted the tradition that the commission for its execution was given to Hubert van Eyck by Jodoc Vyt, and that he presented it to his parish church, now the cathedral of Saint Bavo at Ghent. But this tradition does not repose on any sure foundation. It is not warranted by the inscription on the frame, which does not say that Vyt ordered the picture, but merely that it was completed at his request.[2] It now seems probable that William IV of Bavaria, Count of Holland and Zeeland, gave the commission. His territory was in the diocese of Utrecht and province of Köln, which fully accounts for the prominent position given to the tower of Saint Martin's at Utrecht, as also to the adjacent view of Köln. Ghent was in no way connected with either Utrecht or Köln, but was in the diocese of Tournay and the province of Rheims. Again, the most prominent figure among the Knights of Christ is Saint Martin, the patron saint of Utrecht.

---

[1] Probably by the bolt which kept the shutters from flying open, or by the metal work to which the curtains that protected the exterior were attached.

[2] This inscription cannot have been put on the frame until after the 6th of May, 1432. If one may judge by the lettering, it was not painted by John, but doubtless by order of Vyt; had he given Hubert the commission to design and execute the altar-piece, that fact would certainly have been recorded.

The only saint especially connected with Ghent who is characterised by an emblem is Saint Livin, who was also much venerated in Zeeland. Probably at some time after the death of William IV in 1417 the picture was left on Hubert's hands,[1] and Vyt may have seized the opportunity of making a good bargain by acquiring the painting, on which Hubert continued to work until his death in September, 1426.

Until the sixteenth century the altar-piece was thought to have been both designed and executed by him. Münzer, in 1495, speaks of it as the work of one painter who was buried before the altar, and that painter was certainly Hubert. When the altar-piece was cleaned and restored by Blondeel and Scorel in 1550, the inscription on the exterior of the frame was discovered, and it became known that it was unfinished when Hubert died in 1426, and had been completed by his brother John. Then the apocryphal legend was invented and published by De Heere, and, soon after, amplified. It met with great success and universal acceptance.

Pursuant to the custom prevalent among the painters of that time of introducing their own portraits into the pictures they painted, two of the Just Judges (5) were fatuously fixed upon as being the portraits of Hubert and John.[2] These were copied over and over again and engraved, and figure to this day in most works on Netherlandish art. Later on the frame was repainted, the inscription forgotten, and the credit for the entire work given to John. The inscription was rediscovered in 1824, but, as already stated, with the two first words of the third line partly effaced.[3]

[1] See W. H. James Weale's remarks in the *Burlington Magazine*, vol. VI, p. 249, on the contention of Dr. J. Six, published in the *Gazette des Beaux Arts*, vol. XXXI, 171–187, Paris, 1904.

[2] For remarks on alleged portraits of the Van Eycks, see p. 230.

[3] The damage had no doubt been done before Christopher van Huerne copied the inscription.

Critics have been ever since discussing the part taken by each of the brothers in the work. Waagen, in 1822, was the first to tackle the question, but at the end of more than fourscore years the solution appears to be as far off as ever. Had the altarpiece come down to us in the state in which it was in May, 1432, there would have been a better chance of forming a correct opinion ; but this is, unfortunately, far from being the case.

It was cleaned and renovated by Lancelot Blondeel and John Scorel in 1550,[1] probably with loving care ; but since then it has undergone no less than four restorations. The first, in 1663, was by Anthony Van den Heuvel. In 1822 the four central panels suffered severely from a fire that broke out in the cathedral ; hot ashes fell on the altar, and the panel of the Adoration was split. A man named Lorent was employed in 1825 and 1828 to repair the damage, at the wage of 15 francs a day. He devoted eight days to the Virgin, twelve to the Eternal Father, fifteen to Saint John the Baptist, and eighteen to the Adoration of the Lamb. In 1859 these panels were again restored by Donselaer ; each of these restorations diminished the chance of forming a correct opinion.

It is only within the last few years that the discovery of the Turin miniatures (see p. 4), the critical examination of a certain number of pictures which have come to light, and the inter-comparison of these, have begun to shed fresh light on the subject. Those who have leisure and are curious to learn the reasons for the very various opinions of earlier writers, will find a fair summary of those put forth prior to 1864, in M. Ruelens' *Annotations*, pp. xxx to xxxix, or they can refer to the works enumerated in our bibliography (pp. 287 to 296).

---

[1] According to Mark van Vaernewyck, 1568, it had been previously cleaned by a man who effaced the tempera painting on the predella.

Jodoc Vyt, at whose expense the polyptych was completed by John van Eyck, was the second son of Sir Nicholas Vyt, a Receiver of Flanders, and of Amalberga Van der Elst. He owned several mansions in Ghent, and the lordships of Pamele in Brabant, and Leedberghe. After filling various offices, he was chosen burgomaster in 1433–1434. He married Elisabeth Borluut. They founded, on the 13th of May, 1435, a daily Mass to be said in perpetuity at the altar of the chapel which they had built [1] on the south side of Saint John's church, now the cathedral of Saint Bavo. Jodoc died in or about 1439, his wife on the 5th of May, 1443 ; neither was buried in the chapel they had founded.[2] Vyt's arms were *Or* two bars checky *azure* and *argent ;* his wife's *Azure* three harts salient *or*.

COPIES

Michael Coxcie, as we are informed by De Heere's ode (strophes 21–23), was commissioned by Philip II of Spain to make a copy of the polyptych. To its execution he devoted two years, 1557–1559, and received as remuneration 4000 florins. In 1559 this copy was sent to Valladolid, but was subsequently removed to Madrid and placed in the Old Palace, where it still was at the end of the eighteenth century. Annexed by the French in 1808, it was brought to Brussels by General Belliard. In 1820 the panels were separated ; the two representing the Blessed Virgin and Saint John the Baptist

[1] " In de cappelle ende ten autare die zij met haren goede van nieus hebben doen maken." Extract from the deed of foundation, communicated by M. Victor Van der Haeghen.

[2] For further biographical details regarding the Vyt family, see " Contributions à la Biographie Gantoise," published by V. Fris in *Bulletin de la Société d'Histoire et d'Archéologie de Gand,*" 1907, XV, pp. 85–89.

were in that year purchased by Max Joseph, King of Bavaria, and are now in the Munich Gallery (Nos. 97, 98). In 1823 the panels on which the Eternal Father and the Adoration of the Lamb are painted were bought by the Berlin Museum.[1] The panels forming the shutters were subsequently acquired by the Belgian Government, and are now attached to the four original central panels in the cathedral of Saint Bavo at Ghent. Coxcie's copy does not reproduce the Van Eycks' work entirely, for on the exterior the portraits of Vyt and his wife and the statues of the two Saints John are replaced by figures of the four Evangelists in grisaille, and the angel's salutation and Virgin's reply are omitted. On one of the dexter shutter-panels, moreover, portraits of Coxcie, of Charles V, and Philip II are substituted for three of the Knights of Christ. The other panels are faithfully but superficially rendered. They lack the finish of the originals and the splendour of their colouring. The draperies are simplified, the jewellery poorly copied, and there is a want of air and life in the whole.

A seventeenth-century copy on canvas of the inner portion of the polyptych, formerly in the chapel of the Town-House of Ghent, was sold on the approach of the French army under Pichegru to M. Charles Hisette, from whose widow it was purchased by Mr. Aders in 1819. It was afterwards in the collection of a Mr. Robinson, at whose sale, on the 26th of April, 1839, it was purchased by Mr. Lemme for £99, 15s., and by him was lent to the Exhibition of Art Treasures held at Manchester (No. 375) in 1857. It was subsequently acquired by the Antwerp Museum (No. 413–424). In it the order of the Holy Hermits and the Holy Pilgrims is, judging from a photograph, inverted.

[1] These Berlin copies (No. 525) measure 2.07 × 0.79, and (No. 524) 1.33 × 2.36.

A reduced copy in water-colours, made by Mr. E. Schultz, 1866–68, for the Arundel Society, now belongs to the National Gallery, and should preferably be exhibited in the room occupied by the works of early masters of the School. Another copy of the entire work was in the possession of the late Professor Sepp of Munich. The Berlin Photographic Company have published excellent photo-engravings of all the panels, three-tenths of the size of the originals, and also copies in colour of two of the panels at Berlin.

DRAWINGS

In the Louvre are two silver-point drawings on paper, which Crowe (p. 66) considers to be the original designs for the outermost panels of the upper zone ; the figure of Adam, " a small facsimile of the picture, that of Eve somewhat different, the head more in profile." They are certainly late fifteenth or early sixteenth century copies, wanting in firmness ; the head of Adam is bent slightly downwards, with quite a different expression to that in John van Eyck's painting. At the foot of the sheet is an elegantly draped figure of a woman, and on the reverse six figures : a mother standing with a child in her arms, a man seated on a chair with a volume lying open on his knees, and four women wearing caps of a decidedly German type. Another drawing after the Adam and Eve is preserved in the Library at Erlangen (Kaemmerer, 38). The Berlin Museum possesses an early sixteenth-century sketch of the angel Gabriel.

BIBLIOGRAPHY

In the following notes we have confined ourselves to the mention of articles treating of this altar-piece exclusively, not included in the general bibliography, and to the more important works issued since 1870.

1781. REYNOLDS, Sir Joshua, in his Journey to Flanders in 1781 (Works, II, 254, 1798), says this painting contains " a great number of figures in a hard manner, but there is great character of truth and nature in the heads, and the landscape is well coloured."

1870. "THE ADORATION OF THE LAMB." In *Notes and Queries*, 4th Ser., VI, 385, 550 ; VII, 150.

1872. CROWE, 57 : " The whole of the outer part may have been executed under supervision by the pupils of the Van Eycks. The three great figures of the Father, Mary, and Saint John, and those of Adam and Eve, are undoubted works of Hubert."

1887. BODE, 212 : " There can be no doubt that the composition of the entire work is due to Hubert, who in addition covered all the panels and finished or nearly finished the whole of one row. I recognise his hand and his exclusively in the paintings on the exterior, particularly in the superb portraits of the donor and his wife." He attributes the three figures of God, the Blessed Virgin, and Saint John the Baptist, entirely to Hubert. In the two panels of the angels another hand has added cold tints, violet and rose, to the original warmer flesh tones. Adam and Eve are certainly the work of one hand, whether Hubert's or John's ; the hand of the latter is recognisable in the five lower panels, especially in the central one. Hubert's work is far superior to that of John, who laboured under a great disadvantage in that he had to complete a work already far advanced, and to which, until his brother's death, he had remained an entire stranger.

1887. CONWAY, 133, considers the Adoration panel to be certainly the work of John.

1894. REBER, 104–106. The entire work designed by Hubert. God, the Blessed Virgin, Saint John the Baptist, and the Adoration of the Lamb, with the exception of the landscape, painted by him ; the landscape of this and the other panels by John, who certainly painted Adam and Eve. Is in doubt as to who painted the Annunciation.

1898. KAEMMERER, 10–38, strangely says that the Last Judgment was represented on the predella, for which there is no authority, and where it would have been entirely out of place. He is of opinion that Hubert designed the whole work, and executed the three central figures of the upper zone and the greater portion of the Adoration of the Lamb beneath them ; and that all the rest was executed by John. He says that the shutters on which Adam and Eve are painted are more than 30 centimeters taller than the central panel, which they covered when closed.

1898. LABAN, 33–43, points out that whereas in the upper zone and in the central panel of the lower zone the whole arrangement is at once seen to be strictly symmetrical, the plan adopted in the four shutter-panels of the lower zone is altogether different, in that the means by which symmetry is attained are there ingeniously disguised.

1899. SEECK, 68–70, after a careful examination of the altarpiece, arrives at the following conclusion : the portraits of Vyt and his wife, the five central panels of the upper zone, the Knights of Christ, the Just Judges (with the exception of the bare-headed man in the background, added by John), and the statue of Saint John the Evangelist, were painted by Hubert ; but the base on which the last stands was altered by John. The statue of Saint John the Baptist and the two outer shutters with Adam and Eve, and the reverse, were painted by John ; the remainder partly by Hubert and partly by John. He puts forward a theory (pp. 10, 11) that John was an excellent calligrapher, but that Hubert could not write ; one example that he gives in support of this is the occurrence of the Gnostic Agla,[1] which he thinks has no meaning.

1900. VAN DEN GHEYN, Quelques Documents inédits à propos de deux tableaux célèbres. In *Bulletin de la Société d'Histoire*, Gand, VIII. 201–208. A full account of how the panels now at Berlin came to be sold.

1900. VOLL, 42–62, takes the central figure of the upper zone to be Christ, whereas it is clear that it is a figure of the Eternal Father, the Son being represented by the Lamb, and the Holy Ghost by the Dove. The three central panels, he thinks, were painted by John in his early days, but are now so obscured by dirt and dust that it is difficult to arrive at a positive decision on the point. The two panels with the angels he also

---

[1] See pp. 44 and 155 ; also *Kunstchronik*, N.F., XII, 261.

attributes to John. The splendid portraits of Vyt
and his wife, which he rather depreciates, present the
greatest difficulty to him, and he considers that they
were drawn by Hubert, but entirely coloured by John.
The other panels of the exterior, those of the lower
zone and Adam and Eve, were painted by John after
his return from Spain. In short, John over-painted
all his brother's work, and therefore must be looked
on as the painter of the entire work ! No wonder this
critic considers it a misfortune that the inscription
on the frame was brought to light.

1901. BODE, 127.

1902. LAFENESTRE, 132–135.

1902. HYMANS, 14. The figures of Adam and Eve may
with sufficient probability be assigned to Hubert.

1902. HULIN, Catalogue, 9. There can be no doubt here :
the figures of Adam and Eve are certainly the work
of John, not of Hubert.

1902. C. PHILLIPS, in the *Fortnightly Review*, October, pp.
592–600, says :—

" The conception, and in a great measure the
realisation, of the three great figures above—the
Eternal in the vesture of a Sovereign Pontiff in the
centre, the Virgin, robed and crowned, on His right,
Saint John Baptist on His left—are manifestly Hubert's.
The three figures bear the closest and most unmis-
takable relation to those in the ' River of the Water
of Life.' But surely here the hand of Jan has travelled
over his brother's work, making more wonderful still
the jewels and the robes, but hardening to severity the
majesty of the Eternal, and bringing the Virgin and
the Saint John nearer to earth !

" For the astonishing force and directness, for
courageous facing of material truth, for splendour of
colour and miraculous power of execution, these
'Singing Angels' are the most wonderful section of
the whole work. Nothing in Netherlandish art can
match them.

" The famous inscription on the lower wings of
the altar-piece tells us that—

" ' Pictor Hubertus e Eyck, maior quo nemo
repertus Incepit ; pondus que Iohannes, arte secundus, frater perfecit, Iudoci Vyd prece, fretu . . . '
—that is to say : ' The painter, Hubert van Eyck,

greater than whom there is none to be found, commenced (this picture); the heavy work was, at the request and expense of Jodoc Vydt, completed by his brother John, who in art comes next after him.'

"In taking this inscription into consideration, in estimating it at its true worth as an authority, we must bear in mind that it was put in by John on the completion of his labours, and that he had in view, not only his brother's posthumous fame and his own present artistic position, but the remuneration of his share in the work by the worthy citizen of Ghent, to whom for his piety, and his munificence, and his discernment, the world owes so great a debt of gratitude.

"The 'Adam' and 'Eve' are unmistakably the work of Jan van Eyck: audaciously and naïvely true portrait-figures of a man and a woman as they presented themselves to the steadfast, searching gaze of the mighty realist.

"More unmistakably than anywhere else, save in the 'Adam' and 'Eve,' is the hand and the spirit of Jan to be traced in the magnificent portraits of the donor, Jodocus Vydts, and his spouse Isabella, two of his masterpieces of patient realisation, and, above all, of intense vitality and individual character."

1903. MARKS, 8, praises the wonderfully faithful renderings of the exotic plants represented, which he unhesitatingly attributes to John.

1903. ROSEN, 62–91, enumerates the various trees and plants, and criticises the representation of these and of the rocks and landscape.

1904. WEALE, 26–28.

1905. FIERENS, 176–215, attributes nearly everything to John, but thinks fit to give Hubert the glory of having conceived and designed the three central figures of the upper zone—a concession which, he says, it is difficult to refuse to traditional opinion; but at the same time, one must recognise that only one painter could thus model their draperies and the face of the Virgin, and display such splendid colour, which painter was John van Eyck. He says the altar-piece was designed c. 1420, and satisfies himself as to the date at which, in his view, each panel was painted, the Adoration of the Lamb and the face of the shutters on each side being the first, and the whole of the exterior the last to be executed. He repeats Kaemmerer's statement that the Last Judgment was represented on the predella, giving, however, by mistake Vaernewyck and Van Mander as his authorities.

1905. MUTHER, I, 60, 70–72, attributes the figures of the Eternal Father, the Blessed Virgin, Saint John the Baptist, and the angel musicians to Hubert ; all the rest to John, who he thinks altered Hubert's design.

1905. DURAND-GRÉVILLE. L'Inscription latine du retable de Gand. In *Bulletin de la Société des Antiquaires*, 258–260. Gand.

1906. HEINS. La plus ancienne vue de Gand. In *Bulletin de la Société d'Histoire et d'Archéologie de Gand*, 115–126. The view seen from the window of the Virgin's chamber represents a street in Ghent.

1906. MAETERLINCK. Une œuvre de Van Eyck mimée à Gand au XVe siècle. In *Bulletin de l'Art ancien*, 215–216. An account of a mystery play given at Ghent on the occasion of the joyous entry of Philip III, Duke of Burgundy, after the battle of Gavere, 23 April, 1458. It represented the Adoration of the Lamb as pictured in the altar-piece. The stage was 28 feet high and 53 feet broad. It is interesting to note that the principal Knights of Christ in this play were SS. George, Victor, Maurice, Sebastian, and Quirin.

1907. BERGMANS, P. Représentation du Retable de l'Agneau mystique, en tableau-vivant, à Gand, 1458. Belgium : Fédération Archéologique. *Annales*, XX, ii, 530.

1907. MONCHAMPS, GEORGES. L'Inscription du retable de l'Agneau. In *Leodium*, v, 5–6. Liége.

1907. REINACH, 221, thinks that John's share was confined to the two magnificent portraits of the donors.

1908. ROMÉ, N. DE. La Part d'Hubert van Eyck dans le Retable de l'Agneau Mystique. In *Musée*, v, 56.

1908. WEALE, 56. " After a careful study of all that has been written on the subject, I see no reason for changing my opinion that the only portions of the altar-piece entirely due to John are both sides of the shutters on the face of which Adam and Eve are represented. These and the panels at Berlin are in a better state of preservation than those remaining in the cathedral at Ghent, and therefore offer the least difficulty to those who may wish to try and solve the problem of who painted each portion."

E

1910. REINACH, T. L'Inscription du "Retable de l'Agneau" des frères van Eyck. In *Gazette des Beaux Arts*, 4 P., IV, 5. Accompanied by a photographic reproduction of the inscription.

1911. DOEHLEMANN, 399–401, 405.

1911. VAN DEN GHEYN, Canon G. A propos de la vente des volets de l'Agneau Mystique. In *Bulletin de l'Académie Royale d'Archéologie de Belgique*, IV, 157–182. Anvers.

1912. WEALE and BROCKWELL. There seems nothing material to add to the conclusions arrived at in the past, except to express the belief that, if younger men can manage to spare the time to go through the countless documents that still remain to be explored among the national and municipal archives of Holland and Belgium, persistent effort will in time be well rewarded. It may yet come to be proved that the polyptych was originally commissioned by William of Bavaria for the royal chapel at The Hague. It has not been established that the picture was begun at Ghent, nor have we any record of the year when Hubert first arrived there.

It may be of use to set out the various alternative readings that have been suggested in the first three lines of the inscription (see p. 54) :—

In line 1 : e Eyck, *Eeyck*, and ab Eyck.
In line 2 : *pondus* and opus ; *que* and quod ; *secundus* and secondus.
In line 3 : Frater perfectus ; opus perfecit ; suscepit letus ; frater perfecit ; perfecit letus ; letus perfecit and [*perf*]*ecit*.
Of these the reading we now adopt is here given in italics.

We have printed (p. 54) the fourth line of the inscription in italics to denote that the pigment used differs from that of the first three lines.

A DONER PROTECTED BY SAINT ANTHONY

COPENHAGEN : ROYAL GALLERY

Plate IX

B

By HUBERT

But Left Uncompleted

II. A Donor protected by Saint Anthony

Plate IX

Copenhagen : Royal Gallery (Catalogued, No. 63, as being by Petrus Christus).   Oak.   1 ft. 11¼ in.×1 ft. ¼ in. (0.592× 0.312).   Acquired in 1764.

Dexter shutter of a triptych.   A man of middle age kneeling in the foreground of a landscape, his hands joined in prayer.   He wears a red, loose-sleeved gown trimmed with fur and girt with a belt from which hangs a purse.   He is protected by Saint Anthony, who, clad in a black habit marked with the tau cross and bell, lays his right hand encouragingly on his client's shoulder.   The ground at the foot of the rocks behind the saint, and the hillside on the left, are overgrown with the palmetto. In the background on the extreme left, beyond a line of bushes, is a castle of considerable size, in the entrance and bay window of which, as well as on the open platform, figures of the household are discernible.

On the reverse of the panel was a figure, in grisaille, of the Angel Gabriel, of which very little now remains.

The purse attached to the donor's cincture figures in a portrait attributed to Peter Christus, in the collection of the late Mr. George Salting, and bequeathed by him to the National Gallery (No. 2593) in 1910. It was possibly one of the properties of the Van Eycks, acquired by Christus from John's widow.

This is the dexter shutter of a triptych, of which the exterior represented the Annunciation ; the centre panel of the interior, Our Lady and Child, or some subject from the life of Our Lord; and the shutters, the donors with their patron saints. Above this triptych would have been placed, in accordance with the general custom, a statue of the saint in whose honour the altar was erected. There can be little doubt that it formed part of an altar-piece formerly in the church of Saint Saviour, at Ghent, painted by Hubert van Eyck for Robert Poortier, a burgher of Ghent, and Avesoete his wife, founders of the altar of Saint Anthony in that church, as we learn by their last will dated the 9th of March, 1426, just six months before Hubert's death. At that date the altar itself was not yet completed, and the altar-piece and statue of Saint Anthony were still in master Hubert's workshop.

The will, of March 9, 1426, of Robert Poortier and his wife is preserved in the Archives of the town of Ghent.

1872. CROWE, 143. Much in the spirit of John van Eyck, and perhaps one of the best efforts of Christus.

1875. CLEMENT DE RIS, in *Gazette des Beaux Arts*, 2 P., XII, 408. Fine and firm, energetically modelled and powerfully coloured. In a perfect state of preservation. He adds that, as by that time framed, it was the dexter panel of a diptych, the corresponding part being a mediocre " Holy Family " by an imitator of Van Dyck !

1900. WEALE, in *Revue de l'Art Chrétien*, 5 S., XI, 285 ; in the *Nineteenth Century*, No. 285, p. 789 ; and in *Zeitschrift für bildende Kunst*, N.F., XI, 253–255.

1901. SEECK, in *Kunstchronik*, N.F., XII, 258, says that the treatment of the rocks and vegetation in this picture

THE THREE MARYS AT THE SEPULCHRE

RICHMOND : SIR F. COOK

Plate X

presents close analogy to that of the landscape in the Turin picture of Saint Francis. He believes it to be by Peter Christus, but accounts for its being so far superior to his other works by the supposition that it was painted under Hubert's supervision, and probably not entirely without his collaboration.

1901. WEALE, in *Gazette des Beaux Arts*, 3 P., xxv, 477.

1904. DVOŘÁK, 183, thinks that this picture dates from the middle of the fifteenth century, and accepts its attribution to Peter Christus.

1905. FIERENS, 119, considers the landscape to be very fine, and similar in style to that in the Turin Saint Francis.

1906. VOLL, 47.

III. THE THREE MARYS AT THE SEPULCHRE

PLATE X

Richmond, Surrey : Sir Frederick Cook. Oak. 2 ft. 4 in. × 2 ft. 11 in. (0.715 × 0.89).

Prior to 1472 in the possession of Philip de Commines. In the eighteenth century it belonged to James Wynckelman, Lord of 't Metersche, whose collection was sold at Bruges, May 4, 1770. It was acquired by M. Bernard Bauwens, at whose sale, August 8, 1826, it was bought by a dealer. In 1854 it was in private hands at Antwerp, and was purchased by Mr. William Middleton, of Brussels. At the sale of his collection at Christie's, January 26, 1872 (No. 140), it was bought as a work by " Van Eyck " for £335 by a Mr. Johnson, from whom it was acquired by Sir J. C. Robinson, and from him it passed to the late Sir Francis Cook.

In the centre of the foreground the empty sepulchre is seen with its displaced cover lying slantwise across it. On the cover an angel is seated, wearing an alb and a stole crossed over his breast. He holds a golden sceptre in his left hand, and has

his right raised as he announces the Resurrection of
the Lord.   To the right have just arrived the three
holy women.   Magdalene is pictured kneeling at the
foot of the sepulchre, with one hand resting on the
pot of ointment set on the edge of the tomb, the
other slightly raised in astonishment at the angel's
words.   Her   companions   stand   a   little   farther
back, wrapt in wondering silence.   In front of the
sepulchre two soldiers in armour, and, on the left,
a third, lie fast asleep.   In the foreground palmettos
are growing, and flowering plants, amongst which
are the mullen, teasel, white nettle, and flag-lily.
In the rising background, between brown rocks, a
number of men on foot and on horseback are making
their way along a winding road leading to a fortified
town crowded with numerous houses and towers.
Snow-capped mountains [1] beyond rise to the sky,
relieved here and there by light fleecy clouds and
crossed by a flight of wild geese.[2]   The sun has just
risen, but is hidden from view by rocks on the right ;
the effects of light falling on the towers crowning
the hills on the left—the centre of the town remaining in shade—are admirably rendered.   Oddly
enough, the light in the foreground of the picture
comes from the opposite side, suggestive, perhaps,
of moonlight.[3]   In the lower sinister corner is an
escucheon in grisaille, charged with a chevron
between three escallops and a bordure ; and surrounded by a collar of the Order of Saint Michael.
This was evidently added between 1469 and 1472,
as the Order was instituted by Louis XI of France
in 1469, and the only member of it who bore these
arms was Philip Van den Clyte, better known as

[1] For remarks on the introduction of snow-capped mountains into
Eyckian pictures, see pp. 46, 78, 85, 89, 94, 159, 226.
[2] For remarks on the flocks of wild geese or cranes in paintings by
the Van Eycks, see pp. 48, 78, 89, 94, 130, 227.
[3] For remarks as to the lighting of this and other Eyckian pictures,
see p. 220.

Philip de Commines. His treasonable practices having come to the knowledge of Charles the Bold, his estates were confiscated on the 8th of August, 1472, and all his goods sold.

The picture is not in a perfect state of preservation. The blue drapery of one of the women standing on the right, and the heads of both, have suffered. Portions of the sky and some of the buildings in the background have been overpainted since 1870. The fore part is best preserved.

" Formerly, as shown by the coat of arms in the lower right corner, in the possession of Philip de Commines (1445–1509). The Hebrew inscriptions have been deciphered as : ' Jesus, the man of Ephratha, Messiah, Peter the first . . . apostle John here in the land of Israel in the year of . . .' "— Extract from the private catalogue of Sir Frederick Cook, p. 11.

Exhibited : London : Burlington House, Old Masters, 1873, No. 171 (as the work of John van Eyck) ; Burlington Fine Arts Club, 1892, No. 11 (as John van Eyck (?)) ; New Gallery, 1899, No. 9 (as John); Bruges : Early Netherlandish Masters, 1902, No. 7 (as Hubert, about 1410). London : Guildhall, 1906, No. 1 (as Hubert). London : National Loan Exhibition, 1909–10, No. 75 (as Hubert).

1855. Otto Mündler held this to be an authentic work by John van Eyck. See CROWE, 1857, p. 98.
1872. CROWE, 113. The numerous details of armour are given with extreme care ; the landscape is very attractive.
1873. *The Athenæum*, January 11, p. 55.
1892. *The Academy*, No. 1051, 25th June, p. 619.
1893. TSCHUDI, in *Repertorium*, XVI, 101. The types are those of John van Eyck ; the treatment of the foreground like that of the Pilgrims and the Hermits in the Ghent polyptych ; the colour charming, and the light effects of the setting (!) sun remarkable.

1898. KAEMMERER, 50–52, remarks that in this picture there is much that charms us in the Ghent polyptych, but that the tone is weaker, the perspective of the landscape background unhappy, and the architecture confused. He believes the picture to be an early work contemporary with the Fountain of Living Water, and th nks it may have been painted for the church of the Holy Cross at Bruges, founded by the brothers Peter and James Adornes, after their return from a pilgrimage to the Holy Places in 1427. He says that the arms agree with those of the Honyns, a family allied to the Adornes, and that the picture may have been presented to the church by them. The maternal grandmother of the brothers was a Honyn, but the arms of the two families differ essentially ; Commines bore *Gules* a chevron *or* between three escallops *argent* and a bordure *or*, and Honyn *Sable* a chevron between three escallops *or*, without a bordure.

1899. SEECK, 22, 68. One of Hubert's earliest works. The figures of the angel and the guards give evidence of a rising understanding of living movements to which John never attained. The perspective is faulty ; the feet of the soldier farthest from the front are larger than those of his companion in the foreground.

1899. FRIEDLAENDER, 6, 7.

1900. FRIEDLAENDER, in *Repertorium*, XXIII, 246. Remarkable among the works of Van Eyck.

1900. WEALE, in *Zeitschrift*, N.F., XI, 252, 254.

1900. WEALE, in *Revue de l'Art Chrétien*, 5 S., XI, 253.

1900. *The Athenæum*, May 26.

1900. VOLL, 103–106, assumes this to be a late work, and then goes on to prove, by comparison with John's paintings, that it cannot have been painted by him.

1902. FRIEDLAENDER, in *Repertorium*, XXVI, 68. An early work by John van Eyck, painted before 1425 ; shows closer points of resemblance than any other painting to the panel representing the Adoration of the Lamb.

1902. FRY, in the *Athenæum*, September 20, p. 388.

1902. HULIN says : " This important picture is one of the most precious documents for the history of art. It is clearly by the same hand as the central panels of the Ghent altar-piece. As, on the other hand, it differs in many respects from the authentic works of John, it must, I think, be attributed to Hubert."

1902. GUIFFREY, 474, describes the angel as *blessing* the holy women, and the sun as *setting ! !*

1902. A writer in the *Times Literary Supplement* of November 21, suggests that the view of Jerusalem in the background of this picture was painted from a sketch made on the spot. Mr. A. Marks (1903, January 16) replied that the view could not possibly have been made on the spot, as the walls, pulled down in 1239, were not rebuilt until 1542 ; moreover, the sun is represented as rising in the west. For further correspondence, see the issues of February 27, March 6, and April 3. It seems far more probable that the painter composed his background on slender information 'derived from Ludolph of Saxony, or on some pilgrim's description of the Holy Places.

1902. PELTZER, Alfred. In *Monatsbericht über Kunstwissenschaft*, II, 393.

1903. M., War Hubert van Eyck in Jerusalem ? in *Frankfurter Zeitung*, 24, iv.

1903. WEALE, in the *Burlington Magazine*, I, 42. The rocks and the foliage of the trees, imperfectly rendered, prove this to be an early work.

1903. WEALE, F.C., 12–13.

1903. *The Athenæum*, September 13, p. 356.

1903. ROSEN, 110. The rocks are well painted, not so the pine, the branches of which are represented as springing from the trunk at the same height.

1905. FIERENS, 115, thinks the picture is posterior to the Van Eycks.

1906. VOLL, 47, declares it to be of several decades' later date than the Van der Paele altar-piece.

1907. VISCOUNT DILLON, in private letter, writes : " I am afraid no importance can be attached to the armour. It is pseudo-classic."

1908. BROCKWELL, in the *Athenæum*, April 18, p. 485, says : " Mention might have been made of Filippo Parlatore's *Flora Italiana*, in which the *Chamærops humilis* is fully considered. Moreover, a reproduction of part of Bernardus de Breidenbach's woodcut of the " Civitas Iherusalem " of 1486 would have been welcome."

1908. WEALE, pp. 201–202. " Thought by many to be posterior to the Van Eycks. The writer believes he was the first to suggest that this painting, which shows intense religious feeling, was not painted by John, but by Hubert ; this opinion was fortified, as he pointed out in 1902, by the analogy their lighting presents to that of the miniature of Saint Julian conveying passengers across a river in a storm, in the Turin Hours. The Eyckian authorship has been recognised by many.[1] There are, however, two details in the Richmond picture which militate against the ascription. The sleeping soldier in front of the sepulchre has at his side a helmet with two necklames, a detail which, several of the best authorities on mediæval armour declare, proves that part of the painting to be posterior to 1440 ; the handpiece by his side has also a later appearance."

1912. WEALE and BROCKWELL. The armour here shown was not that commonly worn, but similar to that used in theatrical pageants. It being, as Lord Dillon points out, pseudo-classic, too much stress need not, perhaps, be laid on the deductions which some critics might draw from it in regard to the dating of the picture as a whole.

IIIA. THE THREE MARYS AT THE SEPULCHRE

PLATE XI

A painting of " The Three Marys at the Tomb," clearly derived from this picture, was until lately in the collection of the Countess A. A. Komarowsky at St. Petersburg. It is now in the possession of M. Theobald Heinemann of Munich. It may perhaps have been executed at Granada by Peter Christus II.

1905. NEUSTROIEFF, A. In *Zeitschrift für bild. Kunst*, N.F., XVI, h. ii, 292–3.
1909. WEALE. *Peintres Brugeois : Les Christus*, p. 20–21.

[1] *See* HULIN, 1902, p. 2, No. 7, and DURRIEU, 1903, p. 18.

THE THREE MARYS

Plate XI

PORTRAIT OF A GOLDSMITH

Plate XII

C

By HUBERT or JOHN

IV. Portrait of a Goldsmith

Plate XII

Hermannstadt, Hungary : Gymnasium, Bruckenthal Collection.   Oak. $6\frac{7}{8}$ in. $\times$ $4\frac{1}{2}$ in. (0.174 $\times$ 0.11).[1]

HALF-LENGTH portrait of a rather melancholy-looking man, probably a goldsmith, turned to the right, the .face seen in three-quarters.   He is clad in a brown dress open in front, showing the straight collar of a black tunic.   His head-gear is a scarf of blue silk, the lappets of which, with their edges cut in the shape of foliage, fall in front of his shoulders. In his right hand he holds a ring ; his left hand and forearm rest on the frame.

Dark background ; on it an imitation of Albert Dürer's cipher, and the date 1497, additions probably made by the person who enlarged the panel by adding a strip all round, so that it now measures 21 centimeters by 15 centimeters.

It is a remarkably fine picture, though it has suffered at the hands of a restorer.   The fashion of cutting the edges of the headkerchief into leaf-shapes came into vogue in the Netherlands at the end of the fourteenth century, and died out before 1425.   The back of the panel was formerly painted.

Exhibited : Bruges, Early Netherlandish Masters,

---

[1] This picture is at present lent for a period of two years to the Alte Pinakothek at Munich.

1902, No. 15 (as the work of John).   London, Guildhall, 1906, No. 2 (as by Hubert).

1901. BODE, in *Jahrbuch der kgl. Preussischen Kunstsammlungen*, XXII, 119. The admirable rendering of the personal character, the delicate execution of the drawing, and the beauty of the colour, prove this to be a genuine Van Eyck.

1901. FRIEDLAENDER, in *Repertorium*, XXIV, 480.

1902. HULIN, 15, attributes this portrait to John.

1903. WEALE, in the *Burlington Magazine*, I, 42, attributes the work to Hubert.

1903. FRIEDLAENDER, in *Repertorium*, XXVI, 68, attributes this portrait to John.

1905. FIERENS, 151, compares it with the portrait in the National Gallery, No. 290 (see p. 108), and thinks that, although contemporary, it cannot be ascribed with certainty to John van Eyck.

1906. VOLL, 45.

1906. PHILLIPS, in *The Daily Telegraph*, May 3. " The exquisite sensitiveness of the characterisation, the pathetic character of the piece altogether, point to the elder brother Hubert, as Mr. Weale has already indicated. But the firmness of the modelling, especially the masterly painting of the brow and ear, remind the specialist forcibly of John."

V. OUR LADY AND CHILD, SAINT ELISABETH OF HUNGARY, SAINT BARBARA, AND A CARTHUSIAN

PLATE XIII

Paris : Baroness Gustave de Rothschild.   Oak.
1 ft. 2 in. × 1 ft. 7 in. (0.355 × 0.48).

The scene is laid in a portico or cloister paved with light-blue tiles and slabs of porphyry and verd antique. Five round arches supported by cylindrical columns of green and black marble rest on the low wall which separates the cloister from the outer world. In the centre the Virgin-Mother stands erect beneath a canopy with a cloth of honour

OUR LADY AND CHILD, S. ELISABETH OF HUNGARY, SAINT BARBARA AND CARTHUSIAN

PARIS: BARONESS GUSTAVE ROTHSCHILD

By permission of Messrs. Levy & Co., Paris

Plate XIII

which reaches to the ground, and completely shuts out the view through the central arch. With her right arm she tenderly supports the Divine Infant against her bosom, her left hand retaining His feet.

The Child holds a crystal orb surmounted by a gold cross, and raises His right hand in the act of blessing a Carthusian kneeling in the foreground, his hands joined in prayer. He is protected by Saint Barbara, who has one hand on his right shoulder, while with the other she holds out a palm to the Infant Christ. In a garden of flowers hard by stands her other emblem, a tower with a window of three lights, through which is seen against a blue star-sprinkled background a statue of the god Mars—his name on its base—which has the appearance of an antique bronze.

On the left of the Virgin stands Saint Elisabeth of Hungary (rather than Saint Anne) holding three crowns superposed ; her dress is a grey violet trimmed with white fur, a plain linen coif, and over all an ample black cloak. Saint Barbara is habited in green with a crimson mantle kept in place by a cord attached to its jewelled neckband ; her hair, confined by a cincture of pearls, falls behind her in undulating masses. The Blessed Virgin is represented in a dark-red loose-sleeved dress trimmed with ermine and girt with a green-and-gold sash ; over this she wears a blue mantle edged with gold embroidery studded with precious stones. Her hair, confined by a jewelled band, falls over her shoulders. A rich Oriental carpet with fringed border is spread on the pavement beneath her feet. The cloth of honour behind her, and the canopy above, are of red-and-green brocade, with blue floral ornaments within double ogee-shaped compartments bordered by undulating foliage enwreathed with scrolls bearing the salutation, *Ave, gracia plena.*

The background, seen through the open arches, is an exquisite bit of landscape, through which a broad river winds its way towards the front from distant snow-capped mountains.[1] On the left it skirts the crenelated walls of a city with many churches and towers of an English type of architecture, including an exact reproduction of old Saint Paul's as seen from the south ;[2] the buildings and busy streets are represented with marvellous distinctness. On the river is a boat crowded with passengers to the city, another is moored to the bank ; swans, too, enliven the scene. On the near bank is a country waggon with a party looking out at the side from beneath its canvas covering. In the half-distance the river is spanned by a bridge of seven arches ; numerous horsemen and pedestrians are wending their way across or looking down at the water, in which they are faithfully reflected. In the sky above we espy a flight of wild geese.[3] The outlook through the arch on the extreme right of the panel is on to a thickly wooded hillside, beyond which are buildings, including a church backed by distant mountains.

The Carthusian portrayed may be Dom Herman Steenken, of Zuutdorp, a village to the south of Axel, in Zeeland.[4] He entered the Order at Diest, and, at an early age, was appointed Vicar of the Nunnery of Saint Anne *ter Woestine* (in the desert), near Bruges, an office which he held from 1402 to 1404, and again from 1406 until his death in the odour of sanctity on the 23rd of April, 1428.

We have been unable to find any documentary

---

[1] For snow-capped mountains, see pp. 46, 70, 85, 89, 94, 159, 226.
[2] See the view reproduced in Weale, 1908, p. 186.
[3] For remarks on wild geese, see pp. 48, 70, 89, 94, 130, 227.
[4] This Carthusian is again portrayed in the " Madonna and Child, Saint Barbara, and a Carthusian," formerly in the collection of the Marquess of Exeter, but now in the Berlin Gallery (No. 523B), where it is catalogued as a work by Peter Christus. See p. 170.

evidence as to the date of this picture, which we think must have been painted between 1406 and 1420, certainly before the Rolin altar-piece. Dom Herman wrote a number of books, two of which have been published : " De Regimine Monialium Liber I." and " Sermones quinquaginta super Orationem Dominicam," printed respectively at Audenaerde in 1480 by Arnold De Keysere, and at Louvain in 1484 by John of Westphalia.

A notice of Dom Herman, kindly extracted from the Archives of the Order and communicated to us by Dom Peter Pepin, informs us that he was in the habit of repairing for prayer to a chapel dedicated to Saint Barbara not far from the nunnery.

The Charterhouse of Saint Anne was destroyed in 1578, when the nuns took refuge in Bruges. This picture appears to have come later on into the possession of the Archduke Ernest of Austria, Governor of Belgium from 1592 to 1595.

The panel has been enlarged all round by a thumb's breadth.

1857. MÜNDLER. A very fine authentic piece by John van Eyck.

1872. CROWE, 113.

1894. TSCHUDI, in *Jahrbuch der kgl. Preussischen Kunstsammlungen*, xv, 65–70.

1898. KAEMMERER, 93–97. The landscape has undeniably an Eyckian appearance, but the figures are hard and lifeless. The painter was unable to represent living persons.

1899. SEECK, 18–22, 68. Certainly by Hubert, and earlier than the smaller Berlin picture.

1900. VOLL, 81–84, dates this picture about 1437, and praises highly not only the landscape background, but also the modelling and colour of the figures ; he thinks it is certainly an original work by John.

1900. WEALE, in *Revue de l'Art Chrétien*, 5 S., XI, 285 ; *Zeitschrift für bildende Kunst*, N.F., XI, 254 ; and *Nineteenth Century*, No. 285, p. 789.

1901. WEALE, in *Gazette des Beaux Arts*, 3 P., XXV, 475.

1903. DE MONT, 52, looks on this picture as the work of one of John's pupils, and declares the river and town to be a servile copy of those in the Rolin altar-piece!

1904. KERN, 14, plate viii.

1905. FIERENS, 121. The most remarkable of the pictures attributed to Hubert, for the splendour of its colour and the extraordinary precision of the details of the background.

1907. S. REINACH, Tableaux inédits ou peu connus, 1–7, Paris.

1908. WEALE, p. 186. Although the river in the background has been held to be the Rhine, the cathedral to the left of the river is unmistakably Old St. Paul's seen from the south.

VI. PORTRAIT OF AN ESQUIRE OF THE ORDER OF SAINT ANTHONY (or THE MAN WITH THE PINKS)

PLATE XIV

Berlin : Kaiser Friedrich Museum, (No. 525A). Oak. 1 ft. 4 in. × 1 ft. ½ in. (0.40 × 0.31).

Formerly in the collection of Philip Engels, sold at Köln, May 16, 1867, described in the catalogue (No. 17), as the portrait of a Duke of Burgundy, by Hubert van Eyck. Purchased by Mr. Suermondt of Aachen, for 5500 francs, it was in 1874 bought from him for the Berlin Gallery.

Portrait of a man of about sixty years of age, turned slightly to the right, the face, deeply wrinkled and closely shaven, seen in full light. He wears a loose grey robe, trimmed with fur, just low enough at the neck to let his red satin damask tunic and some fine linen be seen. A high, broad-brimmed fur hat covers his head. Around his neck is the collar of the Order of Saint Anthony, to which is suspended a tau cross with a tinkling bell attached thereto, all of silver, here painted grey with white lights. His hands originally rested on a parapet,

AN ESQUIRE OF THE ORDER OF S. ANTHONY

BERLIN : ROYAL GALLERY

Plate XIV

still discernible under the coat of paint with which it has been covered. He holds a bunch of red-and-white pinks in the right hand, on the fourth finger of which he wears a handsome ring. The background is dark.

The Order of Saint Anthony, founded in 1382 by Albert of Bavaria, Count of Hainault, was originally a military order, to which only noblemen and doctors were admitted. Under Jacqueline of Bavaria, in 1420, it ceased to be a military, and became simply a pious society, and by an ordinance of the chapter dated the 11th of June of that year, it was decided that the tau and bell to be worn by knights and ladies should be of silver gilt, and those by esquires and their wives of plain silver.[1]

Engraved by Gaillard, 1869, H. 0.15, B. 0.17. Facsimile by the Berlin Photographic Company, 1907.

Exhibited : Bruges : Early Netherlandish Paintings, 1867 (No. 3).

The individual here portrayed figures as one of the Kings in an Epiphany picture belonging to Count Landsberg Velen, at the castle of Gemen, Velen, ascribed to the "Master of the Family of Saint Anne," and supposed to have been painted for a member of the Hackeney family, between 1480 and 1510.

1867. E. GALICHON, in *Gazette des Beaux Arts*, XXIII, 484.
1869. W. SCHMIDT, in *Zeitschrift für bildende Kunst*, IV, 357.
1869. BÜRGER (Thoré), in *Gazette des Beaux Arts*, 2 P., I, 7–10, thinks this portrait was painted between 1432 and 1436.
1872. CROWE, 95.

[1] The insignia of the Order are thus described in the statutes : "Ung coller, et pendant à icellui coller une pottence et au debout d'icelle une clocquette sonnant." Portraits of the members formerly adorned the chapel at Barbefosse, and it is possible that this may have been one of them. See MS. in the Bibliothèque Royale, Brussels, Fond Goethals, 707.

F

1874. WOLTMANN, in *Zeitschrift für bildende Kunst*, IX, 195.
1887. BODE, in *Gazette des Beaux Arts*, 2 P., XXXV, 214.
1898. KAEMMERER, 62, dates this portrait *c.* 1433.
1899. SEECK, 26–30, 68, attributes it to Hubert, and thinks it was painted before 1422.
1900. VOLL, 113 119.
1900. KAEMMERER, 72–74.
1901. BODE, 120–122.
1903. DE MONT, 55, dates this portrait 1436.
1908. HYMANS, 48, calls this a portrait of John of Bavaria, notwithstanding that the collar of the order of Saint Anthony shows that the wearer was a simple esquire.
1908. FIERENS-GEVAERT, I, II, maintains that it is a portrait of John of Bavaria, and repeats the contention that it is a fine replica of a lost original.
1912. PHILLIPS in a letter to Brockwell writes : " I am afraid that I agree with Carl Voll in calling in question the ascription of the famous ' L'Homme à l'Œillet ' to Jan van Eyck. The modelling is so utterly different from that of his other portraits, save one other in Berlin. I know this is rank heresy, and that no specialists save Voll accept this view."
1912. WEALE and BROCKWELL. Probably by Hubert, to whom it was assigned at Köln in 1867. There is no record of its having at an earlier period been ascribed to John.

VII. OUR LADY AND CHILD, SAINT KATHERINE, SAINT MICHAEL, AND THE DONOR

PLATES XV AND XVI

Dresden : Royal Gallery (No. 799). Oak. $10\frac{3}{4}$ in. × $8\frac{1}{2}$ in. (0.275 × 0.215) ; shutters, $10\frac{3}{4}$ in. × $3\frac{1}{4}$ in. (0.275 × 0.08).

Formerly in the collection of Everard Jabach ; No. 266 in the inventory drawn up on July 17, 1696, described as by Hubert van Eyck, and valued at 6 livres.

The exterior represents the Annunciation—a general arrangement. On the dexter panel, the archangel, on the sinister, the Blessed Virgin, as two

OUR LADY AND CHILD ENTHRONED

Plate XV

ivory statues on octagonal pedestals in square-headed niches ; Gabriel in an alb and an ample mantle, holding a sceptre, and with his right hand slightly raised as he delivers his message ; Mary, the gathered folds of her mantle in her left hand, raises her open right in token of submission to the Divine will ; the Holy Dove is flying down to her.

Interior. In the nave of a three-aisled building Our Lady sits enthroned in a graceful attitude, with both hands supporting the infant Saviour seated nude on a linen cloth spread over her lap. The Child's left hand rests on His knee ; with His right He holds a long white scroll, bearing the exhortation : *Discite a me quia mitis sum et humilis corde*, in black minuscules with a blue initial. His Mother wears a dress of deep blue, with a jewelled border at both neck and wrists, and over this an ample mantle of deep red crimson edged with gold embroidery interspersed with precious stones. Her long fair hair, drawn back behind the ears and confined by a cincture adorned with rubies, sapphires, and pearls, falls in undulating masses over her shoulders. Two rings adorn the third finger of her left hand. Her feet rest on a rich carpet spread over the throne-steps and pavement. The principals of the throne are crowned by bronze figures. Those in front represent a pelican in its piety and a phœnix ; and those at the back, the sacrifice of Abraham, and David and Goliath. A cloth of honour of rich brocade is suspended by cords from the columns of the triforium ; the pattern is of foliage, flowers, and golden fruit, with greyish-white lions and light-blue unicorns on a black ground. Two rows of cylindrical marble columns, which divide the nave from the aisles, rest on Gothic bases, but are crowned by late Romanesque capitals of interlaced branches of foliage ; above these, on corbels, are statues of saints in tabernacles with crocketed canopies ; the piers in the background have storied capitals. The lancet windows of the clerestory are filled with grisaille glass, those of the aisles with roundels.

On the dexter shutter is a portrait of the donor, presumably Michael Giustiniani, a man of about fifty, kneeling on the pavement, his hands apart, uplifted in prayer. His robe of olive-green, full-sleeved, and with a high collar, is trimmed with fur ; he wears a wig. A deep crimson head-covering with the lappet falling over the right shoulder, a plain gold ring on the little finger of the right hand, and pointed shoes, complete his costume. He kneels, protected by Saint Michael—a manly but youthful figure, with auburn locks and wings of rainbow hue, attired in bronze armour, with a gorgeret and jupon of mail ; his left arm supports his helmet ; his lance rests against his right shoulder ; while a strap across his chest supports a buckler at his back. The capital of the pillar immediately behind him is adorned with a group of warriors, one of whom has probably been suggested by a figure of Bellerophon and the Chimæra, or of Alexander, on some ancient sarcophagus.

On the sinister shutter Saint Katherine, patroness of the learned, is represented standing, reading a book supported on her left hand ; with her right she holds a sword which rests on the pavement, where lies the other instrument of her martyrdom, a wheel of torture. Her dress is of bright blue with close sleeves terminating above the elbows, with long lappets hanging from thence, and over it she wears a sideless robe of ermine with a blue skirt. A richly jewelled coronet confines her fair hair, which is drawn off her forehead and falls on her back. Her only other ornament is a simple necklace with a pendant jewel. A two-light window at her back is filled with roundels, and its traceried head with glass of various colours ; the lower

S. MICHAEL AND THE DONOR   S. KATHERINE

Plate XVI

portion is open, and through this tiny space, about 5 centimeters by 1¼, we are afforded a view, beneath a brilliant cloudless sky, of a town, fields with trees, delicate blue hills, and beyond them sparkling snow-capped mountains.[1]

The frame bears the following texts, painted to represent inscriptions in relief in the hollows of the moldings. On the centre panel :

HEC EST SPECIOSIOR SOLE + SVP[ER] O[MN]EM
  STELLARV̄[M] DISPOSICIONE[M] LVCI
COMPA[RA]TA Ī[N]VĒ[N]ĪT̄[VR] PRIOR: CĀ[N]DOR Ē[ST]
  ENĪ[M] LVC[I]S ETERNE + SPEC[V]L̄[V]M S[I]ÑE
  MACVLA DEI MAIESTATIS +
EGO QVASI VITIS FRVCTIVICAVI SVAVITATE[M]
  ODORIS : E[T] FLORES MEI F[RV]CTVS
HONORIS + HONESTATIS · EGO M̄[ATE]R PVLCHRE
  DIL[E]C[TI]Ō[N]IS + TIMORIS + MAGNITVDINIS +
  S[AN]C̄[T]E SPEI+[2]

On the dexter panel :

HIC EST ARCHANGELVS PRIN-
-CEPS MILICIE ANGELORVM, CVIVS HONOR PRESTAT
  BENEFICA P[O]P[V]LŌRV̄[M] E[ST] OR̄[ACI]O P[ER]-
  DVCIT AD
REGNA CELORV̄[M]. HI[C] ARCHANGEL-
-VS MICHAEL DEI NVNCI[V]S DE A[N]Ī[M]AB[V]S
  IVSTIS, GR̄A DEI ILLE VICTOR IN CELIS RESEDIT
  Ā PACIS.

At the upper dexter angle is an escucheon bearing *Gules* a castle triple-towered *argent,* on a chief *or* an eagle issuant *sable,* Giustiniani.

On the sinister panel :

VIRGO PRVDENS ANELAVIT
AD SEDEM SIDEREĀ[M] VBI LOCVM P[RE]P[ARA]VIT,
  LINQVENS ORBIS AREAM GRANVM SIBI RESERVAVIT
  VENTILĀ[N]DO PALEĀ[M]. DISCIPLINIS EST

[1] See pp. 46, 70, 78, 89, 94, 159, 226.
[2] Wisdom VII, 29, 26; Ecclesiasticus XXIV, 23, 24, *magnitudinis* for *agnitionis* in the Vulgate.

IMBVTA PVELLA CELESTIB(V)S NVDA NVDV̄[M] Ē[ST]
SECVTA CERTIS × [CHRISTI] PASSIB[V]S DV̄[M]
MV̄[N]DA[N]IS Ē[ST] EXVTA, etc.[1]

At the upper sinister angle is an escucheon
bearing *Argent* 21 billets *gules*, on a canton *or* a fess
gules. The shutters have suffered from over-
cleaning.

Etched by Hugo Bürkner.

Medici Print, 1 ft. 2 in. × 2 ft. 1¼ in. (0.35 × 0.64).

1765. Catalogue of the Dresden Gallery. The travelling
altar-piece of Charles V., by Albert Dürer.

1817. Catalogue. German school : by an unknown master.

1840. Catalogue. By Hubert van Eyck.

1846. Catalogue. By John van Eyck.

1872. CROWE, 104–105, attributes the whole to John, and
describes it inaccurately.

1898. KAEMMERER, 78, gives it to John, and dates it
c. 1437.

1899. SEECK, 32, 70, believes it to date from about 1434 ;
the splendid architecture and extremely delicate colour
alone to be John's, everything else copied from Hubert.
He notes that the light falls on Saint Katherine's face,
although she is standing with her back to the window.

1899. PHILLIPS, in the *North American Review*, vol. CLXIX,
says that the St. Michael on the dexter wing shows
identity of handling and treatment with the St. Michael
in the Hermitage at St. Petersburg.

1902. MARKS, Alfred, in *The Athenæum*, December 13, expresses his surprise at the unanimity with which this
picture has been ascribed to John alone. " In this
work," he observes, " the personages dominate their
surroundings, with the result that we have a harmonious whole—one of the most perfect pictures in
the world. I cannot escape the conviction that we
see here the result of the collaboration of the two
brothers." He attributes the figures to Hubert, the
accessories to John.

[1] From the hymn at Vespers in several fourteenth-century Office-
books in use in the diocese of Liége, and in the Breviary of Tournay,
printed at Paris in 1497. The "etc." stands for the final line, " VACUIS
HONORIBUS."

OUR LADY AND CHILD AND CHANCELLOR ROLIN
PARIS: LOUVRE

Plate XVII

1902. WOERMANN, Katalog, gives this work to John.
1903. DE MONT, 23, dates this picture c. 1437.
1904. KERN, 12, plate vi.
1905. FIERENS, 161, considers the Saint Katherine one of John van Eyck's finest creations.
1908. WEALE, p. 196. Most probably painted by Hubert.
    P. 199. Perhaps the most interesting of all the documentarily unauthenticated paintings. It retains its original frame, bearing neither John's name nor his motto.
    P. 200. The work is attributed to Hubert in the 1696 inventory of Jabach's paintings at Limoges.
    Was this triptych left, unfinished, by Hubert and completed by John ? . . . The representation of St. Katherine with an open book in her hand, in addition to the sword and broken wheel, would seem to indicate that the donor was an orator or philosopher.
1910. DURAND-GRÉVILLE, 183. " Nous insistons sur ce fait, que la forme du collet du donateur ne peut guère être posterieure à 1410."
1911. DOEHLEMANN, 403.
1912. WEALE and BROCKWELL. Probably painted by John, but in part from sketches left by Hubert.

VIII. OUR LADY AND CHILD AND CHANCELLOR ROLIN

PLATE XVII

Paris : Louvre (No. 1986 [162]). Oak. 2 ft. 2 in. × 2 ft. ½ in. (0.66 × 0.62).

Formerly in the collegiate church of Our Lady at Autun, in Burgundy.

On the left, the Blessed Virgin is seated on a marble throne with mosaic inlays, furnished with cushions of blue-and-gold brocade. An angel in a blue alb, with beautiful peacock wings, flying down, holds an elaborate gold crown over her head. With both hands Mary supports the Divine Child seated on her right knee. He is nude, holds a crystal orb surmounted by a jewelled cross, and raises His hand to bless the chancellor, Nicholas Rolin, who kneels before Him with joined hands at a prayer-desk covered with blue drapery bordered with red, on which lies his open breviary. He is clad in a robe of dark violet-and-gold brocade trimmed with fur, and wears a wig. Mary, whose hair, parted in the middle, is confined by a black riband and drawn back behind the ears, has a blue dress, almost entirely hidden by the dark crimson mantle which envelops her person and falls with numerous folds and sharp breaks on the pavement. Along its edge runs a text, embroidered in gold, from the Lesson at Matins in the Office of Our Lady, taken from the twenty-fourth chapter of Ecclesiasticus : *Exaltata sum in Libano*, etc.

The figures thus grouped are in a three-aisled hall or portico, into which the broad daylight streams through an arcade of three slightly stilted arches resting on slender cylindrical columns of variegated marble ; above are two windows of coloured glass, the lower portions only of which are seen ; those in the aisles are filled with pearl-white roundels. The capitals of the columns are adorned with interlacements of foliage and animals, and those of the piers in the angles with groups of figures representing the expulsion of Adam and Eve from Paradise, the sacrifice of Cain and Abel, Noe quitting the ark, and the sin of his youngest son.

The pavement is formed of rectangular slabs of stone, alternately plain and adorned with geometrical inlays. The arcade opens on to a garden of roses, lilies, irises, and other flowering plants, with a path through the centre, on which a couple of magpies are disporting themselves ; beyond this five steps lead to a raised terrace with a crenelated wall. Here we see two peacocks basking in the sun, and two men who—one in blue with a red head-dress, and a walking-stick in his left hand, the other in red—are looking down over the battlements at a broad river intersecting a town, the two portions of which are connected by a fortified bridge of seven arches. Beyond the bridge, in mid-stream, is a castled island ; from a distant range of blue mountains, whose snowy summits [1] glisten in the sunlight, the river, enlivened by a variety of craft, flows towards the front with many windings through a lovely country of hills, fields, and meadows. This landscape and the town in the foreground contain an almost incredible amount of detail. Through the arcade on the left may dimly be seen a flock of geese flying in the sky.

The background bears a general resemblance to that of the painting in the Rothschild collection at Paris (see p. 78).[2] The composition was most probably suggested by the scenery about Maastricht ; that town, the suburb of Wyck on the opposite side of the river, and the bridge and island agreeing pretty closely with the picture, so far as their relative position is concerned, but no further, for here evidently, as in all the landscapes of the Van Eycks, the whole is really an original composition, but so skilfully designed as to give the impression of its being a real view.[3]

The effect of the picture is marred by a disagreeable yellow varnish.

Nicholas, son of John Rolin and Amée Jugnot, born at Autun in 1376, lord of Authune (Burgundy), Aymeries and Raismes (Hainault),[4] was created

[1] For remarks on the introduction of snow-capped mountains into paintings by the Van Eycks, see pp. 46, 70, 78, 85, 94, 159, 226.

[2] The details vary considerably ; e.g. the cathedral here having the appearance of a French edifice ; the tower of Saint Martin's cathedral at Utrecht is pictured nearer the river. It is illustrated in Weale, 1908, p. 186.

[3] This background is imitated in the " Annunciation " at one time attributed to Roger De la Pasture at St. Petersburg, and in several other paintings.

[4] The two last fiefs and those of Pont-sur-Sambre and Dourlers belonging to René of Anjou were, when he, by the death of his father-in-

Chancellor of Burgundy and Brabant, December 3, 1422. He married (1) Mary de Landes (died before 1411), and (2) Guygonne de Salins. He founded the hospital at Beaune in 1445, and died January 18, 1462. In his portrait in the altar-piece of the hospital, 1446, he appears as of about seventy years of age.

The chancellor is also represented in a remarkably fine miniature at the head of the first volume of *Les Chroniques de Hainaut* (Brussels : Burgundian Library), a translation from the Latin of James de Guyse by John Wauquelin of Mons, who is represented presenting his work to Duke Philip III, surrounded by members of his court, his son Charles at his left side and the chancellor at his right. Copies of this miniature with modifications occur in several other manuscripts written by Wauquelin, in the Brussels Library, and in the Romance *Gérard de Roussillon*, in the Imperial Library, Vienna (No. 2549).

A pen drawing of the chancellor [1] is preserved in the Town Library at Arras.

1778. COURTÉPÉE, Description du Duché de Bourgogne, Dijon, III, 451. The picture was then in the sacristy of the collegiate church of Our Lady at Autun. The background is described as showing the city of Bruges in perspective, with more than 2000 figures !

1857. CROWE, 96 : "A splendid specimen of John's early and most powerful manner . . . almost equal to the large productions of Hubert. . . . Here John's art is displayed in all its force and weakness ;—admirable when we only look at the characteristic rendering of the scratch-wigged chancellor, or the adumbrations that cover the wondrous details of architecture, or the

law in 1431, became Duke of Lorraine, seized by the Duke of Burgundy, who granted the revenues thereof to his chancellor. Later on René fell into Philip's power and was imprisoned at Lille. On February 4, 1437, before being set at liberty, he sold all his rights to these fiefs to the chancellor.

[1] Reproduced in Weale, 1908, p. 116.

crystalline purity of a distance carried to a horizon of snow mountains miles away; disappointing when we look at the plain mask of the Virgin, or the wooden shape of the aged babe naked on her knee, or the piled and broken drapery that rests on the figures."

1860. WAAGEN, 70. The features of the Virgin are pretty, but of little spirituality of character; the Child, of unusual elegance for the master; the angel, very beautiful; and the portrait of the donor, of astonishing energy.

1866. MICHIELS, II, 297. The town in the background not Bruges, but Maastricht.

1885. GILBERT, 151.

1898. KAEMMERER, 93, dates the picture c. 1437.

1899. SEECK, 23–26, 68, thinks it was painted c. 1422, and that Rolin has the appearance of a man of fifty years of age.

1900. VOLL, 65–70, dates it c. 1425.

1901. BODE, 124, says it was painted c. 1434, certainly not before 1432.

1902. C. PHILLIPS, in *The Fortnightly Review*, October, p. 595: " True, the landscape has many of the characteristics which we shall find to be those of Hubert, and the angel who, floating in mid-air, holds a crown over the head of the Madonna, has no parallel for grace and beauty in the later work of Jan. But the wrinkled Christ, prematurely old and wholly unspiritual, is Jan's very own, the Chancellor Rolin is one of the most wonderful portraits, and the general execution suggests most strongly his hand; though it may well be that the work was executed in the lifetime of Hubert, and under his influence."

1902. MARKS, in *The Athenæum*, December 12, p. 800.

1903. MARKS, 22: " The Louvre picture is certainly the work of two painters. Otherwise we must suppose that the painter, having completed his figures, proceeded to kill them with his accessories. John surpassed himself in painting the accessories of this picture. . . . The winding river can be no other than the Rhine. . . . John shows here, perhaps even more than in the Ghent altar-piece, that he is a great master of landscape painting. . . . The dominant interest of the picture does not centre in the figures."

1904. KERN, 15, plates ix and x, judging by the perspective, considers it to be a work of John's later period.

1904. DVOŘÁK, 191, 216, 219, 241. Indisputably painted by John.

1905. FIERENS, 128–131, dates it c. 1426.

1906. VOLL, 36, thinks the town represented to be Liége, and the picture to have been painted by John, at latest in 1426.

1908. WEALE, 186. The town in the background of the Louvre altar-piece has been declared to be Bruges, Lyons, Maastricht, and Liége ; the river in this and in the Rothschild and Berlin Carthusian panels to be the Rhine, while others say it is the Maas, and Rosen and Voll go so far as to assert that the view is that seen from the citadel of Liége. These contradictory assertions are all alike easily disproved. In the Rothschild panel the cathedral to the left of the river is unmistakably Old St. Paul's seen from the south ; in the Rolin altar-piece a noble cathedral of a decidedly French type occupies a similar position, and the tower of Saint Martin's at Utrecht stands near the bridge.

P. 193. The Rolin panel is anterior to 1430.

P. 199. In some of his earlier pictures, such as the Rolin panel, John has to a certain extent injured the general effect by the multiplication of detail.

1911. DOEHLEMANN, 401–402, 405–406.

1912. KERN, 52, 53.

1912. WEALE and BROCKWELL. Perhaps by Hubert.

The background of a miniature in a Book of Hours (fol. 162) executed c. 1435 for the Bastard of Orleans, John, Count of Dunois, has been admirably adapted from that in the Louvre painting.

1910. BROCKWELL, in The Athenæum, January 1, p. 21 : " The Book of Hours of Jean Dunois, the Bastard of Orleans, which was written and illuminated in Paris ' about 1435,' as the official label states, is also lent by Mr. Yates Thompson [to the National Gallery]. The miniature exposed illustrates one of the Seven Deadly Sins, and is particularly interesting because the distant landscape is identical with the background of the famous ' Virgin and Child with the Chancellor Rolin ' in the Louvre (No. 1986)."

THE VISION OF SAINT FRANCIS
PHILADELPHIA : MR. J. G. JOHNSON

Plate XVIII

IX. The Vision of Saint Francis of Assisi

Plate XVIII

Philadelphia, U.S.A. : Mr. John G. Johnson. Oak. 5 in. ×
5¾ in. (0.125 × 0.145).

Purchased about 1830 by the 1st Lord Heytesbury from a medical man at Lisbon, as an original
work by Albert Dürer. It remained in the collection at Heytesbury until November 4, 1894, when
it was purchased from the 3rd Lord Heytesbury
by the dealers Gooden and Fox. It was by them
sold on December 3, 1894, to Mr. Johnson of Philadelphia for £700.

The picture represents the vision of Saint Francis
on Mount Alverna, when he received the stigmata.
In his treatment of the subject, the painter has not
adhered rigidly to the earlier representations, in
that he has omitted the rays from the Saviour's
hands, feet, and side, to those of the saint, and has
placed the sleeping brother, Leo, on the same plane
as the saint, instead of in the half-distance. In all
earlier Netherlandish pictures the habits of both
the saint and the brother are grey, and the Franciscans were known as the Grey Friars ; but here
the habit is brown, the colour adopted by the reformed Franciscans, a conclusive proof that the
picture was painted in the South of Europe. The
first convent of the reformed Franciscans in the
Low Countries was not founded until the end of
the fifteenth century. It must also be remarked
that the kneeling saint is not an ideal impersonation
of the poor man of Assisi, but the portrait, evidently
true to life, of a sturdy middle-aged man. The
scene is laid in the foreground of an exquisite landscape in a retired spot, shut in on each side by tall

limestone rocks. The saint kneels before a mass of rock, above which, to the right, appears the seraphic vision. Between the rocks we get a view of a river in the half-distance, which bathes the walls of a fortified town with many towers and spires seen in bright sunlight ; on the stream are boats, and on the bank and the bridge giving access to the city gate are innumerable figures on foot and on horseback. In the far-off distance are snow mountains,[1] from whence the river flows with many windings towards the town, and birds are seen in the sky.[2] In the foreground flowers bloom amidst the herbage, while the palmetto grows in abundance at the foot of the rocks, on the summit of the tallest of which are three birds.

Two panel paintings representing Saint Francis of Assisi, said to have been painted by the hand of John van Eyck, were in the second half of the fifteenth century in the possession of Sir Anselm Adornes, lord of Corthuy, Ronsele, Ghendbrugge, &c., a scion of the Genoese family of Adorno, born in 1424, at Bruges, of which town he was burgomaster in 1475. He was assassinated at Linlithgow, on the 23rd of January, 1483. By his wife, Margaret Van der Banck, who died on the 23rd of March, 1462, he had amongst other children two daughters who became nuns : Margaret, who entered the Charterhouse of Saint Anne ter Woestine, and Louisa, a canoness of the abbey of Saint Trudo, both in the immediate neighbourhood of Bruges. Their father, by his will, dated February 10, 1470, bequeathed the two paintings to them, and directed his executors to have the portraits of himself and his wife painted on the shutters of each of the paintings, so that his daughters and other pious people might be reminded to pray for them.

[1] For snow-capped mountains, see pp. 46, 70, 78, 85, 89, 159, 226.
[2] For flights of birds, see pp. 48, 70, 78, 89, 130, 227.

Whether this last direction was carried out we do not know. Both convents were demolished during the troubles in the last quarter of the sixteenth century, and the numerous works of art which they contained either perished or were dispersed. It is possible that the painting in the Johnson Collection may be one of the two pictures of "Saint Francis" by John van Eyck mentioned in Adornes' will.

Exhibited: British Institution, 1865 (No. 41); Burlington House, Old Masters, 1886 (No. 198).

Cleaned by Mr. Roger Fry in 1906.

1857. WAAGEN, 389, writing of the panel, then at Heytesbury, describes it as "delicate in feature and very earnest in expression. . . . In the treatment of the equally delicate, solid, and miniature-like execution, this little picture agrees entirely with the altar-piece in the Dresden Gallery, surpassing it, however, in the depth of the warm tone."

1860. PINCHART, *Archives des Arts, Sciences, et Lettres*, I, 264, translates a passage from the will as follows : "Je donne à chacune de mes filles, Marguerite et Louise, toutes deux religieuses, l'une au couvent des Chartreuses (près de Bruges), et l'autre à Saint Trond, un petit tableau, représentant Saint François, dû au pinceau de Jean van Eyck, et j'ordonne que sur les volets soient peints, avec grand soin, mon portrait et celui de ma femme." Then follow biographical details relating to Anselm Adornes.

1886. ROBINSON, J. C., in *The Times* of February 1, calls it an exquisite little gem by John van Eyck.

1886. WEALE, in *The Times*, February 3, p. 7 : "The pictures could not have been painted by Van Eyck for Anselm Adornes, as the latter was only fifteen years old when the great master died, and I am not aware of any relative of Adornes who belonged to the Order of Saint Francis. It seems to me more probable that these little pictures were executed in Spain, for the reformed Franciscans, distinguished by the brown habit of the choir brothers and the black habit of the lay brothers, was, unless my memory deceives me, not introduced into Flanders until the end of the fifteenth century."

1886. *The Athenæum*, February 6 : "What looks very like Montserrat, with its conventual buildings on the crags, appears in the distance. Mr. J. C. Robinson has recognised certain Spanish herbage in the foreground. The face of Saint Francis is, we think, Spanish, not Flemish."

1886. *The Athenæum*, February 20 : "We must express wonder that *cognoscenti* worthy of the name have ascribed the brilliant and beautiful little picture to Antonello rather than to Van Eyck. . . . The snow-clad hills may be the Pyrenees."

1887. CONWAY, 141, calls it a smaller replica of the Turin picture.

1900. MARKS, in *The Athenæum*, May 26, p. 664 : "I had the kind permission of Sir W. Thiselton-Dyer, the Director of Kew Gardens, to show him a photograph of the picture, when he at once recognised the plant as *Chamærops humilis*, and was good enough to direct me to a book giving the geographical limits of the plant (Willkomm and Lange : *Prodromus Floræ Hispanicæ*). In this work it is stated that the plant grows in Portugal, among other places bordering on the Western Mediterranean. Here, therefore, it may well have been seen by John van Eyck when he visited Portugal in the year 1428. . . . Lord Heytesbury bought his picture in Lisbon."

1906. FRY, in a private letter to Weale : "The repaints in the head of Saint Francis were all taken out [by me], and under them the original work was untouched. Brother Leo's hood, head, and hands were abominably repainted, and the drawing entirely hidden. The original work, admirably preserved, is now alone seen. The added strips have been taken off and the picture restored to its original dimensions."

1908. WEALE, p. 200. The fact that Mr. Johnson's "Vision of Saint Francis" was found at Lisbon seems to have led to the conclusion that it was painted by John during his sojourn in Portugal.

1908. GRANT, J. Kirby, in *The Connoisseur*, September, p. 4.

1908. BROCKWELL, in *The Athenæum*, April 18, p. 485. The Johnson version did not leave England until 1894.

1912. PHILLIPS, in a private letter to Brockwell : "I now

fully believe that the Heytesbury 'St. Francis' now in America is a Hubert van Eyck and *the* original, although the Turin example is very fine."

1912. WEALE and BROCKWELL. The difficulties attending a definite ascription of this small picture to one brother or the other are, in the main, due to (1) our having no knowledge that Hubert was ever in Spain or Portugal, although John was in the Peninsula ; (2) the assumption, based on no sure grounds, that, as the picture was found in Portugal in 1830, it was originally painted there ; (3) the introduction of the brown habit, here worn by Saint Francis ; and (4) the appearance of the palmetto.

Stylistic considerations and the emotion contained in this small masterpiece suggest the genius of Hubert, to whom, on the whole, preference may be given. There is, however, nothing to prevent its having been painted by John, working under the influence of Hubert, or from his elder brother's sketches.

D

By JOHN or HUBERT

X. The Annunciation

PLATE XIX

Saint Petersburg : Hermitage Gallery (No. 443). Dexter shutter of a triptych. Canvas, transferred from the original panel. 3 ft. ¼ in. × 1 ft. 3 in. (0.92 × 0.38).

This painting is said by the dealer Nieuwenhuys to have been found in a church at Dijon, to which it had been presented by Philip III, Duke of Burgundy. Taken to Paris in 1819, it was sold by Nieuwenhuys to King William II of Holland. On the dispersal of that monarch's collection in 1850, it was purchased for the Hermitage for 12,949 francs, equal to £518.

A copy is said by Crowe and by Kaemmerer to have been in the possession of a M. van Hal at Antwerp, and to have been sold there, and afterwards at Paris, in the middle of last century.

In the nave or transept of a lofty three-aisled building the Blessed Virgin is represented standing on the left, behind a prayer-desk, on which an illuminated book lies open. Opposite her the angel, who, bearing a sceptre of crystal and gold, has entered from the side aisle, raises his right hand, and greets her with the salutation : AVE GRĀ PLENA, to whom she, her hands raised apart and with her head slightly inclined, signifies her humble submission to the Divine will by the words : ECCE

THE ANNUNCIATION

SAINT PETERSBURG: HERMITAGE

L. Gecele, Photo

Plate XIX

ANCILLA DŇI ; both inscriptions, the latter being inverted, in detached gold capitals float in the air. Amid seven rays of light, projected from heaven through the clerestory, the Holy Dove flies down to Mary. She is clad in a blue dress trimmed with ermine, open at the neck, girt with a broad sash immediately below the breast, and over this an ample blue mantle with a narrow border of gold. Her hair, confined by a jewelled band, is drawn back off the forehead and falls over her shoulders, leaving the left ear exposed.

Gabriel, who has beautiful peacock-wings, wears, over a tunic of green-and-gold velvet brocade, a cope of dark red and gold, bordered with pearls and precious stones, and kept in place by a circular morse. A jewelled coronet with a cross flory rising from the front confines his hair, which falls in curly locks on his shoulders.

The draperies of both the angel and the Virgin spread around in many folds on the pavement, which is composed of oblong storied panels, separated from each other by bands of undulating foliage of varied design, with the signs of the zodiac in elliptical medallions at the intersections. Those seen are Gemini, Cancer, Leo, Scorpio, and Sagittarius ; while the storied panels show Samson slaying the Philistines with the jawbone of an ass ; Delilah cutting off his hair—DALIDA VXOR S— Samson pulling down the pillars of the temple of Dagon—SAMSON MVLTAS GENTES INTERFECIT Ī 9VIVIO [convivio]—and David cutting off Goliath's head ; Saul, surrounded by his warriors, looking on from his tent. These are accompanied by explanatory inscriptions. In the immediate foreground, on the left, is a wooden stool, with a tasselled red damask silk cushion on it, and beyond it a glass vase with lilies.

The architecture in this picture is remarkable,

but cannot be considered as the representation of any one building, though all the details appear to be correctly drawn. The late Romanesque arcade, with its very stilted arches, seems to have been copied from the arches of an apse, but straightened out ; the capitals of the columns are sculptured with interlaced foliage, those of the piers at the angles with figures. The square-headed triforium, with its row of columns, may possibly have been suggested by the Baptistery at Parma, but more probably by the cathedral of Tournay. The spandrils between the arches at the farther end of the building are adorned with two half-length figures in circular medallions : Isaac on the right and Jacob on the left. In the window above is a full-length figure of Our Lord in a red robe and yellowish-blue mantle, holding a sceptre and an open book. His feet rest on a globe, on which in capital letters is ASIA. Above Him are two seraphim standing on wheels. On each side is a mural painting—that on the right representing the daughter of Pharaoh—PHARAONIS FILIA—and a maiden carrying the infant Moses—MOYSES—in a cradle—F[I]SCELLA ; that on the left, Moses—MOYSES—bending before the Lord—DÑS—and receiving the tables of the law, on which is inscribed the second commandment : *Non assumes nomen Domini Dei tui in vanum.*[1] The compartments of the wooden ceiling are also apparently represented as decorated with paintings.

Exhibited : Bruges, Golden Fleece Exhibition, 1907 (No. 174).

1843. NIEUWENHUYS, I, 2.
1864. WAAGEN, Die Gemälde Sammlung in der K. Ermitage, München, p. 115, gives 1433–34 as the probable date of this painting.
1872. CROWE, 113 : "Though not of John van Eyck's

_____
[1] Exodus XX, 7.

best, this genuine work is full of interest, on account of the finish and variety of its accessories."

1879. CLEMENT DE RIS, in *Gazette des Beaux Arts*, 2 P., XIX, 573.

1883. BODE, Kaiserliche Gemälde Galerie in St. Petersburg, Paris, dates it 1426.

1898. KAEMMERER, 71, suggests that the upper portion may have been added !!

1899. C. PHILLIPS, in the *North American Review*, 712, calls it "an unlovely, yet in detail a wonderfully interesting piece, produced a year or two earlier than the altar-piece in the Bruges Gallery."

1899. SEECK, 70, attributes it to John, and dates it 1437.

1900. KAEMMERER, 70, dates it 1436.

1900. VOLL, 62, believes John to have painted this soon after 1426. He says that we know that John in his younger days spent a long time in France, and gives as his authority (note 39) Laborde, "Les Ducs de Bourgogne" *passim*,[1] and concludes that this picture was painted during a stay in Burgundy, where he must have made Rolin's acquaintance, and received the commission to paint the altar-piece now in the Louvre.

1902. C. PHILLIPS, in *The Fortnightly Review*, October, p. 595 : "But of the dramatic imagination Jan van Eyck, as we know him in his well-authenticated works, has nothing. To him was not given the vision of the poet-painter, that the mind's eye, before the hand sets to work, can see full and complete. . . . Take the astonishingly wrought yet spiritually and physically ugly 'Annunciation' of the Hermitage at St. Petersburg. Seldom has a subject which lends itself to spiritual emotion been so undramatically, so un-spiritually, treated."

1904. KERN, 13, plate vii.

1905. DURAND-GRÉVILLE, 34.

---

[1] This is very vague. We cannot find a single passage to warrant the reference. It is quite possible that John (or Hubert) may at some time have been in Burgundy, but there is not a scrap of documentary evidence to prove it. It is far more probable that the commission to paint the "Madonna and Child with the Chancellor Rolin," in the Louvre, and the St. Petersburg "Annunciation," was given him in Flanders, at Bruges or Lille. The Chancellor was much more there than in Burgundy.

1905. FIERENS, 127, dates this painting *c.* 1427.
1906. VOLL, 36, dates it 1426.
1907. WILLIAMSON, in *The Connoisseur*, XIX, 209.
1907. VERHELST, A., Exposition de la Toison d'Or à Bruges, in *Durendal*, XIV, 515–518.
1907. GREIG, J., in *The Morning Post*, Aug. 16 : " The details indicate extraordinary vision and technical power. . . . The floor is a revelation in artistic verisimilitude, the action of the small figures seen in perspective being expressed with an authority unequalled in art."
1908. SAINTENOY believes this painting to have been executed after 1429, and the background to have been based on Cluniac architecture.
1908. MARKS, in a letter to Weale, October 5, writes : " M. Saintenoy does not touch on one difficult point. John, after the death of Hubert and the completion, six years later, of the Ghent masterpiece, signed his pictures with great insistence. If the ' Annunciation ' was painted by John after 1429, why is it not signed ? "
1908. WEALE, 199 : " If this ' Annunciation ' be compared with that on the exterior of the polyptych, how inferior in expression are the figures here seen, and how inappropriate their surroundings ! "
1912. KERN, 50, plate 20.
1912. WEALE and BROCKWELL. The picture is not now in its original frame, which may at one time have borne the artist's name and date. It seems much more likely to have been painted by John than by Hubert.

B. NICHOLAS ALBERGATI, CARDINAL OF SAINT CROSS, 1432

VIENNA : IMPERIAL GALLERY

From a photograph by E. Bruckmann

Plate XX

E

By JOHN[1]

I. Paintings of which the Date is Known

XI. Portrait of B. Nicholas Albergati
(1375–1443)

Plate XX

Vienna : Imperial Gallery (No. 624). Oak. 1 ft. 2 in. ×
11½ in. (0.35 × 0.29). Head, 6 in. (0.15).

THIS was, in 1659, in the collection of the Archduke
Leopold William, Governor-general of the Low
Countries,[2] then in the Belvedere Gallery,[3] where it
passed for the portrait at an advanced age of Jodoc
Vyt,[4] the donor of the Ghent altar-piece. In the
catalogue of the Imperial Gallery of 1884, Engerth
entitled it " Portrait of the Cardinal of Saint Cross,"
and that title is still preserved in the 1907 catalogue.
In 1898 Kaemmerer threw doubt on the correctness
of this ascription, justly remarking that the portrait

---

[1] The following eleven pictures by John are in all probability here
placed in their correct chronological order.
[2] Inventory, No. 109. " Ein Contrafait van Oehlfarb auf Holcz des
Cardinals von Sancta Cruce. Original von Johann van Eyckh."
Jahrbuch der kunsthistorischen Sammlungen des allerhöchsten Kaiser-
hauses, I, part 2, cxxi, col. 1. Wien, 1883.
[3] Catalogue of 1860 : Early German and early Netherlandish
Schools, Room 2, No. 42.
[4] This ascription was accepted by Passavant (*Kunstblatt,* 1841,
p. 14). Crowe and Cavalcaselle, in 1857, were, I believe, the first to
remark the considerable points of difference in the two portraits, and the
exactness of their observations was confirmed by Hotho, in 1858, and by
Waagen, in 1866

does not bear the slightest resemblance to the monumental effigy of Dominic Capranica, Cardinal of Saint Cross, in the cathedral of Siena ; and no wonder, for the prelate here represented is not Capranica,[1] but Albergati.

This eminent prince of the Church, born at Bologna in 1375, was the son of Peter Nicholas Albergati and Philippa, his wife, only daughter of Dr. Bartholomew Chiopetti. He entered the Order of the Carthusians when in his twentieth year, was successively prior of the monastery of Saint Jerome outside Bologna in 1406, and of the Holy Cross of Jerusalem at Rome in 1407, in which year he was also appointed procurator-general of the Order ; he was rector of the newly founded monastery of the Holy Trinity at Mantua from 1409 to 1416, and again prior of Bologna from 1416 until the end of March, 1417, when he was elected bishop of Bologna. Created a cardinal-priest by Martin V, May 24, 1426, he took for his titular church the Holy Cross of Jerusalem. In his humility he discarded his family arms, and substituted for them a simple cross. A model of all priestly and episcopal virtues, he continued to observe the austere rule of the Carthusians, sleeping on straw, never eating flesh-meat, wearing a hair shirt, and rising at midnight to pray. Nine times he was sent by the Holy See on important embassies,[2] when, dealing with matters involving questions of worldly policy of no

[1] This prelate was created a cardinal-deacon by Martin V, July 23, 1423, but the nomination was not published until November 8, 1430; on the 19th of that month Capranica took for his titular church Saint Mary *in via lata.* It was not until after Albergati's death, in 1443, that Capranica was raised to the dignity of cardinal-priest, with the title of Saint Cross. *See* CHACON, Vitae et res gestae Pontificum Summorum, II, 110, Romae, 1630 ; PASTOR, History of the Popes, ed. ANTROBUS, 2nd ed., I, 261 and 264-266 ; and EUBEL, in *Römische Quartalschrift,* XVII, 274-275. Rome, 1903.

[2] Thrice to France (in 1422, 1431, and 1435), thrice to Lombardy (in 1426, 1427, and 1430), and thrice to the Council at Basel (in 1432, 1434, and 1436).

small difficulty, he invariably displayed consummate prudence combined with perfect uprightness and integrity.[1] Thus in 1431 he was sent on an embassy to the Kings of France and England and the Duke of Burgundy, to try and bring about a general peace.

The Duke, who had started on a journey to Holland, had actually reached Vere, when he was informed of the cardinal's intended visit. He at once returned to Brussels, and sent messengers in every direction to the principal ecclesiastical and lay dignitaries of his dominions, summoning them to him without delay, that the Pope's ambassador might be received with the honour and solemnity befitting his rank and dignity.

The cardinal, accompanied by Amé Bourgois, one of the Duke's councillors and chamberlains, arrived at the Charterhouse of Hérinnes, near Enghien, early in October, 1431. Proceeding to Brussels, he was received there, on the 18th of that month, by the Duke in person, surrounded by his court [2] Thence he returned to Hérinnes, accompanied by Amé Bourgois and master Giles d'Escornaix, provost of Harlebeke, who both escorted him to Ghent, which they reached on the 3rd of November. The cardinal stayed at the Charterhouse there until the 6th. Thence he went to Lille, and later on visited Bruges, where he spent two or three days at the Charterhouse, between the 8th and 11th of December.

The Duke meantime had despatched letters to the authorities of those towns, bidding them receive the cardinal with the honours due to his rank.[3]

[1] Eugenius IV, writing to Charles VII of France, says that he is sending him the Cardinal of Saint Cross, "virum sapientissimum, magnaque auctoritate, ut nosti, et procul ab omni passione remotum, cuius omnes cogitationes, omnia consilia tendunt ad concordiam, ad pacem."

[2] The Archbishop of Köln and the Chancellor of France were also present at this interview.

[3] The accounts of the treasurers of both Enghien and Brussels for this period are lost. In those of the treasurers of Ghent are numerous

One of these letters was probably addressed to John van Eyck, bidding him paint the portrait of the cardinal. However, as his stay in Bruges was of such brief duration,[1] it was obviously impossible to paint it direct from life. Van Eyck was therefore unable to do more than make a careful drawing of his likeness, with such memoranda as would enable him to execute a satisfactory painting. This exquisite drawing, in silver-point on a white ground, is preserved in the royal cabinet of prints at Dresden.[2] At the dexter side are a number of notes disposed in sixteen lines, evidently written with the pencil used for the drawing ; these, partly hidden by the shading of the head, are now unfortunately, owing to the drawing having been exhibited during several years, much faded, with the result that some of the words baffle all attempts to decipher them.[3]

From this drawing the painting was executed. In it the cardinal is seen to the waist, modelled in yellowish tone, with few flesh tints and without any deep shadow. Bareheaded, he wears the *cappa clausa*, a loose crimson robe edged at the neck and arm-openings with white fur, and fastened at the neck by two buttons ; the straight vertical folds of this robe, the arms and hands being unseen, give it

entries of payments to messengers, to labourers for clearing the streets of the town and the road thence to the Charterhouse, for wine and comfits presented to the cardinal, for the hire of horses for the town officials who rode out to meet and escort him, to the town trumpeters, and to the bell-ringers of the seven parish churches. The accounts of the Treasurer of Bruges and of the fabric of the collegiate church of Saint Donatian also contain entries of payments for wine, herbs, spices, and wax-lights presented to the cardinal.

[1] It is uncertain whether Van Eyck was then at Bruges or at Ghent. In either case the time was too short.

[2] H. 0,212 ; B. 0,18. Acquired before 1765. Reproduced by WOERMANN, Handzeichnungen alter Meister im königlichen Kupferstich Kabinet zu Dresden, München, 1896 ; in *Die Insel, Mappenwerk*, Leipzig, 1899; in *Onse Kunst*, I, 4, Antwerp, 1902 ; and in the *Burlington Magazine*, V, 195. London, 1904 ; and in Weale, 1908, p. 60.

[3] So much as can be deciphered is given in Weale, 1908, p. 61.

an elegant bell-shaped appearance. The cardinal's head is turned to the right ; his close-shaven vigorous face, seen in three-quarter profile, with the light falling directly on it, is full of expression. There is quite a charm about the little brownish eyes, which appear to be looking out from beneath the eyebrows with a keen scrutinising glance, while a pleasant playful smile hovers about his closed lips. The numerous wrinkles on the forehead and the folds of skin on the face and on the neck, up to the root of the ear, are marked by fine reddish strokes ; the left ear, seen in light, is admirably drawn. The short scanty grey hairs of his head, in a state of confusion, seem to tremble beneath each other, and the blood to be circulating under the relaxed skin and in the veins of the pupils of his eyes. The background is dark, but lighter and bluish near the head.

As compared with the drawing, the painting is less lifelike and individualistic ; this is especially the case with the mouth and the lower portion of the face. It seems as if Van Eyck endeavoured to embellish the form of the head so that it should appear less heavy and broad.

1857. CROWE, 88, rightly describes the drawing as the original beautiful design.

1897. FRIEDLAENDER, in *Repertorium*, xx, 71.

1898. KAEMMERER, 70–72, looks on the drawing as evidence that John's usual method was not to paint portraits direct from life. This, however, was certainly an exceptional case, when it was impossible to do so.

1902. ROOSES, in *Onze Kunst*, I, 3–8. The writing is no doubt in John's own hand.

1904. WEALE, 190–198, establishes the identity of the cardinal portrayed, and the date of the drawing.

1908. WEALE, 196. The earliest portrait proved to have been painted by John.

XII. Portrait of a Man, 1432

Plate XXI

London : National Gallery (No. 290). Oak. 1 ft. 1¼ in. × 7¼ in.
(0.336 × 0.188).

Bought in 1857 from the landscape painter Carl Ross, at Munich, for £189, 11s.

Portrait of a dark-complexioned man with blue eyes, of about forty-five years of age, standing at a window-opening. Turned to the right, close shaven, with his face seen in three-quarters, he wears a dark red dress with full sleeves trimmed with sable, and fastened in front by two buttons. His head-covering is formed by a green scarf, the long lappet of which hangs down in front of the right shoulder, the other end just reaching to the left. In his right hand he holds a roll of manuscript, while his left forearm rests on a parapet of yellowish stone, bearing on the front, in Greek characters, what is supposed to be his Christian name, *Tymotheos*, and beneath this in capital letters incised in the stone, " léal sovvenir," showing that this portrait was painted for presentation to a friend, or more probably was a gift from the painter, who has written at the foot in calligraphic characters :

" *Actū año Dñi* 1432, 10 die Octobris, a Ioh. de Eyck."

It is not known whom this portrait represents ; certainly not a Fleming, perhaps a Greek, possibly a humanist, apparently an intelligent, though by no means a handsome man, who, in spite of his angular features, heavy jaw, thick lips, prominent cheekbones and up-turned nose, is a charming figure. The modelling is excellent, the colour rich and simple, but very harmonious and well relieved by the dark

PORTRAIT OF A MAN (LÉAL SOUVENIR) 1432

LONDON : NATIONAL GALLERY

Plate XXI

background. The under side of the panel, painted to imitate jasperated porphyry, bears, near the top,

the cipher ⚷ of an early Italian, probably Venetian, owner. This cipher may recall the name of Gregorius de Gregoriis, the late fifteenth and early sixteenth century Venetian publisher. Several old copies of the portrait are said to be in existence.

1854. FOERSTER, in *Kunstblatt*, October 19, p. 373.
1872. CROWE, 94. The drawing is careful; the painting blended to a fault.
1898. KAEMMERER, 60, thinks " Léal souvenir " was the man's own motto, and that " Tymotheos " can scarcely be conceived to be his name.
1904. DVOŘÁK, 196.

A silver-point drawing (H. 0.21 ; B. 0.14) in the Print-Room of the Berlin Museum, which bears a slight resemblance to this portrait, is ascribed on insufficient grounds to John van Eyck.[1] It formerly belonged to the poet Adolphus Hilarius ; was in the collection of William Mayor (died 1874), and was acquired by the Museum at a sale in Munich, June 19, 1897 (No. 244).

XIII. OUR LADY AND CHILD, 1433

PLATE XXII

Ince Hall, Ince Blundell, Liverpool : Mr. C. J. Weld-Blundell.
Oak. 8¾ in. × 6 in. (0.225 × 0.15).

The scene is laid in a room dimly lighted from the right by a window glazed with tiny lozenges and a border of red, white, blue, and white. In the centre the Virgin Mother enthroned with the Child on her knees, His lower limbs partly covered with

[1] Reproduced in WEALE, 1908, p. 64.

the white linen cloth on which He is seated. With
both hands He is turning over the leaves of an
illuminated manuscript which His mother holds
before Him with her left hand. She wears a full
loose dress of blue material, with jewelled neckband
and white fur trimming at the cuffs and the hem of
the skirt, confined at the waist by a broad red belt
studded with gold, and over all an ample crimson
mantle, the folds of which spread over the ground
on all sides. Her luxuriant light-brown hair, confined by a circlet of pearls with a jewel in the centre,
falls over her shoulders in wavy tresses. A rich
cloth of honour of green and gold brocade hangs
from a red-fringed canopy high up above her head.
On a table before the window stands a metal vase
with crystal cover, while on the window-sill are a
couple of oranges and a goblet half full of wine. A
tall pricket chandelier with a taper and two sconce
branches, and a white metal pot with brass mountings
are placed on a low aumbry on the Virgin's left ; in
its lock is a key, to which three others are attached.
A rich carpet spread beneath Mary's feet contrasts
well with the sombre floor ; to the left is a large
brass pan.   In the upper part of the background on
the right, close to the cloth of honour, is the signature :

COPLETṼ ĀNO D and on the opposite side   ᴀᴧᴄ
ℳ ᴄᴄᴄᴆ xxx ɪɪᴊ John's device, which ap- ɪхн
ꝑ ɪoнᴇᴍ ᴅᴇ ᴇʏᴄ pears here for the first хᴀɴ
ʙʀᴠɢɪѕ time.[1]

This picture is a marvellous example of John's
talent both as regards finish of detail and vigorous
treatment of colour. The Virgin's expression is
pleasing and not without dignity ; that of the
Child, happy and playful. The disposal of the
oranges and the metal and crystal vessels so as to

[1] Weale, in 1906, was the first to give the correct date, 1433.

OUR LADY AND CHILD, 1433

INCE HALL

Plate XXII

catch the light from the foreshortened windows on the right, and the manner in which the master has concentrated his powers upon depicting every little detail as perfectly as possible, is nowhere more noticeable than in this, probably the first picture completed by him after settling in Bruges. Unfortunately, the panel is covered with a thick coat of varnish, and in addition is slightly warped, which has led to a general cracking of the surface.

Exhibited : London : Old Masters, Burlington House, 1884 (No. 267) ; Burlington Fine Arts Club, 1892 (No. 14) ; Guildhall, 1906 (No. 3).

1854. WAAGEN, III, 249.
1857. CROWE, 338–341.
1883. *Athenæum*, October 6, p. 440.
1893. TSCHUDI, in *Repertorium*, XVI, 101, says the letters of the signature are uncertainly drawn, and have probably been copied from the original frame.
1906. FRIEDLAENDER, in *Repertorium*, XXIX, 574, thinks the inscription has been copied from the original frame. He evidently had not remarked that the date is 1433, not 1432.

An old copy of this picture (Oak. H. 0.368 ; B. 0.277) was formerly in private hands at Messina, where it was bought by the Duke of Verdura for 50 ounces (£25) ; his collection was sold at Rome in April, 1894, when this panel was bought in at 1200 lire (£48) ; it now belongs to his daughter. The inscription, occupying a similar position, is identical with that on the Ince Hall original.

Another weaker copy is said to be in the Museum at Catania.

On the upper part of the back there is what appears to be a contemporary note that the panel was pledged on the 2nd of July, 1619, for 3 ounces 15, or 60 scudi—" 1619 a 2 Luglio questo quadro di Luciano Costa e stato in pegno per oz. 3—15 Scudi (?) 60."

XIV. PORTRAIT OF A MAN, 1433, IN ALL PROBABILITY JOHN VAN EYCK'S FATHER-IN-LAW

PLATE XXIII

London : National Gallery (No. 222).   Oak.   13 in. × 10¼ in. (0.332 × 0.261) ; within the frame, 10½ in. × 7½ in. (0.266 × 0.19).

Formerly in the collection of Thomas, Earl of Arundel. It was at Amsterdam in 1655, in the possession of the Countess of Arundel ; in the inventory of her pictures it is described as " Ritratto de Gio. van Eyck de mano sua." It was later in that of George Alan, Viscount Midleton of Peperharrow (died 1848), at whose sale, July 31, 1851, it was purchased by the picture-dealer Farrer for £315. Purchased by the Trustees from H. Farrer, in 1851, for £365.

The bust of a man, apparently a well-to-do merchant of about sixty-five years of age. He is clad in a dark dress, the fur collar of which just covers the lower part of his face, but shows a little linen at the throat. His head-covering is a rich red scarf wound in a very artistic manner, its ends piled up at the top of the cranium. The closely shaven face, wearing a bright expression, is seen in three-quarters turned to the right, the eyes looking to the left. This, one of the best of John's portraits, is delicately painted in a reddish-brown tone, the modelling of the left cheek in shadow is most successful, its elevations and hollows, the pleats of the eyelids and at the root of the nose, and the veins and wrinkles of the forehead, being rendered with absolute faithfulness. The framework, which is original, is formed by four mitred pieces of molding glued to the face of the panel and secured by wooden

PORTRAIT OF A MAN 1433
LONDON : NATIONAL GALLERY

Plate XXIII

pegs, and painted to imitate marble. The upper border bears the painter's motto : " ALS IXH XAN " ; at the foot is his signature, with date : " JOHES DE EYCK ME FECIT ĀNO M°CCCC° 33° 21 OCTOBRIS."

1854. WAAGEN, I, 348.
1904. WEALE, 249.
1905. DURAND-GRÉVILLE, in *Les Arts Anciens de Flandre*, I, 23–25, takes this to be a portrait of John van Eyck, by himself, when about forty-seven years of age.
1905. FIERENS, 146, esteems this one of John's best portraits.
1906. VOLL, 43–44. Drapery of head-dress very clumsy ; cannot be of the fifteenth century.
1909. RUPP, 480–484.
1909. WEALE, in *The Burlington Magazine*, XIV, 360.
1909. BROCKWELL, in *The Athenæum*, April 3, p. 416.
1910. WEALE, in *The Burlington Magazine*, XVII, 177 : " Judging by the painting, the man appears to have been about sixty or sixty-five years of age in October 1433, consequently he would have been between thirty-three and thirty-eight when Margaret was born in 1406." The strong resemblance between the features of the two persons has been confirmed by Dr. Oswald Rubbrecht, who has made a special study of the recurrence of features in families, and holds the view that the man in this picture is to be identified as the father of Margaret van Eyck.
1910. DURAND-GRÉVILLE, 125 : " Si l'*Homme au turban* de la National Gallery, comme nous le croyons prouvé malgré les doutes un peu hâtifs émis à ce sujet, est bien l'auto-portrait de Jean, agé de 47 à 48 ans en octobre 1433, et si l'un des *juges integres* est bien le portrait de Jean à l'âge approximatif de 35 ans, on arrive à 1420 ou 1421 pour la date d'exécution de ce portrait et du volet qui le renferme." This view may be dismissed without comment.

H

XV. Portraits of John Arnolfini and Joan
Cenani, his Wife, 1434

Plates XXIV and XXV

London : National Gallery (No. 186).   Oak.   2 ft. 9¼ in. ×
2 ft. ½ in. (0.845 × 0.624).

Acquired after 1490 by Don Diego de Guevara,[1]
councillor in 1507 of Maximilian and the Archduke
Charles, and major-domo of Joan, Queen of Castile.
He added shutters to it, on the outer side of which
were painted his arms and motto.   Before 1516 he
presented it to Margaret of Austria, Governess of
the Netherlands.[2]   At her death, in 1530, it passed
into the possession of Mary of Hungary, and it
figures in the inventory of her property in 1556.[3]
It was subsequently taken to Spain.   In 1789 it

[1] See p. 199.

[2] " Ung grant tableau qu'on appelle Hernoul le fin, avec sa femme
dedens une chambre, qui fut donne a Madame par Don Diego, les
armes duquel sont en la couverte du dit tableaul.   Fait du painctre
Iohannes.   [En marge : il a nécessité d'y mettre une serrure pour le
fermer ; ce que Madame a ordonné faire.]"   Inventaire des Peintures,
etc., de Marguerite d'Autriche, dressé en 1516.   Lille : Archives of the
Department of the North, B 3507, p. 209.

" Ung aultre tableau fort exquis qui se clot a deux feulletz, ou il y a
painctz ung homme et une femme estantz desboutz, touchantz la main
l'ung de l'aultre ; fait de la main de Iohannes ; les armes et devise de
feu don Dieghe es dits deux feulletz ; nomme le personnaige, Arnoult
fin."   Inventaire des painctures, etc., appartenans a madame Marguerite,
d'Austriche, dressé en son palais de Malines le 9 Juillet, 1523.   Paris :
Bibliothèque Nationale, Collection Colbert.

A similar description of the picture is given (No. 133) in the
" Inventaire des Tableaux, Livres, Joyaux et Meubles de Marguerite
d'Autriche, fille de Marie de Bourgogne et de Maximilien, Empereur
d'Allemagne, fait et conclus en la ville d'Anvers le xvii d'Avril
mvc"xxiiii."   See Revue Archéologique, Paris, 1850-51, VII, p. 57.

[3] " 85. Cargasele mas una tabla grande con dos puertas, con que se
cerrava, y en ella un ombre e una muger, que se tomaban las manos, con
un espejo, en que se muestran los dichos ombre e muger, y en las
puertas las armas de don Diego de Guebara ; hecha por Juanes de Hec,
anno 1434, segun pareçe por el dicho ynbentario."   Simancas : Royal
Archives.

JOHN ARNOLFINI AND WIFE 1434
LONDON: NATIONAL GALLERY

Plate XXIV

was in the palace of Charles IV, at Madrid.[1] A
little later it fell into the hands of General Belliard
or one of the other French generals. In 1815
Major-General Hay, who had been wounded at the
battle of Waterloo, found it in the apartments to
which he was removed at Brussels. After his
recovery he purchased and brought it to England ;
in 1842 it was acquired by the Gallery for the
moderate sum of £630.

The picture represents a Flemish interior, a
quadrangular room seen in perspective. In the
centre stand a newly married couple. The man,
apparently about thirty-five years of age, is tall
and slight, and has a grave and thoughtful countenance ; he holds his right hand raised in an im-
pressive manner ; while the bride has laid hers in
his left, stretched out towards her. He wears a
close-fitting dress of two shades of black, the sleeves
of which are fastened at the wrist with a red cord.
Over this is a sleeveless tunic of claret-coloured velvet
trimmed with sable fur, reaching to a little below
the knees. Black hose and boots and a large
Italian hat of plaited straw dyed black, complete
his costume. A ring adorns the second finger of his
right hand.

The lady, some years younger than her husband,
is attired in a loose light-green dress, trimmed and
lined with white fur, and confined immediately
below the breast by a rose-coloured cincture embroidered with gold. She has gathered up the front
of her skirt into a mass of stiff folds, displaying a
blue under-dress, the tight sleeves of which are

[1] *See* Justi in *Zeitschrift für bildende Kunst*, XXII, 179, Leipzig, 1887,
who quotes from the Inventory of Paintings in the Royal Palace of
Madrid in 1789 (No. 871). It was then kept " in an unworthy chamber
which it was in those days customary to fit out with numerous good
pictures . . . How this picture, ' the jewel of John van Eyck's art,'
found its way, together with numerous other paintings, mostly of small
value, over the Pyrenees, will always be a mystery."

edged at the wrist with gold lace. Her hair, confined in a caul of red network, is drawn back from off her forehead into two horns, over which is thrown a beautifully frilled kerchief of fine linen. A double string of pearls passes twice round her neck, and a couple of rings adorn the fourth finger of her left hand. At her feet in the foreground is a lively little griffin terrier or Bolognese dog, painted with marvellous accuracy.

From one of the beams of the ceiling in the middle of the room hangs a six-branched chandelier of brass, terminated by a lion's head with a ring in its mouth ; one of the candles is burning. On the right is an aumbry with a couple of oranges on it, a third lying on the sill of a window immediately above it. The upper part of this window is filled with pearl-white roundels ; the shutters of the lower portion, which is not glazed, are open, disclosing a cherry tree covered with fruit, and a glimpse of clear blue sky. On the left, at the farther end of the room, is a bed furnished with a coverlet and hangings of rich crimson. By its head stands an armchair with upright back terminated by cresting and a figure of Saint Margaret triumphing over the dragon, from which a dusting-brush is suspended. On the bedside carpet, which is adorned with flowers and crosses, lie a dainty pair of red shoes, while on the floor, in the foreground to the right, are two pattens of white wood with black leather latchets. Along the farther wall is a bench furnished with a crimson cover and a couple of cushions.

Above the back, terminated at each end by a carved monster, hangs a circular convex mirror in a carved frame adorned with ten little medallions, in which are painted a series of miniatures, commencing at the foot with the Agony in the Garden of Olives, followed by the Betrayal, with Saint Peter cutting off Malchus's ear, Christ being led before

MIRROR, AND SIGNATURE OF JOHN VAN EYCK, 1434

LONDON : NATIONAL GALLERY

Plate XXV

Pilate, the Scourging at the pillar, the Carriage of the cross, Calvary, the Deposition, the Entombment, the Descent into Limbo, and the Resurrection.

In the mirror are seen faithfully reflected, not only the two figures and that portion of the room comprised in the picture, but an oak portal beyond projecting into it, in which two persons are standing, —apparently John van Eyck, dressed in blue, and a youth in scarlet. A string of amber beads with a green silk tassel at the end hanging from a peg to the right of the mirror is reflected on the grey tinted wall. On the wall above the mirror is written, in a highly ornate hand—

"Iohannes de Eyck fuit hic 1434."

The colouring of this marvellous interior is full of vigour and blended with the utmost care. The flesh tints are admirable, and in their rendering show a remarkable transparency of shadow. The picture, in short, is an exquisite gem in the finest state of preservation save in one place, across the mirror.

The back of the panel is painted on a chalk ground.

John Arnolfini settled in Bruges in 1420. Both he and his wife became members of the confraternity of Our Lady of the Dry Tree. They lived in the Coopers' Street, in a picturesque house, pulled down to make room for the present ugly theatre. There Arnolfini, who had been knighted by Duke Philip, and made one of his chamberlains, died on the 11th of September, 1472. He was buried at the Austin Friars', in the chapel of the Lucchese merchants, where he and his brother Michael had founded a Mass to be said daily for the repose of their souls. Joan, who survived her husband, was still living in 1490 ; she was eventually buried in the church of the Rich Clares.

Medici Print, 1 ft. 8½ in. × 1 ft. 3¼ in. (0.52 × 0.38).

Another portrait of John Arnolfini is in the Berlin Gallery (No. 523A) ; see p. 146.

1568. VAERNEWYCK, chap. xlvij, the earliest author who mentions this picture, says that Mary of Hungary saw it when in the possession of a barber, to whom she gave in exchange for it a place worth a hundred florins a year.

1604. C. VAN MANDER, 119, repeats this idle tale.

1847. CARTON, 309, misreads the inscription thus : JOHNINES DE EYCK, HIC. 1438, which, he says, has no sense, and makes him doubt the authenticity of the picture ! !

1852. VIARDOT, Les Musées d'Angleterre, 29, Paris, describes the picture as a scene of chiromancy, and says that the man is trying to read in the lines of the lady's outstretched hand the future of the babe whose birth she is expecting !

1854. WAAGEN, I, 348, repeats Vaernewyck's story, and considers the figures to be the portraits of John van Eyck and his wife.

1855. LABORDE, La Renaissance des Arts à la Cour de France, II, 601–604, Paris, entitles the picture La Légitimation. The man, he says, is solemnly holding up his right hand to attest, in the presence of a crowd of witnesses flocking in at the front door, that the child whose birth the lady is evidently (!) expecting is his, and that with the view of accentuating this fact Van Eyck surrounded the convex mirror with ten others of much smaller size, each reflecting the scene in exact perspective, varied according to its position, with a minuteness and fidelity which are most remarkable ! !

1856. PINCHART, in Revue Universelle des Arts, III, 124, Paris.

1861. WEALE, Notes, 22–28, refutes the misstatements of previous writers.

1862. LOFTIE, 135.

1872. CROWE, 94, 99–101.

1875 The Saturday Review, August 28.

1883 WEALE, 63–65.

1887. JUSTI, Alt Flandrische Bilde in Spanien. In Zeitschrift für bildende Kunst, XXII, 179–180.

1891. LAURIE, 392.

1900. VOLL, 8–16.

1900. EASTLAKE, 108.
1902. C. PHILLIPS, in *The Fortnightly Review*, October, p. 594 : " The ' John Arnolphini and his Wife ' realises in the presentment, hand in hand, of the quaintly costumed Italian merchant and his not specially well-favoured young wife, a moment of unusual solemnity, of mystic union between the couple. Can it be doubted, by those who have carefully and sympathetically considered the picture, that it is intended to commemorate the condition of the wife, so clearly indicated, not less by her form and attitude than by the expression of the husband, in whom a moment of the holiest emotion, though it is made manifest neither by word nor gesture, transfigures to a solemn beauty a countenance of an almost grotesque ugliness ? "
1903. F. WEALE, 20.
1904. WITT, 16–20.
1904. BOUCHOT, 238–240, questions the authenticity of the inscription, which he mistranslates, and says that the painting, described in the inventory of Margaret of Austria as a large picture, is probably still in Spain, and cannot be this ! " Large " and " small " are relative terms, and this is correctly set down as " large " by comparison with those preceding it in the inventory.
1904. KERN, 9, plate iv, shows that John had not completely mastered the laws of linear perspective when he designed this picture.
1908. BROCKWELL, in *The Athenæum*, April 18, p. 485. "We are under the impression that Mr. Weale some years ago satisfied himself that the picture when in Spain hung in the lavatory of the royal palace."
1911. BROCKWELL, in *Notes and Queries*, February 25, p. 147.
1912. KERN, 30, plate i.
1912. BROCKWELL, in *The Morning Post*, July 4.

A curious imitation of this picture (Oak. H. 0.45 ; B. 0.24) signed *Godefridus Iohannis fecit anno* 1581, was in the possession of the late Rev. James Beck.

XVI. Our Lady and Child enthroned, Saint Donatian, Saint George, and the Donor, Canon George Van der Paele, 1434

PLATE XXVI

Bruges : Town Gallery. Oak. 4 ft. × 5 ft. 2 in. (1.22 × 1.57). The figures about two-thirds life-size.

Originally over the altar of Saints Peter and Paul in the collegiate church of Saint Donatian at Bruges ; [1] removed to the sacristy before 1778 ; taken to Paris by the French in 1794 ; brought back by the Allies in 1815, and deposited in the Gallery.

The scene is laid in a circular Romanesque building, or in the apse of the transept of a church, but not in that of Saint Donatian nor of any known Romanesque church.[2] The Blessed Virgin is seated on a throne beneath a canopy furnished with a handsome cloth of honour of woollen material with a rich pattern of foliage and flowers on a blue ground. The front principals of the throne are adorned with figures of Adam and Eve in niches, and surmounted by sculptured groups representing the death of Abel, and Samson tearing the lion in pieces. A beautiful carpet covers the steps of the throne and part of the pavement of blue-and-white Spanish—probably Valencian—tiles. The Virgin's robe of blue, cut square at the neck, is bordered with a jewelled band ; over it she wears a large red mantle lined with olive green, and bordered with precious stones between

---

[1] CROWE (1872, p. 108) and KAEMMERER (1898, p. 66) say that this picture was commissioned for the high altar of the church. It was not placed over the high altar until after 1578, when the silver-gilt reredos given by Margaret, Countess of Flanders and Artois, was broken up and melted.

[2] See the illustrations in James ESSEX, *Journal of a Tour through part of Flanders in August,* 1773, edited by W. M. Fawcett, Cambridge, 1888, p. 13 ; and J. GAILLIARD, *Inscriptions funéraires de la Flandre Occidentale,* 1, plate 2. Bruges, 1861.

OUR LADY AND CHILD, SS. DONATIAN AND GEORGE, AND CANON G. VAN DER PAELE, 1436

BRUGES : TOWN GALLERY

Plate XXVI

two rows of small pearls. Her long crimped hair, confined by a jewelled circlet of gold, falls in undulating masses over her shoulders. With her right hand she supports the Divine Child seated nude on a fair linen cloth spread over her knee. With His right hand He is holding a parakeet, and with His left accepting a bunch of flowers from His mother.

On the right stands Saint Donatian, seen in profile, vested in a splendid cope of blue-and-gold velvet brocade, the orfreys of which are embroidered with figures of the Apostles in canopied compartments ; a circular morse of gold set with precious stones keeps the cope from slipping from the shoulders. A richly jewelled cloth-of-gold mitre, and gloves over which he wears several rings, complete his costume. With his right hand he supports the emblem which characterises him—a wheel with axle and spokes complete, on the rim of which stand in a circle five lighted candles. With his left he holds with its veil an archiepiscopal cross, a splendid specimen of goldsmith's work.

To the left, opposite Saint Donatian, the donor, Canon George Van der Paele, is represented kneeling under the protection of his name-saint. He is vested in a red cassock and large-sleeved surplice, with an almuce of grey fur thrown over his left arm. In his right hand he holds a double eye-glass, and with his left supports open before him his breviary with its forel of sow-skin.

Saint George stands behind him clad in a complete suit of armour, with the word ADONAI inscribed across his gorget. A lance with pennon, bearing *Argent* a cross *gules*, rests against his left shoulder. He raises his helmet to salute the Divine Infant as he presents his client.

The apse is formed by a series of round arches supported by cylindrical columns, the capitals of which are carved with interlaced foliage and animals,

while those of the pillars on the farther side of the
ambulatory are storied ; the windows between the
latter are filled with roundels.

Realism prevails throughout this picture, which,
with the exception of the Ypres triptych (see
p. 122), is the largest work by the master. The
most pleasing figure is that of Saint Donatian, a
dignified court prelate, with a noble head of in-
tellectual type ; but even here we have not the
slightest attempt at idealisation. The Virgin Mother
is represented as a woman of about thirty, utterly
lacking in refinement ; while the Child, a puny
infant, short and attenuated, and curiously aged,
is apparently frightened at the sight of Saint George,
an awkward conscript, who is doffing his helmet with
a trivial expression utterly devoid of religious
feeling.

The portrait of the canon is that of a man of
marked individuality, but obviously infirm. He
had been installed in his canonry on the 20th of
August, 1410, and had for many years been in constant residence at Saint Donatian's, where he
founded two choral chaplaincies, one on the 13th
of September, 1434, the other on the 8th of May, 1441.
He also presented the church with some relics of
Saint Christopher and Saint Ursula in a reliquary
of silver gilt with a cylindrical turret of rock crystal,
adorned with his arms and surmounted by a figure
of Saint George and a crucifix. He died at an
advanced age on the 25th of August, 1443, having
been very infirm during the last ten years of his
life. He was buried in the grave of his brother,
Canon Jodoc, in the nave, on the north side of the
altar of Saints Peter and Paul, between the tomb of
his uncle, Jodoc Van der Paele, also a canon, and
that of Margaret, Countess of Flanders. His grave
was covered with a slab of blue stone adorned with
his effigy in sacerdotal vestments within a border

inscribed : " Hic iacet dominus Georgius de Pala canonicus huius ecclesie qui obiit anno Domini M cccc xliij," with the evangelistic animals and his mother's arms.

The altar-piece still retains its original frame, with the following legends ; of these the one at the top runs :

HEC EST SPECIOSIOR SOLE + SVPER OMNEM STEL-
LARVM DISPOSICIONEM LVCI COMPARATA INVENITVR
PRIOR : CANDOR EST ENIM LVCIS ETERNE + SPEC-
VLVM SINE MACVLA DEI MAIESTATIS.[1]

On the right side :

SOLO P[AR]TV NON[V]S FR̄[ATRV]M
MERS[V]S VIV[V]S REDDIT[VR]
ET RENAT[VS] ARCHOS P[AT]R̄[V]M
REMIS CONSTITVITVR
QVI NV̄[N]C DEO FRVITVR ;[2]

and on the chamfer :

S[AN]C̄[̣TV]S DONACIANVS ARCHIEP̄[ISCOPV]S.

On the left side :

NATVS CAPADOCIA
X̄PO MILITAVIT
MUNDI FVGIĒ[N]S OCIA
CESVS TRIVMPHAVIT
HIC DRACONEM STRAVIT ;

and on the chamfer :

S[AN]C̄[TV]S GEORGIVS MILES X̄PI.

---

[1] The little chapter at Lauds on the feast of the Assumption, in the Breviary according to the use of the church of Saint Donatian. The same inscription is found on the panel (2) of the Blessed Virgin of the Ghent polyptych (see p. 41), and also on the frame of the Dresden triptych (see p. 85).

[2] Compare the third and fourth Lessons at Matins on the feast of Saint Donation, in the same Breviary.

At the foot, in minuscules :

Hoc op[us] fecit fieri mag[iste]r Georgi[u]s
de Pala hui[u]s ecclesi[a]e canoni[cu]s p[er]
Iohanne[m]
de Eyck pictorē[m] : et fundavit hic duas
capell[an]ias de gremio chori domini m°
ccc°xxxiiii° : c[om]p[le]t[um] añ[no] 1436.

At each angle is an escucheon, those at the
upper right and lower left angles bear, *Sable*, two
peels in saltire *or* between four loaves *argent*, Van der
Paele ; and those at the upper left and lower right
angles, *Argent*, on three chevrons *azure,* twelve
fleurs-de-lys 5, 5 and 2 *or*, within a bordure engrailed
gules, Carlyns.[1]

The picture has been damaged by cleaning and
clumsy retouches ; the drapery of the Virgin's
dress is partially destroyed ; the Child's right foot
has also suffered ; the white shame-cloth about his
loins is a late addition ; and the whole is covered
with a thick cloudy varnish. The background is
well preserved.

Exhibited : Bruges, Early Netherlandish Masters,
1902 (No. 10). For details of the copy, in the
Antwerp Museum, of this picture, see p. 178.

1769. DESCAMPS, 274, describes the picture thus: "L'Adora-
    tion des Rois (!) ; les têtes sont avec peu ou point
    de sécheresse, surtout celle de l'évêque S. Donas dans
    la manière de Gérard Douw " (! !).
1798. Sir Joshua REYNOLDS, in his " Journey to Flanders
    in 1781 " (Works, II, 1798), says : " The figure of the
    canon has great character of nature, and is very
    minutely painted."
1861. WEALE, Catalogue, 12–17.
1872. CROWE, 108–109 : " A curious instance of the
    painter's occasional descent to a lower level of treat-

---

[1] The arms of his mother, in their usual place. Kaemmerer's
statement, that the Carlyns family contributed to the cost of the painting,
is without foundation.

ment than that observable in the common run of the works of the time. . . . The colour is not handled with the painter's habitual breadth, and traces of manipulation obtrude in all parts. The figures are drawn with less than usual ability ; most of the faces are insipid in expression, and the hands are stiff and long ; tints no longer melt into each other, and the colour, instead of being rich and giving to the flesh a plump and pleasant aspect, has a hard and red appearance. . . . St. Donatian is the most remarkable of the persons in the composition ; his pious and noble head rivets the spectator's attention, and keeps it from the overloaded ornaments of a splendid cope and stole ; but the figure of St. George is trivial and awkward."

1876. FROMENTIN, 427–430 : " Par la mise en scène, le style et le caractère de la forme, de la couleur et du travail, il rappelle la *Vierge au donateur* (the Rolin altar-piece) au Louvre. Il n'est pas plus précieux dans le fini, pas plus finement observé dans le détail. . . . Mais ici tout est plus large, plus mûr, plus grandement conçu, construit et peint. Et l'œuvre en devient plus magistrale en ce qu'elle entre en plein dans les visées de l'art moderne. . . . Le chanoine est incontestablement le plus fort morceau du tableau. . . . C'est un vieillard. Il est chauve. . . . Ce gros visage flasque et rugueux est une merveille de dessin physionomique et de peinture. . . . La tonalité du tableau est grave, sourde et riche, extraordinairement harmonieuse et forte. . . . En vérité, quand on s'y concentre, c'est une peinture qui fait oublier tout ce qui n'est pas elle et donnerait à penser que l'art de peindre a dit son dernier mot, et cela dès la première heure."

1878. WEALE, *Bruges et ses Environs*, 4e édition, 51–56.

1902. JORISSENNE, in *Compte rendu du Congrès de Bruges*, 11–13.

1902. HULIN, 10. This picture has furnished the formula for the composition of a number of paintings by masters working at Bruges.

1903. FRIEDLAENDER, 2. Of all John's works this had the greatest influence on the development of painting at Bruges.

1911. DOEHLEMANN, 402–403.

1912. KERN, 34, plate ii.

The type of the Virgin is reproduced (1) on an early sixteenth-century diptych in the Bartels Collection at Cassel ; (2) on a diptych dated 1523 in the Provincial Museum at Hanover ; (3) on an altar-piece, c. 1515, at Ince Hall, exhibited, with an ascription to Mabuse, at the Guildhall, 1906, No. 60 ; (4) in a somewhat later picture exhibited, with an attribution to John van Eyck, by the late Mr. J. Fletcher Moulton at the New Gallery in 1899, No. 82 ; and (5) in a Madonna and Child, in a rather poor state of preservation, which was in the collection of Mr. Charles Hamilton Walker, and in 1905-6 passed through the hands of Mr. A. H. Buttery, Messrs. P. & D. Colnaghi and Herr Bœhler, of Munich, as being of the school of Van Eyck.

The Virgin and Child reappear on a small panel in the collection of the Earl of Northbrook, the original frame of which is said to have borne the date 1437 (see p. 160).

The figure of Saint Louis of Toulouse presenting a donor, in an early sixteenth-century picture in the Museum at Avignon (exhibited at Paris, 1904, No. 85), bears in pose and gesture a curious resemblance to the Saint George here, which certainly influenced the unknown painter. The pose and several details of the gold statuette of Saint George, executed by Gerard Loyet of Bruges, 1466-1471, for Charles the Bold, and by him presented to the cathedral of Liége, betray the same influence.

For the copy in the Antwerp Museum of the full picture at Bruges, and a somewhat similar copy formerly in the Wynn Ellis Collection, see p. 164.

For the portrait of the Canon only at Hampton Court, see p. 151.

JOHN DE LEEUW, GOLDSMITH, 1436
VIENNA : IMPERIAL GALLERY
From a photograph by F. Bruckmann

Plate XXVII

XVII. Portrait of John De Leeuw, Goldsmith, 1436

PLATE XXVII

Vienna : Imperial Gallery (No. 625). Oak. 13 in. × 11¼ in. (0.33 × 0.28). Head, 4 in. (0.10).

First mentioned in Mechel's catalogue of the Belvedere Collection, 1783, p. 157, No. 28. Taken to Paris by the French in 1809 ; brought back by the Allies in 1815.

Half-length portrait, about half life-size, of a man of thirty-five years of age, on a dark-green background ; the face beardless, seen in three-quarters turned to the right, with small deep-set grey eyes looking straight at the spectator, short nose, fine upper lip, and a long chin. The broad forehead and keen glance of the eyes convey the impression of a highly intelligent man with an energetic will. He wears a dark fur-trimmed gown and a black cap ; his hands are placed before his waist ; between the thumb and forefinger of his right hand he holds a ring, as if showing it. The head is modelled with John's usual care, but the beauty of the face is somewhat marred by the same unpleasant reddish flesh tint that characterises the figures in the Bruges altar-piece, painted about the same time ; the hands, too, are rather weak, as if hurriedly drawn. The frame, which is original, bears the following inscription :

> IAN DE (a lion sejant on a square base with a step)
> as a rebus) OP SANT ORSELEN DACH
> DAT CLAER EERST MET OGHEN SACH . 1401.
> GHECONTERFEIT NV HEEFT MI IAN
> VAN EYCK WEL BLIJCT WANNEERT BEGAN . 1436.

John De Leeuw, the person here portrayed, was a wealthy craftsman, born October 21, 1401, who, after holding minor offices in the Gild of Gold- and Silver-smiths of Bruges in 1430–31 and 1435–36, was chosen dean in 1441. The lion sejant is the mark he used for stamping his works, and here stands for his name, which, if written, would have added 65 to the first chronogram. An interesting entry in the accounts of the treasurers of the town informs us that when Duke Philip, after a long absence in Germany, returned to Bruges in 1455, the inhabitants decorated the fronts of their houses, and that the town council awarded prizes to those whose houses were decorated and illuminated with the greatest taste ; these prizes were supplied by De Leeuw, who was paid 36s. gr. for them.

The date of De Leeuw's death is not known ; his name occurs for the last time in the accounts of the treasurer of the town of Damme for the year 1459.

The picture has suffered by cleaning, and, doubtless owing to the colour having less intensity and charm than usual, it has received but scant notice from writers on the master's works.

1557. VAN VLAENDEREN, "Kronyk," folio 50, in the description of the pageant of 1458 refers to "Meester Jan de Leeu."

1858. HOTHO, II, 187, says that the ring in De Leeuw's hand is probably a wedding-ring.

1882. WOLTMANN, II, 19, and 1891, REBER, 107, call De Leeuw a canon !

1898. KAEMMERER, 73, says that De Leeuw had this portrait painted to present to his bride. This is fancy : he had been married some years, and had at least two children.

1899. SEECK, 28, 70. The hands are weak ; the little finger of the right hand crooked, like a claw. Calls the ring a betrothal ring.

1900. VOLL, 97–100, devotes four pages to throwing doubt on the authenticity of this work. His conclusion is that the portrait is either a forgery or a copy dating from the end of the fifteenth century.

SAINT BARBARA 1437

ANTWERP: MUSEUM

From a photograph by G. Hermans

Plate XXVIII

1901. BODE, 118–119, refutes Voll's arguments.
1903. F. C. WEALE, 23.
1904. WEALE, *Burlington Magazine*, v, 192. His name occurs in a document dated July 20, 1456.
1909. RUPP, 488–491.

XVIII. SAINT BARBARA, 1437

PLATE XXVIII

Antwerp : Museum : Van Ertborn Collection (No. 410). Oak. 12¾ in. × 7¼ in. (0.322 × 0.186).

This picture became the property of M. Joz. Enschedé of Haarlem on June 24, 1769, and was sold by him in 1786 to a dealer, P. Yver, and by the latter to Ploos van Amstel. After his death it was sold at Amsterdam, March 5, 1800, for 35 florins 18 sols to M. Oyen, from whose widow it was purchased in 1826 by M. F. van Ertborn, and by him bequeathed to the Antwerp Museum.

Saint Barbara, seated in a meditative mood on a hillock in the foreground, is turning over the leaves of a book which rests on her knees. In her left hand she holds a palm. Her ample wide-sleeved dress, open in front with a large turned-down collar, is confined at the waist by a plain cincture ; its long skirt covers the ground around her in broken folds. Her hair, confined by a plain riband, falls on her back ; a jewel is suspended to the string of pearls which encircles her neck. In the mid-distance a beautiful octagonal tower [1] is in course of construction ; on its summit four masons are working ; a fifth, near the crane by which a carved stone is being hauled up, stands looking down at the master-mason, who is giving him directions. Near him

[1] This does not represent the tower of a church dedicated to Saint Barbara, as stated by a writer in the *Messager des Sciences* (Ghent, 1839, p. 57), but is simply the emblem characterising this saint. Ignorance of this has led some to describe the picture as Saint Agnes.

I

beneath a shed are sculptors at work, while labourers around are busily employed mixing mortar and bringing them materials, two with a bier and one with a barrow ;—an interesting picture, showing how building operations were carried on in the fifteenth century. Behind the saint four women are passing to the right, where a group of men are conversing ; farther away are buildings with a fortified wall. Four men on horseback are coming in single file down a winding road, beyond which are a wood and a picturesque mountain covered to its summit with buildings. To the left is rising ground with fields, trees, and water ; high up in the air is seen a flight of wild geese.[1] The sky is coloured, the rest of the picture merely drawn, but with the greatest care and minuteness.

At the foot, in capital letters, " IOĦES DE EYCK ME FECIT, 1437."

Facsimile engraving by Cornelius van Noorde, 1769. Copies in the Museums at Bruges and Lille ; mistaken by De Montaiglon and Voll for drawings, though their real character was pointed out by Schnaase in 1834.

Exhibited : Bruges, Early Netherlandish Masters, 1902 (No. 11A).

1884. HYMANS, in the commentaries appended to his translation of Van Mander's " Book of Painters," p. 40, identifies this Saint Barbara with a panel representing a woman in the foreground of a landscape, in the possession of Luke De Heere, described by Van Mander as only a preparation for a painting, but exceedingly pretty.

1901. *Petite Revue Illustrée de l'Art en Flandre*, March 15, Ghent, on the engraving by C. van Noorde in the Bruges Gallery.

1903. SCHUBERT, 38–42, is of opinion that in this work the Eyckian landscape attained its highest perfection !

[1] For critical remarks on the flocks of geese or cranes in paintings by the Van Eycks, see pp. 48, 70, 78, 89, 94, 227.

1909. HOLMES, C. J., *Notes on the Science of Picture-Making*, pp. 194–195 : " The unfinished picture of *St. Barbara* by John van Eyck in the Antwerp Gallery shows clearly how the Flemish masters worked. The design was first carefully drawn on the gesso ground, perfect in all its details, and the painting was then executed piece by piece, each part being finished before the next was started. The panel was sometimes toned with a wash of pale colour, often a flesh tint, before the actual painting was started. This tone served to fix the lines of the drawing, and to modify the extreme whiteness of the gesso. When finished, the painting was exposed to the sun, not so much to dry the pigment as to extract the excess of oil, which otherwise would have accumulated near the surface in course of time, and would have given the work a yellowish tone. The bleaching action of sunlight upon the oils used in painting is not always remembered."

1911. DOEHLEMANN, 406.

XIX. OUR LADY AND CHILD BY A FOUNTAIN, 1439

Antwerp : Museum : Van Ertborn Collection (No. 411). Oak. 7½ in. × 4¾ in. (0.19 × 0.122).

This picture was in the possession of Margaret of Austria, Governess of the Netherlands. In the inventory of her collection in 1516, it is described as " Une petite Nostre Dame, faite de bonne main, estant en un jardin ou il y a une fontaine ; "[1] but, more fully, in that drawn up in her palace at Mechlin, on July 9, 1523, as " Ung aultre petit tableau de Nostre Dame tenant son enfant, lequel tient une petite patenostre de coral en sa main, fort anticque, ayant une fontainne empres elle et deux anges tenant ung drapt d'or figure derriere elle."[2]

[1] "Inventaire des Peintures, etc., de Marguerite d'Autriche, dressé en 1516." Lille : Archives of the Department of the North, B 3507.

[2] "Inventaire des Peintures, etc., de Marguerite d'Autriche, dressé en son palais de Malines, le 9 Juillet 1523." Paris : National Library, Colbert Collection. In the margin : " Donné par ordonnance de ma ditte dame à son trésorier général, Jehan de Marnix."

Margaret subsequently gave it to her treasurer-general, John van Marnix.

In 1830 it was in the possession of the parish priest of Dickelvenne (East Flanders), from whom it was purchased by M. F. van Ertborn, and by him bequeathed to the Antwerp Museum.

Our Lady stands on a grass plot in the open air, tenderly pressing the Infant Jesus to her breast with both hands. The Child with His right hand embraces her affectionately, and with His left stretched out behind Him holds a tasselled chaplet of red coral beads. Two angels with peacock wings, in flowing albs, one vermilion, the other violet, hold up a cloth of honour of red-and-gold brocaded damask, the end of which covers the ground on which the Virgin stands. She is draped in an ample blue mantle, which falls about her feet in rather stiff folds. Her light-brown hair, parted in the middle and confined by a narrow band of pearls, is drawn back behind the ear, making the forehead and temples appear unusually large. On the right, in the immediate front, stands a metal fountain with a circular basin, into which water of crystalline purity falls from four jets. In the background we see on each side of the suspended cloth a low bank faced with masonry, and covered with fine grass and flowering plants : daisies, violets, lilies of the valley, yellow water-flags, and a thick hedge of purple roses and lilies.

The frame, painted to imitate reddish-grey marble with white veins, bears the following in-scription in capital letters :

ALS IXH XAN

JOĦES DE EYCK ME FECIT + CPLEVIT (complevit) AÑO 1439.

The picture is in perfect preservation save for a small patch on the Child's head.

MARGARET VAN EYCK 1439
BRUGES : TOWN GALLERY
By permission of A. Dalet

Plate XXIX

Exhibited, Bruges, Early Netherlandish Masters, 1902 (No. 13).

1905. FIERENS, 163, rightly notes that this picture has a character quite exceptional in the series of John van Eyck's works. He thinks it was based on the Madonna by Stephen Lochner, in the Diocesan Museum at Köln, which he dates *c.*1435; but that painting is certainly of later date.

A beautiful copy of this picture adorns a Flemish Book of Hours formerly in the possession of Mr. Edwin H. Laurence, of Abbey Farm Lodge, Hampstead; and an early pen drawing of it on paper is preserved in the Print Room of the Kaiser Friedrich Museum, Berlin, 7120 (1878).

The Berlin Gallery and the Metropolitan Museum at New York possess paintings with figures of the Madonna closely resembling this.[1]

XX. PORTRAIT OF MARGARET VAN EYCK, WIFE OF THE PAINTER, 1439

. PLATE XXIX

Bruges : Town Gallery. Oak. 12¾ in. × 10¼ in. (0.32 × 0.26).

Formerly in the possession of the Bruges Gild of Painters and Saddlers, and exposed in their chapel annually on Saint Luke's Day, at other times kept in their archives. Owing to the existence of a heavy mortgage on the property of the gild, it escaped being taken to Paris in 1794. Later it was found in the fish-market at Bruges by Mr. Peter van Lede who, in 1808, presented it to the town.

Half-length portrait, the face turned to the right seen in three-quarters. The lady, attired in her best, wears a loose-sleeved gown of scarlet cloth trimmed with grey fur, girt under the breasts with

[1] See pp. 172 and 174.

a sash of green silk woven in chevrons. A crespine head-dress, over which is a white linen kerchief with a ruche of the same material, completes her costume. Her hands are superposed before her, displaying her wedding-ring on the fourth finger of the right hand.

Though painted with great minuteness, and marvellous delicacy and finish, the effect of this evidently perfect likeness is the same whether viewed closely or from a distance. John has not flattered his wife, but has portrayed her with the insight born of intimate acquaintance. Her features are not attractive, and her head-dress does not improve her appearance ; but she was evidently an intelligent woman, and a competent housewife, with a clear steady eye and a firm mouth, showing that she had a will of her own.

The frame, painted to imitate marble, bears the following inscriptions in capital letters : at the head,

"cō[n]ivx m̄[ev]s ioh[ann]ēs me c̄[om]plevit an̄[n]o 1439° 17 ivnii " ;

and at the foot :

"etas mea triginta triv̄[m] an[n]orv̄[m]. als ixh xan."

The reverse of the panel is painted in imitation of porphyry.

Lithograph by A. Toupey, 1907 (H. 0.216 ; B. 0.168).

Exhibited, Bruges, Early Netherlandish Masters, 1902, No. 12.

1769. Descamps, 306, says that this portrait was exhibited annually on St. Luke's Day in the chapel of the Painters' Gild, but fastened with a chain and padlock, as the companion painting, John van Eyck's own portrait, had been stolen. Every attempt has been made to verify the truth of this statement, which appears to be a fiction.

1857. CROWE, 89–90. The hand is, perhaps, the most complete and perfect John van Eyck ever executed.

1900. BOUCHOT, " Les Femmes de Jean van Eyck," in *Revue de l'Art Ancien*, VII, 405.

1902. GUIFFREY, 472 : " Le morceau de reception de van Eyck dans la Corporation " ! ! A nonsensical statement. Van Eyck was not a member of the gild, and the custom of presenting a diploma work was nonexistent.

1902. LAFENESTRE, in *Revue des Deux Mondes*, 5 P., XI, 140.

1902. FRY, in *The Athenæum*, Sept. 13, 356.

1902. HYMANS, L'Exposition des Primitifs Flamands à Bruges, 17–18.

1903. WEALE, F. C., 24–25.

1905. FIERENS, 165.

1906. VOLL, 34–35.

1910. VOLL, 21–27.

XXI. OUR LADY AND CHILD, AND THE DONOR, 1441

PLATE XXX

Kessel-Loo : M. G. Helleputte. Oak. Triptych : arched top. Centre, 3 ft. 10 in. × 3 ft. 3 in. (1.72 × 0.99) ; shutters, 3 ft. 10 in. × 1 ft. 4¼ in. (1.72 × 0.41).

The scene is laid in a vaulted portico of Romanesque architecture, the columns of which are richly sculptured with birds, monsters, and interlaced work. In the foreground on the left stands the Blessed Virgin with the Divine Child on her right arm, and with her left hand tenderly supporting His legs. Her long hair, parted down the middle and confined by a jewelled circlet of gold, is drawn back behind the ears and falls on her shoulders in undulating masses. Posed in a very graceful and dignified attitude, she is enveloped in an ample mantle of crimson cloth, which, kept in place by two tasselled cords, falls over her feet and on to the pavement behind her ; its embroidered border, adorned with pearls and precious stones, bears at the foot, where it becomes much broader, a verse from the twenty-fourth chapter of Ecclesiasticus :

"[Ante] SECVLA [creata sum et usque ad futurum secu]L[um non desinam et] IN [habitatione sancta] CORAM IPSO MINISTRAVI ET SIC IN SION FIRMATA [sum]."

The Child, quite nude, clutches the embroidered neck-band of His mother's dress, and with a gracious inclination of His head extends His right hand towards a priest who kneels before Him praying from an open book in his right hand. On a fluttering scroll, one end of which the Child holds, are the words :

"*Discite a me quia mitis sum et humilis corde iugum enim meum suave est et onus* meum leve."

The priest, a provost of Saint Martin's at Ypres, is vested in a rochet and a cope of blue-and-gold brocade, the orfreys of which are embroidered with figures of the Apostles beneath canopies. A circular morse of gold with three statuettes beneath a triple canopy keeps the cope in position. With his left hand the provost grasps the emblem of his office, a staff adorned with a diaper of fleurs-de-lys within lozenges surmounted by statuettes of saints in tabernacles, and crowned by a large crescent encircling a group representing the charity of Saint Martin.

The pavement of the portico is composed of stones of various colours arranged in a geometrical pattern. The background, seen over the parapet of the portico, is a far-receding landscape traversed from right to left by a river enlivened by boats, swans, &c. The ground on the near side is covered with vegetation and a variety of flowers ; here to the right and close to the river-bank is a hostelry with figures ; while on the left is a man on horse-back. Across the river and to the right is a castle

OUR LADY AND CHILD AND NICHOLAS VAN MAELBEKE, 1441

KESSEL-LOO : M. G. HELLEPUTTE

Plate XXX

flanked at the angles by square towers ; while on
the left are several houses, and the quay, on which
we see a number of persons on horseback and on
foot near a road that winds across a hilly country
dotted over with numerous buildings and figures,
and stretching far away to distant mountains.
Every detail of this landscape is treated with
marvellous care and finish.

On the frame, inscribed in capital letters, here
given *in extenso*, is the antiphon :

"SANCTA MARIA SVCCVRRE MISERIS IVVA PVSIL-
LANIMES : REFOVE FLEBILES : ORA PRO POPVLO :
INTERVENI PRO CLERO : INTERCEDE PRO DEVOTO
FEMINEO SEXV : SENTIANT OMNES TVVM IVVAMEN
QUICVMQVE CELEBRANT TVAM COMMEMORATIONEM.
HEC VIRGO MARIA EX SEMINE ABRAHE ORTA : EX
TRIBV IVDA : VIRGA DE RADICE IESSE : EX STIRPE
DAVID : FILIA IHERVSALEM : STELLA MARIS : AN-
CILLA DOMINI : REGINA GENTIVM : SPONSA DEI :
MATER CHRISTI : CONDITORIS TEMPLVM : SANCTI
SPIRITVS SACRARIVM."

The shutters are divided both on the inner and
outer side into two zones. In the lower half of the
dexter shutter, Gedeon, clad in a suit of steel armour,
stands on a rocky hill, holding with both hands a
lance. He has bared his head in presence of the
angel who stands beneath an oak tree on the right
and is addressing him ; on the frame below is the
legend " vellus gedeonis." The burning bush is
figured in the upper zone as a tall, smooth-trunked
tree, the branches of which fill the entire breadth of
the panel with a dense mass of foliage. A half-
length figure of the Eternal within an aureole appears
surrounded by tongues of fire springing from the
foliage. He is crowned with a tiara, and vested in
an alb and a cope of cloth of gold fastened by an
oval morse adorned with a ruby surrounded by nine
pearls. His right hand raised in the act of blessing,

He holds in His left an orb with a slender crystal cross terminated by gold fleurs-de-lys. At the foot of the tree is a plot of grass and flowers, bordered by a path and a bed with a row of shrubs, beyond which is a moat with ducks and swans. On the farther side are houses and gardens, an inn, a large pond with a variety of waterfowl, and a turreted castle with a man on a ladder repairing the roof. Away across the pond are numerous buildings with figures in the open spaces between them, and beyond these a forest stretches away to mountains in the distance. On the molding separating these two zones is the legend, "rubus ardens et non comburens."

In the lower half of the corresponding sinister shutter, Aaron, clad in a green cope, is represented standing before an altar with a budding rod in his right hand. On the frame at the foot we read, "virga aaron florens." The closed door of the sanctuary, spoken of by the Prophet Ezechiel, is figured in the upper portion of the panel as a rectangular tower flanked at the angles by cylindrical turrets ; the gables and the ridge of the tiled roof are crowned by an elegant open-work cresting of metal ; similar cresting at the foot of the roof is carried round the turrets. The door itself is bordered by broad bands of metal-work set with precious stones connected by horizontal bands of similar design. The archivolt of the doorway is adorned with twelve statuettes of prophets. Above it, in a canopied tabernacle, is a figure of the Synagogue, blindfolded, holding the tables of the Law upside down, and a banner, the staff of which is falling to pieces. On brackets at each side of this are statues of Moses and prophets, and above these, immediately below the roof, a series of statuettes in tabernacles. In the foreground at the foot of the tower, lilies and other plants are flowering right up to the very door.

On the right is a pretty piece of landscape. The molding separating these two zones bears the legend, " porta ezechielis clausa." Both shutters are filled at the head with open-work tracery enclosing figures : the fall of our first parents ; an angel with a flaming sword standing at the entrance to Paradise, the angel Gabriel and the Blessed Virgin.

On the exterior of the shutter are grisailles : at the head, three angels blowing trumpets, and a fine half-length figure of the Blessed Virgin and Child. appearing within an aureole. At the foot, full-length figures of the Sibyl pointing up to the apparition, and of the Emperor Octavian contemplating it with hands uplifted in prayer. The explanatory legends are : " ara celi—maria—sibilla —octauianus."

This triptych, had it been completed, would have been John's masterpiece. It was undertaken at the request of Nicholas van Maelbeke, who, as twenty-ninth provost of Saint Martin's abbey, governed it from 1429 until his death in 1445. It was then, though unfinished, placed over his tomb in the choir of the church. Luke De Heere, in the poem he composed in 1559, mentions it (strophe 19), as also Mark van Vaernewyck in his *Nieu tractaet* (strophe 126), published at Ghent in .1562 ; the latter describes it accurately in his *Spieghel der Nederlandscher Audtheyt*, printed in 1574. He says that " the picture, of which the shutters are unfinished, is well deserving of admiration ; that it was painted by master John van Eyck, and has the appearance of being a heavenly rather than a human work." Guicciardini, Vasari, and Van Mander all make mention of it. Sanderus, who was a canon of Ypres, describes it in 1718 as being then in the choir, and the archdeacon Van der Meesch drew the attention of the two Benedictines, Dom E. Martene and Dom Durand, to it, as they tell us in their

Voyage littéraire, published in 1717. Between 1757 and 1760 the triptych was removed from the church into the episcopal palace, and a copy of the central panel, in the possession of the late Mgr. Felix de Bethune (d. 1908) at Bruges, was placed in the Lady Chapel. After the capture of Ypres and the sack of the palace by the French Republicans, the triptych was sold for a song to a butcher, and by him to a M. Waelwyn of Ypres. He parted with it to Mr. Bogaert-Dumortier of Bruges, from whose heirs it was purchased for 6000 francs by M. Désiré Van den Schrieck of Louvain. At his death, in 1857, it became the property of his son-in-law, M. F. Schollaert, Vice-President of the Belgian Chamber of Representatives, after whose death it passed into the possession of M. George Helleputte, his son-in-law.

The authenticity of the picture is incontestable. It is confirmed by two contemporary documents, one, a pen-and-ink drawing (H. 0.278 ; B. 0.18) in the Albertina at Vienna, formerly catalogued as an original drawing by John van Eyck, but now attributed, without a particle of evidence, to Peter Christus.

Another smaller copy (H. 0.135 ; B. 0.15), in silver point, formerly in the collection of Mr. de Franck at Graz, belongs to the Germanic Museum at Nürnberg, where it is attributed to Roger De la Pasture. These drawings represent the central panel only. The first is in a good state of preservation ; the other has suffered slightly. The following points should be noted : (1) The band which confines the Virgin's hair in both drawings is quite simple, whereas in the picture it is adorned with jewellery as in the Ince Hall panel and the Bruges altar-piece ;ʼ (2) the embroidery of the neck-band of the Virgin's dress and of the border of her mantle are non-existent ; (3) the shoe and patten of the .

Virgin's left foot, shown in the drawings, are in the painting hidden by the border added to the mantle; (4) the scroll held by the Child in the drawings is simpler than in the picture, and bears no legend.

In the Albertina drawing the figure of the provost is merely sketched ; he has a large tonsure, but neither moustache nor beard ; the features, too, have much more distinction ; the folds of the cope and the outline of the morse are merely indicated, but there is no trace of the design of the brocade, nor of the storied orfreys. The vaulting of the portico, plain in the drawings, is decorated in the painting. Lastly, the landscape background is not even indicated in the drawings, but if compared with the landscape in the Saint Barbara, its authenticity will be apparent. And, noteworthy above all, this is the earliest picture of the school, and the only one by John van Eyck in which the linear perspective is perfect,—a fact which, notwithstanding its sad state, lends this picture great importance.

A passage said to have been extracted by M. Lambin from a " Memorial " of the community of Grey Friars of Ypres, and published by Carton in 1848, may be translated as follows :—

" In the year 1445 master John van *Eycken*, a famous painter, painted at Ypres that excellent picture which was placed in the choir of Saint Martin's as a memorial of the reverend Sir Nicholas *Malchalopie*, *abbot* or provost of Saint Martin's monastery, who lies buried there before it."

This is said by Carton to be an extract from a contemporary chronicle of the Grey Friars' convent at Ypres,[1] and to prove that the triptych was commenced in 1445, that it was still unfinished when the provost died in 1447 (*sic*), and that the painter was John van *Eycken*. It is highly improbable that any one living at Ypres in the fifteenth century, much

---

[1] LABORDE, *Les Ducs de Bourgogne*, I, cxx, warned students against attaching any value to this extract.

less a contemporary, would distort the name of Van Maelbeke, one of the principal families of the locality, or would call the provost of Saint Martin's an abbot, or say that the picture was painted at Ypres. The note was probably not written until long after 1559, when, on the creation of the see of Ypres by Pope Paul IV, Saint Martin's ceased to be a monastic church, and became a cathedral. The phrase *abt ofte proost* looks as though copied from the 1574 edition of Mark van Vaernewyck's *Historie van Belgis*, and " painted in Ypres " is a strange expression for a resident to use, who would surely have written *here* or *in this town*. The wording of the note, too, betokens an eighteenth- rather than a fifteenth-century origin. Most of the critics who have dealt with this triptych since 1848 have relied on this document as the basis for their rejection of the Eyckian origin of the picture. We think its utter worthlessness is now established.

There can be no doubt that everything seen in the Vienna and Nürnberg drawings, and probably the landscape background and the pavement, were painted by John van Eyck, and that the copies belonging to Mgr. F. de Bethune and to the Town Museum at Ypres show the additions made in the sixteenth century, probably about 1560. The re- presentations of the burning bush and of the closed door of Ezechiel are the portions of the shutters on which Van Eyck had worked most ; a careful examination of these discloses many beauties. In the nineteenth century, shortly previous to 1830, M. Alphonse Bogaert, of Bruges, scrubbed the picture, and then attempted to restore it. In 1858 M. Heris, of Brussels, cleaned it again. Later on, when in the Schollaerts' possession, it was hung in a sitting-room too near a stove, and became blistered ; the damage was very carefully repaired by M. L. Lampe, in 1901.

As to the date at which the first attempt to complete the central panel was made, some evidence may be gathered from a painting representing one of Nicholas van Maelbeke's successors, kneeling before the Infant Jesus seated on His Mother's lap. This panel must have been painted at Ypres, as there is in the background a view of the bridge over the Yperleet, and of the street leading from it past the front of Saint Martin's church. The provost in this picture holds the same staff as his predecessor, and if the details of the vestments, &c., be compared, it will be seen that it cannot be many years posterior. The immediate successors of Van Maelbeke were Lambert Van der Woestine, 1445–1456 ; Nicholas van Dixmude, 1456–1464 ; Walter Thoenin, 1464–1474 ; and Nicholas van Dixmude, 1474–1482. The only masters who are known to have flourished at Ypres during that period are John Perrant and George Uutenhove.

Exhibited in the Loan Exhibition of Old Masters at Bruges, in 1867 (No. 4), and again in 1902 (No. 14), and at the Guildhall, London, in 1906, (No. 7) ; in the last instance as " the last work of the painter."

1863. RUELENS, CIV–CXIII, gives a summary of the various opinions as to the date of the picture, and suggests that Carton's document is of much later date than 1445, and merely the echo of a local tradition. He, however, sees no trace of John van Eyck's hand in the picture, and believes it to be of a later period.

1902. WEALE, in *Revue de l'Art Chrétien*, 4 S., x, 1–6.

1902. HULIN, Catalogue Critique, 14, thinks the picture to be an original altered at the end of the sixteenth or in the seventeenth century, and repainted once or twice in the nineteenth.

1903. FRIEDLAENDER, in *Repertorium*, XXVI, 69, calls it a sad, but nevertheless an insufficiently esteemed relic of an original by John van Eyck.

1905. FIERENS, 169, considers the authenticity of the picture to be indisputable, and that there are few of

John van Eyck's pictures of which the history is so well established, but that owing to restorations there is no trace left of his work.

1906. PHILLIPS, in the *Daily Telegraph*, May 3 : " It was once that great master's, the documentary evidence on the point of authorship being pretty conclusive ; but hardly a square inch of his own brush-work remains, and the central panel, glowing with restorations of the very worst and most sacrilegious kind, looks, to tell the truth, absolutely grotesque. With the wings Van Eyck never had anything to do."

1906. VOLL, 264.

F

By JOHN

II. Paintings of Uncertain Date

XXII. Our Lady and Child

Frankfort : Städel Institute (No. 98), under the title of the
" Madonna of Lucca." Oak. 2 ft. 1¾ in. × 1 ft. 7½ in.
(0.655 × 0.495).

Formerly in the possession of Charles Louis,
Duke of Lucca ; was in 1841 in the hands of the
dealer Nieuwenhuys at Brussels, from whom it was
purchased by William II, King of Holland, at
whose sale in 1850 it was acquired by the Institute
for 3000 florins.

In this, as in the picture at Ince Hall, the scene
is laid in a room of small dimensions, lighted by a
window on the right. The Virgin-Mother is seated
on a high-backed carved oak throne, with bronze
lions surmounting the principals. From a fringed
canopy attached to the ceiling hangs a cloth of
honour, with a green-and-gold pattern of foliage,
and white and red flowers on a blue ground, with
a border of white with a red stripe. She wears a
blue dress, the full sleeves of which are lined with
white fur, and over this an ample crimson mantle
with a bejewelled border of gold embroidery. Her
flowing light-brown hair, drawn back off the temples
and confined by a narrow band adorned with pearls,
falls over her left shoulder. With her right hand

she supports the Child, seated nude on a linen cloth spread on her lap, and gives Him the breast with her left. He holds an orange in His left hand, and lays His right on His Mother's arm. Two rings are on the fourth finger of the Virgin's left hand. In a niche on the left is a brass basin, and on a shelf above it a bottle of water and a brass candle-stick. Opposite this a round-headed window glazed with pearl-white roundels, letting in a moderate amount of light, but enough to make the lions and vessels glitter ; on the sill are a couple of oranges. The throne-steps are covered with a rich carpet which extends to the front, leaving the pavement of white tiles with a blue design visible at the sides.

Etched by J. Eissenhardt.

1872. CROWE, 113, dates this picture 1439.
1898. KAEMMERER, 87, dates it 1436.
1899. SEECK, 22, 70, dates it 1433.
1900. WEIZSAECKER, Catalogue, gives the date of its exe-
      cution as between 1435 and 1440.
1900. VOLL, 70, about 1433.
1903. DE MONT, 55, gives 1432–33 as the date of this
      painting.
1904. KERN, 9.
1908. WEALE, 201. " Certainly by John."

XXIII. PORTRAIT OF JOHN ARNOLFINI

PLATE XXXI

Berlin : Kaiser Friedrich Museum (No. 523A). Oak. 11½ in. × 8 in. (0.29 × 0.20).

Formerly in the collection of the Earl of Shrews-bury at Alton Towers, sold July 6, 1857 (No. 76), when it was described as being much injured and repainted. It was purchased for £37 by C. J. Nieuwenhuys, at the sale of whose collection, July 17, 1886, it was said to be (No. 67) the por-trait of John van Eyck by himself. It was then

JOHN ARNOLFINI

BERLIN : ROYAL GALLERY

By permission of the Berlin Photographic Co.

Plate XXXI

acquired by M. Sedelmeyer, the Paris picture dealer, for £399, and shortly afterwards sold by him to the Berlin Gallery.

Arnolfini is represented turned slightly to the right, his face, close-shaven, seen in three-quarters. He is clad in an olive-green robe trimmed with brown fur, fitting close at the neck with stand-up collar ; a scarlet headkerchief completes his costume. He has small bluish-grey eyes ; his left arm rests on the sill of a window ; his right hand, in which he holds a folded letter with an illegible superscription, is laid upon his left ; a ring adorns the little finger. The luminous flesh tones of the face and the green and red of the costume on the unrelieved dark background make a striking and delightful picture.

For the portrait of John Arnolfini and his wife, painted by John van Eyck in 1434, now in the National Gallery, see p. 114.

Facsimile coloured reproduction by the Berlin Photographic Company.

Etching by Alb. Krüger, 1887.

1887. TSCHUDI, in *Jahrbuch der königlich Preussischen Kunstsammlungen*, VIII, 172–174.
1887. BODE, in *Gazette des Beaux Arts*, 2 P., XXXV, 214.
1893. SEDELMEYER, Catalogue of 300 Paintings, No. 31, p. 43.
1898. KAEMMERER, 101, 104, comparing this portrait with that of 1434 in the National Gallery, arrives at the conclusion that Arnolfini's married life was not happy. This rash judgment is, he thinks, confirmed by the fact that he and his wife were not buried in the same grave, nor even in the same church. Both John and his brother Michael were, as Lucchese merchants, buried in their chantry chapel, in the vault reserved as their exclusive resting-place.
1899. SEECK, 26–30, 53, comparing this with John's dated portraits, is of opinion that it was painted in 1433.
1900. VOLL, 74–75, dates this portrait 1437–1439.
1908. WEALE, 201. " Certainly by John."

XXIV. PORTRAIT OF SIR BALDWIN DE LANNOY, LORD OF MOLEMBAIX

PLATE XXXII

Berlin : Kaiser Friedrich Museum (No. 525G), under the title of "A Knight of the Golden Fleece." Oak. 10¼ in. × 7½ in. (0.26 × 0.195).

Formerly at Modena, in the collection of the Marquess of Coccapane. Brought to London and unsuccessfully offered to the National Gallery. It was then bought by Messrs. P. and D. Colnaghi, who sold it to the Berlin Gallery in 1902.

Half-length portrait of a man ; the face, seen in two-thirds in full light turned to the right ; the eyes looking straight out, away from the spectator. He wears a robe of violet-purple damask, with yellowish-green sprays of foliage, trimmed at the neck and wrists with reddish-brown fur ; under the robe a close-fitting tunic with a collar open in front, showing a little fine white linen. He has a large felt hat, of the same shape as that worn by John Arnolfini in the picture at the National Gallery (see p. 114). He holds with both hands a white wand, the symbol of his official position of chamberlain at the Duke's court. A ring adorns the little finger of his right hand, and upon his shoulders hangs the enamelled gold collar of the Order of the Golden Fleece, of which he had been created a knight by Duke Philip on its institution, January 10, 1430. The collar, a work of the Bruges goldsmith, John Peutin, was delivered to him on Saint Andrew's Day, 1431. Hence it would appear that this portrait was painted after that date. However, it may possibly have been executed some years previously, and the collar added later on. He was one of the members of the embassy sent to Alphonsus V

G

PAINTINGS OF DOUBTFUL AUTHENTICITY

XXV. THE PORTRAIT OF CANON GEORGE VAN DER PAELE

Hampton Court Palace, No. 287 (272) [452]. Canvas, 1 ft. 4¾ in. × 1 ft. 3¾ in. (0.42 × 0.40).

The canon is here portrayed in a greenish-brown cassock trimmed with brown fur. Bluish-black background.

In the collection of King James II, it was described (No. 39) as "a fat man's head, bald, with a double chin."

At the time when John van Eyck was commissioned to paint the altar-piece the canon had become so feeble that the Chapter dispensed him from attendance in choir.[1] He may have felt unequal to support the fatigue of a long sitting to the painter, but as he had been in constant residence ever since Van Eyck had settled in Bruges, the latter must have seen him frequently enough to be able with the aid of this study to give a satisfactory presentation of the head in the altar-piece.

1885. C. JUSTI, in *The Academy*, June 20, p. 445: "On my last visit to Hampton Court I was struck by the resemblance of this head to that of the Canon Georges de Pala in the well-known altar-piece of John van Eyck

---

[1] 1434, 9 Septembris, "Indulserunt domini quod attenta infirmitate et senectute suis, inscribatur ad omnia lucra, sive veniat ad ecclesiam, sive non." Acta Capituli IV, fol. 218 v°. Bruges : Episcopal Archives.

in the Academy at Bruges. The likeness, as a photo-graph now shows me, is indeed perfect. The eyes, where the spirit of life seems all but extinct, yet looking wearily upwards ; the very thin, horizontal lips ; the dried-up and pointed ear—all agree.

"The head at Hampton Court was probably the life-size study for the figure in the altar-piece, and is, in this respect, unique. It is painted in a reddish-yellow mezzo-tinto, quite monochromous, very firm in design and modelling, showing Van Eyck's grandeur and broadness in conception and treatment of a counte-nance, before proceeding to the super-position of microscopic details, of local colour, of light and shadow."

1886. K. CHYTIL, in *Zeitschrift für bildende Kunst*, XXII, 146–148.

1886. JUSTI, in *Zeitschrift für bildende Kunst*, XXII, 251.

1898. KAEMMERER, 68. A later superficial copy of the portrait in the Bruges altar-piece.

1898. E. LAW, " Royal Gallery of Hampton Court," p. 102, catalogues it as " Head of an Old Man," by an un-named artist.

1900. VOLL, 126. A work dating from the end of the sixteenth century. The technique exhibits none of John's peculiarities ; the modelling is weaker and flatter. Nevertheless, the first impression of its truth-fulness to life is overpowering. The original must have been Van Eyck's grandest portrait.

1905. FIERENS, 158, had evidently never seen this picture, as he refers to it as the head of the Blessed Virgin in the Paele altar-piece, and says it is only a copy.

1907. Reproduced in Arundel Club Portfolio (No. 6) as the work of John van Eyck, without any critical com-ment.

1908. WEALE, 84. " This is most certainly an original study from life, not a copy of the portrait in the altar-piece."

1911. LAW, *Historical Guide to Hampton Court*, p. 83, quotes Weale, 1908, p. 84, and describes the picture as " one of the very few genuine pictures by Jan van Eyck in England."

1912. PHILLIPS, in a private letter to Brockwell : ". I find it impossible to believe in the Hampton Court ' Van der Paele.' Though very clever, it is empty and life-less compared to the original, and not really a sketch at all. It is probably a student's copy. There is nothing similar to it in Flemish art of the fifteenth century."

The head of the canon reappears in " The Mass of Saint Gregory" in the Prado Gallery at Madrid, No. 1943 (1864), where it is now catalogued as a work of the sixteenth-century Flemish School; in the past it was variously assigned to Van Orley or Adrian Isenbrant, and by others considered as a copy after Gossart.

XXVI.–XXVII. CALVARY AND THE LAST JUDGMENT

St. Petersburg: Hermitage Gallery (No. 444). Shutters of a triptych. 2 ft. ½ in. × 10 in. (0.62 × 0.25). Canvas, transferred from panel.

These panels were purchased in Spain by the Russian ambassador Tatistcheff, who in 1845 bequeathed them to the Gallery. The central panel, representing, it is said, the Adoration of the Magi, had been previously stolen. Until 1861 both were ascribed to John van Eyck ; they were then, on the authority of Dr. Waagen, attributed to Peter Christus, but in 1887 they were reassigned to John, to whom they are still attributed in the official catalogue.

Calvary. On the slope of a hill stand three tall tau crosses, that in the centre with the title-board facing the front. Our Lord, fastened to it with three nails, has just expired. There surrounds it a crowd of men, judges, soldiers, and others, six or seven of them on horseback. Amongst them a man carrying the reed and sponge ; on the right, the blind Longinus on horseback, aided by another man, has just pierced the Saviour's side. To the right and left of the Redeemer are the two thieves, each blindfolded and fastened by five cords to a cross facing towards the centre; the penitent hanging quietly; the other, on the left, struggling desperately, but in vain. At the foot of the hill in the immediate foreground, the Virgin-Mother, overcome with grief, is tenderly supported by Saint John, with the three holy women in close attendance; to the left, Magdalene praying with arms uplifted towards the Redeemer; beyond her, a turbaned woman stands compassionately contemplating the group around the Virgin-Mother.

The Last Judgment. Our Lord, seated on the rainbow, is draped in an ample mantle which leaves His feet exposed. From the wounds in these and in His outstretched hands proceed rays of glory; just below these, in detached letters, runs the invitation: " VENITE BENEDICTI PR̄IS [Patris] MEI." Two angels hovering in the background bear the holy cross with the title-board; another, on the right, carries the lance and crown of thorns; and a fourth, on the left, three rods with the reed and sponge. Beyond these, on each side, are four angels blowing long trumpets. On the right of our Lord His Blessed Mother, with her right hand on her breast and her left upraised, is begging mercy for a number of suppliants sheltered beneath her mantle; opposite her, on the left, is Saint John the Baptist praying; beyond each of them a choir of adoring angels. Immediately below our Lord's feet a crowd of virgins, facing the front, are singing the praises of God; on each side the Apostles, clad in white robes, headed by Saint Peter, are seated on two benches,— on the end of that to the right is carved the fall of our first parents. Two angels are leading in two groups of the elect: on the right, a pope, a cardinal, a couple of bishops, priests, monks, friars and hermits; on the left, a crowd of laymen, headed by an emperor, a king, and a count. Below, the earth and the sea are yielding up their dead. In the centre stands Saint Michael, a noble figure with out-stretched peacock-wings, with buckler and sword upraised ready to smite the enemy of mankind. The oval buckler, charged with a cross, bears in Greek characters the legend:

"ΑΔΩΓΑΥΙ [? Adonai or Adoravi] ΤΕΤΓΡΑ
ΜΑΘΩΝ
ΑΓΛΑ." [1]

and his armour is covered with mystical inscriptions. He is barefooted ; his flowing, curly locks are retained by a jewelled circlet surmounted by a cross. Beneath his feet a weird spectre of Death, with outstretched legs and arms, and huge bat-like wings, over-shadows the abyss of hell, in which a multitude of the damned, falling head foremost in dire confusion, are being tortured by hideous demons. On the Death's wings are the legends, " CHAOS MAGNVM " and "VMBRA MORTIS," and the fearful sentence, " ITE VOS MALEDICTI IN IGNEM ETERNVM," accom-panied by fiery darts from above.

The original frames of these shutters, of gilt wood, bore the following inscriptions. On that representing Calvary :

" DOMINVS POSVIT IN EO INIQVITATEM OMNIVM NOSTRVM : OBLATVS EST QVIA IPSE VOLVIT : ET NON APERVIT OS SVVM : SICVT OVIS AD OCCISIO-NEM DVCETVR : ET QVASI AGNVS CORAM TONDENTE SE OBMVTESCET : PROPTER SCELVS POPVLI MEI PERCVSSI EVM : ET DABIT IMPIOS PRO SEPVLTVRA : ET DIVITEM PRO MORTE SVA : TRADIDIT IN MORTEM ANIMAM SVAM : ET CVM SCELERATIS REPVTATVS EST : ET IPSE PECCATA MVLTORVM TVLIT : ET PRO TRANSGRESSORIBVS ROGAVIT." [2]

[1] The four Hebrew letters comprising the holy name Jehovah. As to " agla," see pp. 44, 62.
[2] Isa. LIII, 6, 7, 8, 12.

On the frame of the Last Judgment :

" ECCE TABERNACVLVM DEI CVM HOMINIBVS : ET
HABITABIT CVM EIS : IPSI POPVLVS EIVS ERVNT :
ET IPSE DEVS CVM EIS ERIT EORVM DEVS : ET
ABSTERGET DEVS OMNEM LACRIMAM AB OCVLIS
EORVM : ET MORS VLTRA NON ERIT : NEQVE
LVCTVS : NEC DOLOR ERIT VLTRA.[1] DEDIT MARE
MORTVOS SVOS.[2] CONGREGABO SVPER EOS MALA
ET SAGITTAS MEAS COMPLEBO IN EIS : CONSV-
MENTVR FAME : ET DEVORABVNT EOS AVES
MORSV ARI [AMARISSIMO] : DENTES BESTIARVM
[IM]MITTAM IN EOS CVM FVRORE TRAHENTIVM
SVPER TERRAM ATQVE SERPENTIVM.[3] DEDIT MORS
MORTVOS."

The Berlin Gallery contains (No. 529B) a much-enlarged version of this Last Judgment by Peter Christus ; it is signed, and dated 1452 ; it measures 4 ft. 5¼ in. × 1 ft. 10 in. (1.34 × 0.56).

1841. PASSAVANT, in *Kunstblatt*, No. 3, attributes these pictures to John van Eyck.

1858. HOTHO, II, 169, thinks they may have been painted before 1426 by either Hubert or John, as both brothers are, he says, represented standing at the foot of the Cross.

1887. C. JUSTI, in *Zeitschrift für bildende Kunst*, XXII, 244, gives these pictures to John.

1899. PHILLIPS, in the *North American Review*, 713–714, says : " These panels must for the present be put in a class by themselves, or rather with a restricted group of similar works among which are to be numbered . . . the Berlin Calvary, the Three Marys at the Sepulchre, the Saint Francis receiving the Stigmata, and the Fountain of Living Water. These paintings reveal a deeper pathos than the calm Jan van Eyck had hitherto seemed to have at command, and with it a mode of handling not quite so minute and searching in every particular. The Saint-Petersburg Calvary and Last Judgment are not only beyond reasonable doubt John van Eyck's own, but they must, as creations of absolute originality, be counted among the

[1] Apoc. XXI, 3, 4.   [2] Id. XX, 13.   [3] Deut. XXXII, 23, 24.

most wonderful things of the Netherlandish school at this period. Hardly again has the Crucifixion been imagined with this rugged force and grandeur, with this power of intense individualisation which yet robs the world-tragedy of none of its significance."

1902. PHILLIPS, in *The Fortnightly Review*, October, p. 597 : " In my opinion the first in order of date in the series of extant works by Hubert van Eyck. Less certain, less developed in technique, than any of the above panels—in some respects still timid and primitive— they are among the most sublime inventions of the elder Netherlandish art."

1903. DE MONT, 49, says that these two panels most certainly have points of resemblance to Hubert's paintings, but not the slightest to any of John's authentic works.

1905. FIERENS, 118. The architecture in the background, the group of holy women, and the accoutrements of some of the soldiers, remind one of " The Three Marys " ; the horses seen in profile are not without analogy with those in the Turin Hours. The Last Judgment is a bold and original conception. The angels with draperies terminating in broken folds, and some of the blessed, recall the Ghent altar-piece.

1906. VOLL, 269, dates these paintings *c.* 1450.

1908. WEALE, 201. " In the writer's opinion, the work of a contemporary of the Van Eycks brought up in the same surroundings. The figures are less dignified in type than those of Hubert, but there is much dramatic force and deep pathos in both pictures. The painter was probably a North Netherlander ; the Calvary shows so many points of resemblance to the Turin miniatures that he may possibly have designed or executed some of them."

XXVIII. CHRIST ON THE CROSS, THE BLESSED VIRGIN, AND SAINT JOHN

Berlin : Kaiser Friedrich Museum (No. 525F). Linen, transferred from the original panel. 1 ft. 5½ in. × 1 ft. (0.44 × 0.30).

This picture, which was formerly ascribed to Roger De la Pasture, was at one time in the possession of Dr. Noel Walker, of Chelsea, who in the middle of the nineteenth century lived for a time at Florence. In 1897 it came into the hands of the late Mr. Buttery, who sold it to the Kaiser Friedrich Museums-Verein. It is in fairly good condition, but has sustained a few slight restorations, rendered necessary by small pieces of the paint becoming detached in the process of transference from the panel.

In the centre of the immediate foreground rises a tall tau-shaped cross, the beam of which extends almost the full width of the picture ; the large board above it, with the title in three languages, reaches nearly to the head of the frame. To this cross the Saviour is fastened by three nails. His head is bent forward to the right, as if He had cast a last dying look on His Mother. The expression is striking. His dark hair hangs down as if dank from sweat on each side of His face ; blood drips from the wounds in the hands, and, trickling down the forearms, falls from each elbow, and in an abundant stream from the side and feet to the foot of the cross. The foreground is strewn with stones, with here and there a bone. On the right the Virgin-Mother stands with head bowed down and hands interlaced in deep but resigned grief ; a linen kerchief with gaufred edge envelops her head and throat ; over it she wears a light-coloured mantle, the ample folds of which are gathered up under her right arm, showing the dark-blue dress beneath. On the left, the beloved disciple, his head turned away, is wiping his tears with the back of his left hand, and with the other holding up the pale red mantle he wears over his dark violet tunic. Beyond them are numerous figures. The half-distance is filled with a thick growth of bushes with light dotted foliage; in the middle are figures going away towards the gate of a walled city with numerous square and circular towers, and a lofty rectangular building crowned with five cupolas ; in the distant background is a double range of snow mountains.[1] On the left the view is shut out by a hill with a pine tree, some cypresses, and a windmill on the farther side. On the right is a tall tree with bare branches, about which hover a number of starlings. Overhead a clear sky, with small bright floating clouds to the left.

A picture exhibited at Madrid in May 1911 (No. 26), and illustrated in the Catalogue of Primitive Spanish Pictures in the collection of Señora Doña Trinidad Scholtz-Hermensdorff (No. 26), seems to be a copy of the present work.

1898. TSCHUDI, in *Jahrbuch der königlichen Preussischen Kunstsammlungen*, XIX, 202–205.
1899. FRIEDLAENDER, in *Repertorium*, XXII, 411.
1900. WEALE, in *Revue de l'Art Chrétien*, 5 S., XI, 285.
1903. ROSEN, 98–105, notes that the branches of the pine are incorrectly represented as springing from the trunk at the same height. Regards the work as posterior to the Van Eycks.
1906. VOLL, 48, believes this panel to have been painted in the second half of the fifteenth century, and possibly copied from a lost work by Hubert or John.
1908. WEALE, 201. " Thought by many to be posterior to the Van Eycks."

XXIX. OUR LADY AND CHILD

London : Earl of Northbrook, (No. 25.)   Oak.   10½ in. × 7½ in.
(0.265 × 0.19).

Formerly in the collection of E. Joly de Bammeville (No. 29), sold 12 June, 1884, to Nieuwenhuys, from whom it was purchased in 1857 by Mr. Thomas Baring for £120.

[1] See p. 226.

The Blessed Virgin, three-quarters length, is seated facing the spectator, beneath a canopy with a cloth of honour of olive green diapered with flowers, bordered with a narrow scarlet band. She wears a dark blue dress and a crimson mantle, both having richly jewelled borders. Her long hair, which falls in undulating masses over her shoulders, is confined by a band fastened above the forehead by a jewel composed of a ruby surrounded by pearls. With her right hand she supports the Divine Child seated nude on a linen cloth. He is accepting from His Mother a bunch of red-and white pinks, and with His right hand holds the wing of a struggling parakeet. This little picture is said to have been dated 1437 on the original frame. The back of the panel is painted to imitate stone.

Exhibited : London, Burlington House, Old Masters, 1872 (No. 234); 1894 (No. 180). New Gallery, 1899 (No. 69). Bruges : Early Netherlandish Masters, 1902 (No. 11).

1889. WEALE. A descriptive Catalogue of the Collection of pictures belonging to the Earl of Northbrook, 24, No. 25.

1902. HULIN, 11. A° copy of much later date than 1437 ; it seems to be of the fifteenth century.

1903. FRIEDLAENDER, in *Repertorium für Kunstwissenschaft*, XXVI, 67. A weak little picture.

1903. WEALE, in the *Burlington Magazine*, I, 48.

1908. WEALE, 202. " There is no sufficient reason for doubting the date 1437, said by Nieuwenhuys to have been inscribed on the original frame."

1912. DURAND-GRÉVILLE, 88, claims that the Madonna and Child at Vienna, which he illustrates, is by the same hand. The latter would, however, seem to have had a Colognese or Rhenish, rather than an Eyckian, origin.

XXX. Saint George

St. Petersburg : General Plaoutine.   Wood.   *c.* 6½ in. ×
c. 5 in. (*c.* 0.17 × *c.* 0.12).

The present writers have no knowledge as to the
pedigree of this picture, which they have not seen,
but it is worth noting that a picture of this subject
was in June 1445 acquired by Alphonsus V of
Aragon.   That picture is dealt with among the
lost paintings (p. 198).

Saint George on a grey horse, with a very small
head, prancing towards the left ; a greenish-brown
dragon before him is pierced behind the head with
the spear.   The saint, in steel armour flecked with
bright white lights, wears a fluttering crimson scarf.
To the right is the princess in blue-and-gold brocade
with scarlet over-sleeves.   Fantastic overhanging
rocks in the background and a distant city with
water.   Blue graded sky.

1902. PHILLIPS, Claude, " Impressions of the Bruges Exhibi-
tion," in *The Fortnightly Review*, October, p. 598 :   " To
Hubert van Eyck may be assigned a beautiful little 'St.
George,' hardly known, I fancy, to the student, which
I happened to see a few years ago in the collection of
General Plaoutine at St. Petersburg."

1912. Sir Claude PHILLIPS has very kindly sent the joint-
authors the following note on the picture :   " It is twelve
years since I saw the ' St. George.'   It impressed me as
being a Hubert van Eyck of the type of the Turin and
Milan miniatures, and the St. Petersburg ' Crucifixion '
and ' Last Judgment.'   I believe you do not agree in
giving the two latter to Hubert."

1912. Mr. E. R. D. MACLAGAN, to whom we are indebted for
the approximate measurements and the description,
has been good enough to write us as follows :—

" My notes were written from memory after an
inspection under difficulties.   The technique is purely
that of a MS. miniaturist carried out in ' oil,' and

L

very fine indeed. Reminiscent of the Turin Hours in
some of the last Eyck-like pages, but the types of the
faces do not fit in with any genuine work."

XXXI. HEAD OF A MAN

Berlin : Kaiser Friedrich Museum (No. 523c).   Oak.   4½ in. ×
3½ in. (0.115 × 0.088).

Purchased in 1895 at Florence.

Bust of a man, the face seen in three-quarters,
turned slightly to the right.   He has the stubble of
a brown beard, small eyes, and broad rosy cheeks,
and wears, over an underdress, of which only the
stand-up collar is seen, a dull lilac-red robe trimmed
with fur, and a dark-green headkerchief, the lappets
of which fall behind his ears.

This does not appear to be a portrait, but most
probably the head of a figure out of some large
composition.

1899. SEECK, 23.
1900. VOLL, 122.   Not by Van Eyck.
1901. BODE, 131.   Like the head of one of the figures in
    the "Fountain of Living Water"; the flesh tone, owing
    to over-cleaning, is not so red as usual.

XXXII. PORTRAIT OF A MIDDLE-AGED MAN

Philadelphia, U.S.A. : Mr. John G. Johnson.

Bust-length portrait of a man seen three-quarters
to the right.   He wears a plain robe, the edge of
which is trimmed with fur.

This portrait is said to be by John van Eyck,
but has not been seen by the writers.

1908. GRANT, J. Kirby, in an article on the pictures in the
    collection of Mr. J. G. Johnson, in *The Connoisseur*,
    September, p. 4.

XXXIII. PORTRAIT OF A MAN

In the collection of Herr Reinhold von Liphart, Ratsdorf, near Dorpat.

A Man in a dark-red mantle and black cap. A small portrait.

1900. *Zeitschrift für bildende Kunst*, 273.

H

COPIES, VARIANTS, DERIVATIVES, AND IMITATIONS

XXXIV. OUR LADY AND CHILD ENTHRONED, SAINT DONATIAN, SAINT GEORGE, AND THE DONOR, CANON GEORGE VAN DER PAELE

Antwerp Museum : Van Ertborn Collection (No. 412), as an old copy. Canvas, transferred from wood. 3 ft. 8¼ in. × 5 ft. 1 in. (1.20 × 1.54).

The original of this picture is in the Bruges Gallery. For critical notes on it, see p. 120.

A fairly close copy of the late fifteenth or early sixteenth century. It was formerly in the church at Watervliet (East Flanders).

A copy of the Virgin and Child with the canon was in 1852 in the Quédeville Collection.

A copy of the picture was formerly in the Wynn Ellis collection and sold at Christie's in the second portion of the collection on May 27, 1876 (No. 29), to " Johnson," for £31, 10s. It may well have been one of the 403 pictures bequeathed by Mr. Wynn Ellis, of Tankerton Tower, Kent, and of Cadogan Place, to the National Gallery in 1875 ; of that number only 94 pictures were accepted.

1907. VOLL, Vergleichende Gemäldestudien, München, 58–67. A careful comparison of the copy in the Antwerp Gallery with this. The many little discrepancies are pointed out and shown to prove that the Antwerp panel must belong to a date when the Eyckian methods were on the wane.

XXXV. The Vision of Saint Francis

Turin : Royal Gallery, No. 187 (313), and catalogued as the work of John van Eyck. 11¼ in. × 13¼ in. (0.28 × 0.33).

The same composition, with some slight differences, as the picture in the collection of Mr. J. G. Johnson at Philadelphia.

For historical details, see p. 93.   The saint's face, less lifelike, has a pleasanter look ; his tonsure is larger, and more of Brother Leo's face is seen ; the habits of both friars are grey.   Strange to say, the brother, who, having his legs crossed, shows in the Heytesbury-Johnson picture the sole of his left foot, has here two right feet ; and the birds seen in the sky in that painting are not to be found here.

At the beginning of the last century this panel belonged to a secularised nun of Casale, in Piedmont. After forming part of the collection of Professor Bonzani, and of Signor Fascio, Mayor of Felletto in Canavese, it was in 1860 acquired by the Turin Gallery from Luigi Fascio of Casale.

1883. Hymans, in *Bulletin des Commissions royales d'Art et d'Archéologie*, XXII, 108–116, describes the Turin panel as surprisingly beautiful, and of such perfection in the details as was never surpassed (!) by any artist of the fifteenth century.

1897. Jacobsen, in *Archivio Storico dell' Arte*, S.2, III, 208, calls the Turin picture a successful imitation of later date.   The formation of the rocks and the colouring of the foliage with little touches of the brush recall Bles, and the delicate rosy tone with a tinge of violet reminds one of (the pseudo-) Mostaert.

1899. Reber and Bayersdorfer, X, 79, describe it as " The Stigmatization of St. Francis," by a scholar of John van Eyck.

1900. Voll, 109, calls the Turin panel a pretty, sympathetic picture, but cannot discover in it any direct conformity with the character of John's authentic works. He thinks it belongs to a later period, because the saint is kneeling on both knees, and with his hands not outstretched to receive the stigmata. He also considers the landscape romantic, and to be contemporary with Dürer.

1901. BODE, 129, considers the Turin panel to be the original, and the smaller panel a replica executed in Van Eyck's workshop!

1902. C. PHILLIPS, in *The Fortnightly Review*, October, p. 596. The Turin picture is " a somewhat larger repetition, less fine in quality, and less undoubtedly original " than the painting in the Johnson Collection.

1903. ROSEN, 105–110, 133, calls the Turin picture a pretended Van Eyck, and says the landscape resembles those by Bouts, but cannot be by him because the plants are not so well painted.

1908. WEALE, 200. " It appears to the writer to be an enlargement of later date. Since 1885, several critics have expressed the gravest doubt as to its Eyckian authorship. But though differing on some points, they appear to agree that the colouring, and the manner in which the foliage of the trees is painted, point to a date posterior to the Van Eycks. Brother Leo has two right feet, from which it would appear that the painter had failed to remark that, in the smaller picture, the person in question has his legs crossed and shows the sole of his left foot. Durand thinks this the result of mere distraction on the part of Van Eyck. The palmettos are poorly painted, Rosen (1903, pp. 105–109) says, from dried plants brought to Bruges by a sailor!—but they were, most probably, merely copied, as was the V-shaped flight of geese."

A picture of " St. Francis of Assisi and another Franciscan in the Desert," in the Prado Gallery at Madrid, No. 1617 (1525), which was formerly ascribed to Albert Dürer, but now is catalogued under the name of Joachim Patenir, is evidently based on Van Eyck's composition. It is on oak and measures 1 ft. 6¾ in. × 1 ft. 2¼ in. (0.47 × 0.36).

XXXVI. Our Lady and Child in a Church

Berlin : Kaiser Friedrich Museum (No. 525c).   Oak.   12½ in. ×
5¾ in. (0.31 × 0.14).

Formerly in the Suermondt collection at Aachen ;
purchased for the Gallery in 1874.

In the nave of a three-aisled cruciform Gothic
church with an apsidal choir and ambulatory, seen
from the left, the Blessed Virgin, clad in a red dress
and greenish-blue mantle, with an elaborate gold
crown on her head, stands holding the Divine Child
on her right arm, and retaining His feet with her
left hand.   From the waist down He is enveloped
in a long white cloth, the end of which hangs in
front.   With His right hand He clutches the neck-
band of His Mother's dress.   The sun, shining
through the clerestory and the windows of a side
chapel behind the Virgin, produces a fine effect of
light and shadow.   A sculptured stone screen of
three bays surmounted by a rood with statues of the
Virgin and Saint John, and furnished with a brass
Gospel lectern, separates the nave from the choir,
within which stand two angels singing from a book.
On an altar in the side bay to the right is a statuette
of Our Lady on a metal pedestal between two
candlesticks.   The sculptured tympanum of this
bay represents the Annunciation ; that of the
central bay, the Coronation of Our Lady.

The original frame, painted in imitation of stone,
bore in capital letters : "MATER HEC EST FILIA
PATER HIC EST NATVS QVIS AVDIVIT TALIA DEVS
HOMO NATVS."   At the foot : "FLOS FLORVM
APPELLARIS."

1855. LABORDE, *La Renaissance des Arts à la Cour de
France*, 1, 604–607 (Paris), says that the panel in

Cacault's possession was purchased from his house-keeper for 50 francs.

1869. BÜRGER, in *Gazette des Beaux Arts*, 2 P., I, 12, says this picture is the one which belonged to M. Nau.

1872. CROWE, 115 : "Suggestive of doubt. . . . There is a reminiscence of Van Eyck in the type of the heads, and something to recall memories of the Madonna of Dresden, but that the tones are less silvery and the *impasto* is heavier. . . . The way in which the effect of light is brought out reminds us of the later Dutch masters. . . . Is not this a skilful copy by a master like De Hooch ? "

1887. BODE, in *Gazette des Beaux Arts*, 2 P., XXXV, 216. A genuine work by John. The Child is very small, and poorly modelled, and there is a want of decision in the folds of His Mother's dress ; but these are the result of a restoration of the whole of the lower portion of the picture.

1898. KAEMMERER, 76–80. A masterpiece as regards both the lighting and the production of an impression of space, but the weak character of the draperies is against its being attributed unreservedly to John. A free copy is in the Ponzoni Collection at Cremona.

1899. SEECK, 41, 70, notes that the architecture of the church is wholly in the Pointed style, without any ad-mixture of Romanesque ; for this and other reasons he dates the picture *c.* 1440.

1902. PHILLIPS, in the *Fortnightly Review*, p. 598 : "A puzzling work, which I am strongly inclined to assign to Hubert, and not to Jan."

1902. HULIN, 2, 118, attributes this picture to Hubert.

1903. DE MONT, 18, says : "Painted between 1432 and 1480 ; the Blessed Virgin an imitation of one of the virgin-martyrs in the Adoration of the Lamb."

1904. KERN, 14, puts its date *c.* 1436.

1905. FIERENS, 162. The most remarkable of many copies of a lost original.

1906. VOLL, 39, says the church represented is Saint Denis, and dates the picture *c.* 1432.

1908. WEALE, 200. "A doubtful work. The writer be-lieves it to be a copy of a lost original by Hubert. The deep poetic feeling shown is a sufficient proof that he designed it. The copy in the Doria Collection shows more of the arcade on the left and the third bay of the rood screen, with the Nativity in the tympanum, and sepulchral brasses and slabs in the pavement." These details are not in the Berlin panel, but must have been in the original painting.

Several copies of this picture, evidently the dexter panel of a diptych, are known : one formerly in the possession of F. Cacault, who was the representative of France at Naples, Florence, and Rome, was sold at his death for 17 francs to an architect named Nau at Nantes. Laborde, who saw it, gives its dimensions as 43 centimeters by 25. Another copy, dated 1499, painted for Christian De Hondt, abbot of the Cistercian monastery of Our Lady of the Dunes (H. 0.31 ; B. 0.15), is now in the Van Ertborn Collection at the Antwerp Museum. Another, painted c. 1505 for " Messer Antonio Siciliano," was in 1530 in the house of Gabriel Vendramin, at Venice, and is now in the Doria-Pamphili Gallery at Rome.

A finely executed pen drawing (H. 0.30 ; B. 0.14), the lower left corner repaired, in the collection of Count Louis Paar, was sold at Vienna, February 21, 1896, No. 326. Another in pen and bistre on paper (0.43 × 0.23) was lent to the Grosvenor Gallery Winter Exhibition, 1878–9, No. 630, by Sir J. C. Robinson, and is reproduced in Kaemmerer's *Hubert und Jan van Eyck*, p. 77.

XXXVII. OUR LADY AND CHILD, SAINT BARBARA, AND A CARTHUSIAN

Berlin : Kaiser Friedrich Museum (No. 523B), catalogued as the work of Peter Christus. Oak. 7¾ in. × 5¾ in. (0.195 × 0.14).

Formerly in the Marquess of Exeter's collection at Burleigh House, Stamford. Sold at Christie's, June 9, 1888 (No. 288) for £2625, to C. Fairfax Murray ; it subsequently passed to the Berlin

Gallery. In the sale catalogue, the picture was described as the work of John van Eyck.

On the left Our Lady stands, holding in her arms the Infant Jesus, on whom she gazes with an expression of deep love. The Child, a crystal orb in His left hand, has His right raised in the act of blessing a Carthusian, the identical monk portrayed in the Rothschild picture, only older here by some years.[1] Here too he kneels under the protection of Saint Barbara, who has her right hand on his shoulder and her left extended to a tower with three windows, her distinctive emblem; this tower, square and crenelated, is crowned by a metal spire. The Virgin-Mother wears a full-sleeved blue dress trimmed with ermine, and a crimson mantle with a simple border of gold, secured by a cord fastened to two jewels. Her hair, confined by a cincture of pearls, is drawn back behind the ears, and falls over her shoulders. The monk, the hood of his cowl thrown back, kneels with his hands joined in prayer, whilst Saint Barbara, in a red dress girt with a gold cincture, is almost completely enveloped in a green mantle; her hair, also held back by a band of pearls, falls behind. These figures are beautifully grouped in a brightly lighted, lofty portico with two open pointed arches on the right behind Saint Barbara, and two round arches in the background supported by square piers and a column of verd antique, the bases of which rest on a low wall. Above these are two windows with borders of coloured glass; in front of these, and immediately over Our Lady, hangs a circular, conical canopy of a gauzy material, with a red, green, and white fringe. The pavement is composed of rectangular slabs of stone, some with coloured inlays, but mostly plain. The capital of the column on which the round arches rest is sculp-

[1] For the "Madonna and Child, St. Elisabeth of Hungary, St. Barbara, and a Carthusian" in the Rothschild collection, see p. 76.

tured with·interlaced foliage, that of the pier to the right with a group of figures.

Through the central arch a sunlit landscape is seen, and in the foreground, a town composed of innumerable houses, with a wonderful variety of street-fronts and gables, some roofed with red tiles, others with bluish slates. Through the town runs a river, lined on either bank with an avenue of trees. A wooden bridge connects the two portions of the town ; beyond it we descry a water-mill and a house resting on arches of masonry ; farther off still, a bridge of seven arches, with a lofty square tower at each end in immediate connection with the ramparts ; on both bridges are a number of persons, whose faces and figures are reflected in the running water beneath. A small boat is being propelled single-handed beneath the more distant bridge ; three more boats are visible still farther away, while churches and other buildings dot the well-wooded landscape through which the river runs towards the front. An equally minute landscape is seen through the arches behind Saint Barbara ; it comprises a flower-garden, and beyond it a market-place with a cross, many houses, and numerous shops displaying a variety of wares ; the streets are thronged with people ; in the background a windmill and the rampart with its fortified wall. The atmosphere is clear, birds are fluttering about, and a few light, fleecy clouds float across the limpid blue sky.

Exhibited : Leeds, 1868 (No. 533) under the title of " The Virgin appearing to St. Bruno."

1815. BLORE, *Guide to Burghley House, Northamptonshire, the seat of the Marquis of Exeter*, Stamford, p. 57.
1838. WAAGEN, *Works of Art and Artists in England*, III, 277.
1854. WAAGEN, III, 406. In the tone and treatment it has the greatest resemblance to the masterly picture in the Louvre.
1857. CROWE, 341–345 : " A symmetrical and beautifully

ordered composition, perfectly balanced in every part—
the figures being so marshalled, and the accessories so
arranged, as to give the picture an uncommon degree
of simplicity and grandeur. . . . The monk is a splendid portrait, and a marvel for nature and severity ;
the head being as fine in details as it is able in the
mass. . . . A small masterpiece, comparable only to
the best part of the greatest work of John van Eyck."
1889. TSCHUDI, in *Jahrbuch der kgl. Preussischen Kunstsammlungen*, X, 154–165, and XV, 65.
1898. KAEMMERER, 95–97, finds the figures hard and life-
less, and considers this picture to be by Peter Christus.
1900. VOLL, 119. Probably by Peter Christus, whose work
it most closely resembles.
1904. KERN, 15, plate XII. On account of the accuracy of
the linear perspective gives this to Peter Christus.
1904. TSCHUDI, *Die Gemälde Galerie der Kgl. Museen zu
Berlin : Die altniederländische Schule*, 10–11, gives
reasons for ascribing the picture to Peter Christus.
1906. VOLL, 46. Painted late in the fifteenth century.
1908. WEALE, 201. "Doubts have been expressed as to
whether this panel was painted by either of the Van
Eycks. These doubts are founded on the linear perspective, and on the windows being glazed with lozenges
instead of with roundels. The occurrence of a statue
outside the porch, as in Mr. Salting's portrait attributed
to Peter Christus [bequeathed to the National Gallery,
No. 2593, in 1910] and the metallic look of the hair, are
given as reasons for assigning this painting to him."
1912. WEALE and BROCKWELL. The painter of this work
must have seen the Rothschild picture and based his
design upon it. Late ; dry ; probably by Christus.

XXXVIII. OUR LADY AND CHILD BY A FOUNTAIN

Berlin : Kaiser Friedrich Museum (No. 525B), as " The Madonna
of the Rose-hedge." Oak. 1 ft. 10½ in. × 1 ft. 4¼ in.
(0.57 × 0.41).

Purchased at Florence by Otto Mündler, who in
1866 sold it to Mr. Suermondt of Aachen, from whom
it was acquired by the Gallery in 1874.

Our Lady, seen full face, is represented standing in front of a low wall of masonry, the top of which, level with the soil behind, is overgrown with turf ; beyond this is a carefully painted hedge of roses in bloom, and yet farther back palm-trees, citrons, cypresses, and evergreen oaks. The Virgin is enveloped in an ample mantle of brownish red, which, but for a small portion of the body and left sleeve, entirely covers her blue dress trimmed with white fur, and falls in elegant folds about her feet. Her head, covered with a transparent white kerchief, is bent lovingly over the Child, whom with both hands she clasps to her bosom. He with His right arm embraces her, while with His left hand, thrown back, He holds a spray of flowers. The heads of both Mother and Child are encircled with luminous nimbs. On the right stands a bronze fountain, into the basin of which fall four jets of water. A clasped book in a black forel lies on the wall to the left. The foreground is thickly covered with herbage and flowering plants.

This picture recalls the "Madonna by the Fountain" in the Antwerp Museum (No. 411), described p. 131.

Exhibited :   Bruges :   Early   Netherlandish Masters, 1867 (No. 2).

1872. CROWE, 115. "Of doubtful genuineness. The characteristic ugliness of the Virgin's face and Infant's form as surely points to the hand of a disciple, as the broken character of the drapery, the toneless colour, and false perspective."

1898. KAEMMERER, 108. The work of an unknown imitator of John van Eyck, who has given the Virgin's features a coarser appearance, suppressed the angels, and substituted roses and trees for the cloth of honour.

1899. SEECK, 35, 69, deems this to be a copy of a lost original by Hubert.

1908. WEALE, 202. "In the writer's opinion, the copy of

a lost picture. The southern trees are more accurately painted than in the polyptych, and are not copied from it."

XXXIX. Our Lady and Child

New York : Metropolitan Museum (No. 262). Oak. 1 ft. 10¾ in. × 1 ft. (0.575 × 0.307).

From the collection of William II, King of Holland, at whose sale in 1850 it was purchased by the dealer Nieuwenhuys for 600 florins. It was subsequently acquired by Mr. A. J. B. Beresford Hope, at whose sale, May 15, 1886 (No. 30), it was purchased by Lesser, the dealer, for £315. It shortly afterwards passed into the hands of Sedelmeyer, the Paris picture-dealer. Eventually Mr. H. G. Marquand presented it in 1888 to the Metropolitan Museum.

A copy or an imitation of this picture was in the possession of Mr. David Sellar, of Princes Gate.[1]

The figures are almost identical with those in John van Eyck's Virgin by the Fountain, of 1439 (see p. 131), in the Antwerp Museum, save that the position of the Child's left hand is altered. The accessories differ entirely, for here Our Lady is represented standing on the footpace of a throne placed in a late Gothic tabernacle, the pilasters of which are adorned with statuettes of Moses and a prophet and of two female figures symbolising the Church and the Synagogue, the one holding a cross and a chalice, the other the tables of the Law and a banner, the staff of which is falling to pieces.

From a canopy attached by cords to the but-

[1] This does not seem to have been included among the pictures in the Sellar collection shown at the Grafton Galleries in 1898. It may, however, have been one of those pictures the acceptance of which, on the recommendation of Sir E. J. Poynter, P.R.A., was refused by the Committee of the Guildhall.

tresses of the tabernacle a cloth of honour of brocaded damask reaches to the ground. On the front of the canopy is embroidered in gold capitals : DOMVS DEI EST ET PORTA CELI ; while the upright of the foot-pace bears the inscription : +IPSA EST QVAM PRE-PARAVIT DOM[INV]S FILIO DNI MEI. The colour is colder than in John's authenticated paintings, and the architectural details are certainly not earlier than the second half of the fifteenth century. The picture probably dates from about 1460.

Exhibited : Manchester : Art Treasures, 1857, No. 384 ; London : Burlington House : Old Masters, 1871, No. 273.

1843. NIEUWENHUYS, *Description de la Galerie de Tableaux de S. M. le Roi des Pays-Bas*, Bruxelles.
1857. WAAGEN, *Galleries and Cabinets of Art in Great Britain*, 190 : " This admirably preserved picture displays in full measure the solidity of execution of John van Eyck. There is every evidence of its being an early picture by him."
1872. CROWE, 114 : " The colour of the various parts is thin and cold, grey in shadow, and wholly without glazing ; the handling is mechanical ; the forms of the Virgin and Infant are feeble."
1895. BODE, in *Zeitschrift für bildende Kunst*, N.F., VI, 17. Not by John's own hand.
1898. KAEMMERER, 108, mentions Peter Christus as possibly the painter of this picture.
1908. WEALE, 202. Certainly the work of an imitator.

XL. THE FOUNTAIN OF LIVING WATER

Madrid : Prado Gallery, No. 1511 (2188), as the work of John van Eyck. Panel, o ft. × o ft. (1.81 × 1.30).

From the Hieronymite convent of Our Lady of Parral, near Segovia ; removed to Madrid from the sacristy in 1836, and placed in the National Museum, and removed thence to the Prado in 1872.

This altar-piece in composition somewhat resembles the Ghent polyptych. It is divided into
stages corresponding with the general plan of
Netherlandish sculptured altar-pieces, as also with
that adopted by the playwrights of mediæval
Mystery-plays, for which the Low Countries were
so long celebrated.

In the uppermost of three stages the Eternal
Father is seated on a throne in a tabernacle surmounted by a lofty pinnacled canopy adorned with
seventeen statues of prophets. He is clad in
imperial robes, with a crown on His head and a
sceptre in His left hand, the right raised in the act
of blessing. At His feet reposes the Lamb, and
on the principals of the throne, the evangelistic
animals. On the right and left are the Blessed
Virgin and Saint John the Evangelist, both seated
reading. From beneath the throne of God flows
a stream of crystalline purity down through a flowery
meadow into an octagonal canopied well in the
lowest stage. On its surface float innumerable
hosts. In the meadow are seated six angels, three
on each side of the stream, playing diverse instruments of music—an organ, a monochord, and a viol ;
a mandoline, a psalterion, and a harp—and beyond
them, in the lowest story of the lofty turreted
pediments which enclose the scene, two choirs of
angels are singing hymns of praise. One of the
singing angels on the left holds a scroll bearing the
words : *can.* 4. *Fons ortorum puteus aquarum
vivencium.*

On the right of the fountain stands a pope holding
a tall cross, and pointing to the well of grace ; behind
him a cardinal, a bishop, an emperor, a king, and six
other ecclesiastics and laymen, those in the foreground kneeling on the tiled pavement, the others
standing. On the left are a crowd of Jews, one of
whom, a venerable old man, kneels with a staff in

his right hand ; a high priest, blindfolded, from whose grasp the broken staff of a banner (bearing a pseudo-Semitic inscription) is falling to the ground, seems to be remonstrating with the kneeling man on whose arm he lays his left hand. Of eight other Jews, two are falling to the ground in consternation ; a third is walking proudly away ; the others, with hands to their ears, or rending their garments, are fleeing from the source of grace.

Chromolithograph by R. Soldevila, 0.36 × 0.33.

This work is an old copy of a lost original (see p. 202) which adorned the chapel of Saint Jerome in the cathedral of Palencia, where it still hung in 1783, as recorded by Ponz, who describes it.

The original disappeared at some period before 1815.

1853. PASSAVANT, *Die Christliche Kunst in Spanien*, 127, Leipzig, attributes this painting to Hubert.

1858. HOTHO, II, 73, also ascribes it to Hubert, and dates it between 1413 and 1418.

1869. BURGER, in *Gazette des Beaux Arts*, 2 P., I, 10. After a careful study of this picture on several occasions, he expresses his absolute conviction that it was painted by John. He informs us that he saw at Paris, in the hands of the dealer Haro, an old copy.

1879. WOLTMANN, II, 25, believes it to be a copy painted c. 1450.

1875. MADRAZO, "El Triunfo de la Iglesia sobre la Sinagoga," in *Museo Español de Antigüedades*, IV, 1–40, Madrid. He attributes this picture to John van Eyck, and says it was given to the convent of Parral in 1454 by Henry IV, son of John II of Castile, and he quotes a manuscript *Fundacion del Parral* in the Provincial Library at Segovia, in which, at fol. liv, this painting is described as *Un retablo rico da pincel de Flandes que tiene la ystoria de la Dedicacion de la Yglesia.*

1885. F. SCHNEIDER, "Das Eyck'sche Bild im Museum zu Madrid," in *Der Kunstfreund*, 246. Berlin.

1887. L. SOLVAY, *L'Art Espagnol*, 94–96. Paris.

M

1887. BODE, 210, is of opinion that it is a copy of a lost picture by Hubert.

1893. HYMANS, in *Gazette des Beaux Arts*, 3 P., IX, 380, finds this painting cold, and says that Van Eyck can have had nothing to do with either its composition or execution.

1898. KAEMMERER, 48, concludes from the dogmatic (!) appearance of the picture, that the commission for its execution must have been given by some eminent Spaniard, and thinks it may have been painted by Peter Christus.

1899. SEECK, 22, 68, thinks it most likely to be a copy of an original by Hubert.

1900. WEALE, in *Revue de l'Art Chrétien*, 5 S., XI, 284, and *Gazette des Beaux Arts*, 3 P., XXV, 477.

1901. BODE, 131, not by Christus.

1902. C. PHILLIPS, in *The Fortnightly Review*, October, p. 598, says : " By far the most important of the works which Mr. Weale has ascribed—and, I think, rightly ascribed—to Hubert van Eyck is 'The River of the Water of Life' (Rev. XXII, 1), formerly in the Cathedral of Palencia, and now lost to the world. . . . Here we have Hubert *tout pur*, and the man who could easily pass on from it to that still greater masterpiece of realisation and expression, the 'Adoration of the Lamb.' "

1907. E. BERTAUX, in *Revue de l'Art ancien et moderne*, XXII, 252.

1908. JUSTI, *Miscellaneen aus drei Jahrhunderten Spanischen Kunstlebens*, I, 295–307.

1908. WEALE, in *Burlington Magazine*, XIV, 113–114.

1908. D. E. TORMO Y MONZÓ, in *Boletin de la Sociedad Castellano de Excursiones*, Valladolid.

1908. WEALE, 202. " It is very difficult to say whether it is a copy of a lost original by Hubert van Eyck, or an early work by a contemporary Netherlander painted in imitation of the Ghent polyptych. It has been attributed to Louis Dalmau of Valencia, and we have positive evidence that the painter was in 1431 sent by Alphonsus V of Aragon to Flanders." The technique, however, is quite different. Dalmau may have sketched the figures, but he certainly did not execute this painting. " It is not at all clear why Alphonsus sent him to Flanders, but it was probably to purchase pictures.

. . . M. Tramoyeres Blasco thinks that Dalmau remained at Bruges until after John van Eyck's death, July 9, 1441, but of this there is no proof. The panel painted by him for the magistrates of Barcelona in 1443 affords sufficient evidence that he did not acquire the Eyckian technique, though there can be no doubt that he saw and admired the singing angels on the upper dexter shutter of the Ghent polyptych. It is, on the other hand, quite clear that the painter of the Madrid panel, whether he was a Netherlander or a Castilian, must have spent some time at Ghent to attain the degree of perfection which that picture displays. The tabernacle-work which encloses and crowns the painting is evidently a wooden construction."

1909. PHILLIPS, in *The Daily Telegraph*, January 29: "Hubert's greatest work, after the world-famous ' Adoration of the Lamb,' wholly planned and partly executed by him, was the ' Fountain of Living Water,' of which a copy hangs in the Prado Museum of Madrid. The original adorned the chapel of St. Jerome in the Cathedral of Palencia, where it hung as lately as 1873."

1910. J. SIX thinks the original was painted at the end of the fourteenth century.

XLI. THE HOLY FACE

John van Eyck is said to have painted a representation of the Holy Face. The original is now lost. The four following pictures may be copies or variants of such an original.

Munich : Royal Gallery, No. 99 (643). Oak. 1 ft. 7¾ in. × 1 ft. 2¼ in. (0.50 × 0.37).

Formerly in the Boisserée collection.

The head of Christ seen full face ; the hair, parted in the middle, falls in long curly locks on the shoulders and breast ; the beard is forked ; the cruciform nimbus floriated. The gold border of the red robe bears what is apparently meant for

. . . . . Eloy Agla. Dark background, on which, above the nimbus, A and ⲱ. The frame, original, painted to imitate stone, bears at the head PRIMVS NOVISSIMVS, and at the foot VIA VITA VERITAS. The back of the panel is painted black.

This, formerly attributed to Memlinc, is in the writers' opinion, the earliest and best copy of a lost original probably painted by Hubert.

1906. VOLL, 44, considers this painting to be the best representation of a lost original by John.

XLII. THE HOLY FACE

Berlin : Kaiser Friedrich Museum (No. 528). Oak. 1 ft. 8¼ in. × 1 ft. 3½ in. (0.51 × 0.39).

Originally in a convent at Burgos, afterwards at Segovia and in the Solly collection ; acquired in 1821.

A similar representation to that at Munich, but the inscription on the neck-band of the robe is + REX + REGVM +. Bluish-green background, on which A and ⲱ above, and their Latin equivalents, Ī and F̄ for *Initium* and *Finis* below the arms of the nimbus. The frame, original, painted in imitation of yellow marble, bears at the head : VIA VERITAS VITA ; and at the foot : PRIMVS ET NOVISSIM'. Above the latter, in minuscules : *Johēs de Eyck me fecit et apleuiit anno* 1438 31 *Ianuarij*. It is inscribed on the front to the left : "AME (or ALS) IXH XAN."

1858. HOTHO, II, 192, thinks this was painted by John after the Eternal Father by Hubert at Ghent.
1860. WAAGEN, 71, says that this painting shows how closely John adhered to the early type, while developing his warm and powerful colouring and peculiar mastery over detail.

1872. CROWE, III, accepts this painting as being by John, who, he says, in attempting a subject above his strength, was even less successful than his brother.

1887. BODE, 214. The least precious of John's works; the charming colour does not compensate for the want of feeling for nature.

1898. KAEMMERER, 99, doubts its authenticity.

1899. SEECK, 10, 27, 33. A free copy of the head by Hubert at Ghent; the weakest and least important of all John's works; the signature indubitable.

1903. MARKS, 25. "The signature is manifestly not genuine, the device having been copied by some one who did not know the meaning of the words."

1906. VOLL, 43, thinks this work was painted c. 1500.

XLIII. THE HOLY FACE

Bruges : Town Gallery. Oak. 12¾ in. × 10¼ in. (0.325 × 0.26).

Presented in 1788 by M. Joseph De Busscher.

A similar representation ; the robe bordered at the neck with gold lace studded with pearls and precious stones. Enclosed within a painted imitation of a molded stone frame with inscriptions in the hollows. At the head : *Ihesus via : Ihesus veritas : Ihesus vita.*

·IHESVS VIA·   ·IHS VERITAS·
·IHESVS VITA·

At the foot : *Speciosus forma præ filiis hominum. Als ikh kan. Iohannes de Eyck inuentor anno 1440, 30 Ianuarii.*

SPECIOSᵒ FORMA PFILIIS HOĪM   ·A'IE·IXH·XAN·

· Johes de eyck Inuentor· anno· 1440· 30 January ·

The third figure of the date may have been a 2, but more probably a 4. This painting is hard, cold, and dry, and destitute of feeling. The original doubtless had a molded frame painted to imitate stone. The painter of this copy evidently did not comprehend John's device. On the reverse of the panel is the device of the painter of this copy, or of an early owner, and the date 1637.

1833. PASSAVANT, 352. Wanting in perfection, and appears doubtful.

1834. SCHNAASE, 342. The colour falls short of the Eyckian standard, and the employment of *inventor* appears strange.

1847. KUGLER, 109; shows a want of skill in the handling.

1857. CROWE, 103. A superficial imitation.

1858. HOTHO, II, 164. A late copy.

1866. MICHIELS, II, 225. Posterior to 1550, and destitute of merit.

1872. CROWE, 123. Apparently a reduced facsimile of the 1438 painting at Berlin.

1899. SEECK, 27. The weakest and most insignificant of all John's works.

1905. FIERENS, 124, thinks it does not deserve the absolute disdain meted out to it by certain critics.

XLIV. The Holy Face

Innsbruck : Professor Dr. Egon von Oppolzer.   Oak.   15½ in. × 11¼ in. (0.395 × 0.285).

Formerly in the Abel collection at Stuttgart ; sold as a work of Roger Van der Weyden, at Köln, October 9, 1863, for £20, 10s., to Mr. John M. Parsons (d. 1870). It afterwards came into the possession of Mr. von Oppolzer at Munich, at the sale of whose collection, December 3, 1905, it was purchased by Dr. Egon von Oppolzer for £392, 10s.

A similar representation to those referred to above ; the robe dark red, bordered at the neck with a narrow band of plaited gold lace. Blue ground with A and ʊ above the nimbus. A late fifteenth-century painting in excellent preservation.

1863. WEALE, in *Le Beffroi*, I, 349.
1906. R. VON LICHTENBERG and E. VON OPPOLZER, Katalog.

XLV. A Donor

Leipzig : Town Museum (No. 511).   Oak.   10½ in. × 7¾ in. (0.264 × 0.195).

Bequeathed to the Museum in 1878 by Madam Amelia von Ritzenberg.

Portrait of an elderly man in a wig, praying with his hands joined and raised ; the face, turned to left, seen in three-quarters, small eyes, thick lips, and a long broad nose. He wears a green fur-trimmed robe.

1890. BREDIUS, in *Zeitschrift für bildende Kunst*, N.F., I, 129.

1900. VOLL, 121–122.   Not by Van Eyck.
1901. BODE, 120.
1907. HYMANS, in *Gazette des Beaux Arts*, 3 P., XXXVIII, 207, calls this man a canon, but his dress is that of a layman.

XLVI. PORTRAIT OF AN ECCLESIASTIC

New York : Mr. J. Pierpont Morgan.   3¾ in. × 3¼ in.
(0.095 × 0.085).

Formerly in the collection of Thomas Howard, Earl of Arundel, and in that of his widow. It belonged later to Lord Henry Thomas Howard Molyneux Howard, and remained in the possession of his descendants at Greystoke Castle, Penrith, until 1909, when it was purchased by Mr. J. Pierpont Morgan.

A fragment of a large panel picture or of the dexter shutter of a triptych, representing little more than the head of a donor, a canon in a blue cassock trimmed with fur, and a pleated lawn surplice, kneeling and protected by his patron saint, probably one of the apostles, whose hand rests on the donor's head ; only the hand of the saint and part of his purple mantle, lined with green, are seen. The donor has hazel eyes and grey hair ; his face is admirably modelled, and the pleats of the flesh are marked by fine strokes ; the colour, though rather cold, is brilliant and harmonious ; the entire fragment is in excellent preservation.

Engraved in reverse, when in Lord Arundel's possession, by Wenceslaus Hollar, who omitted the patron saint's hand, added hands to the figure of the donor, represented his head as cleft by a sword, and then published the print (H. 0.093 ; B. 0.057) as a true likeness of Saint Thomas of Canterbury (see Weale, 1908, p. 170).

The head has also been engraved in reverse, without the sword, within an oval, by L. Vorsterman, with the legend : *Effigies S. Thomæ Cantuar. Archiepi. Mart.*

Exhibited : British Institution, Ancient Masters, 1858 (No. 125). Guildhall, Netherlandish Masters, 1906 (No. 6).

1858. G. SCHARF, Artistic and Descriptive Notes of the Pictures in the British Institution, 32–33, says that "this picture may possibly be assigned to Justus of Ghent," *i.e.* Jodoc van Wassenhove.

1898. KAEMMERER, 56.

1904. WEALE, in the *Burlington Magazine*, VI, 249.

1906. FRIEDLAENDER, in *Repertorium für Kunstwissenschaft*, XXIX, 574, calls this portrait a dry, cold work, which has nothing to do with John van Eyck.

1910. WEALE, in the *Burlington Magazine*, XVII, 177, holds that this is the picture which, under the title of " Un ritratto di homo in profill, disegno de Jan van Eyck," was in the possession of the Countess of Arundel, widow of Thomas, Lord Howard, Earl of Arundel and Surrey, at the time of her death at Amsterdam in 1655. Another picture in the Countess's possession was the " Portrait of a Man," now in National Gallery (No. 222) (see p. 112).

XLVII. AN OLD MAN

Collection of Mr. Alfred Brown.   Oak.   10 in. × 8 in. (0.254 × 0.201).

From the collection of James Osmaston.

Half-length portrait of an old man turned slightly to the left, seen nearly full face, looking up, with his hands joined in prayer ; the modelling of these is weak. He has thin grey hair ; the beard closely shaven, but with stubble on chin, and rather feeble blue eyes. He is clad in a loose red dress trimmed with fur. His head-dress is not seen, but its lappet hangs down in front from his left shoulder.

Dark-grey background, over-painted.

This portrait certainly dates from the third quarter of the fifteenth century.

Exhibited: Burlington House, Old Masters, 1879 (No. 218); Guildhall, Netherlandish Masters, 1906 (No. 4).

1906. FRIEDLAENDER, in *Repertorium für Kunstwissenschaft*, XXIX, 574. A good work dating from *c.* 1450, in manner near to Dirk Bouts, especially in the form of the hands and the truthful expression of the lean head.

1906. PHILLIPS, in *The Daily Telegraph*, May 3rd: "We must wholly decline to accept it as by either brother; it is of later date, and probably the old copy of a work not John van Eyck's."

XLVIII. CALVARY

Museo Civico, Padua (No. 349). 1 ft. 5¾ in. × 1 ft. (0.45 × 0.30).

Formerly in the possession of a lawyer named Rossi at Padua, by whom it was bequeathed to Dr. Antonio Guglielmini, who in turn bequeathed it in 1894 to the Padua Gallery. In the archives it is described as " the work of a celebrated Flemish painter," and on the back it is marked with Patenir's name written in pencil! It has been described also as a copy by Niccolò Giolfino after a work by Lucas van Leyden. Such a picture, it was held, had been formerly in the Palazzo Dondi dall' Orologio at Padua.

These facts were first published by Frida Schottmuller in *Jahrbuch der Preussische Kunstsammlungen*, Berlin, XXIII, 33–35.

XLIX. Calvary

Venice : Collection of Baron Franchetti. Oak. 1 ft. 5¾ in. ×
1 ft. (0.45 × 0.30).

Formerly in a private collection at Padua, from which it was acquired by its present owner about 1895. What appears to be an unfinished copy of this is the preceding picture now in the Museo Civico at Padua (No. 349) (see p. 186).

1905. BODENHAUSEN, writing in the Berlin *Jahrbuch*, XXVI, 111–115, on " Paintings from the Workshop of Hubert van Eyck," claimed that this was the original of the picture described in the Berlin *Jahrbuch*, XXIII, 33, three years earlier. He described the Franchetti painting as being "not an original by either of the brothers Van Eyck," adding that, according to the discoveries made up to date, it is impossible to ascertain the identity of its painter, who was obviously inspired by Hubert van Eyck."

1912. Sir Claude PHILLIPS, in a private letter, expresses the opinion that this picture is " of the school of Hubert—especially the landscape—but it shows no connection with John van Eyck."

L. Portrait of a Monk

Montauban : Musée Ingres. Panel, 10¼ in. × 7½ in. (0.26×0.19).

Neither of the present joint-authors has inspected this picture, which, judging from the illustration in Durand-Gréville (p. 95), seems to be of little importance. However, for the purposes of reference it may be worth " listing " here among copies, derivatives, and imitations of Eyckian originals.

1910. DURAND-GRÉVILLE, p. 95 : " Le ' Portrait de Moine ' en buste du Musée Ingres, à Montauban, a été signalé pour la première fois par le Dr. A. Bredius, qui l'attri-

buait à Memling.   M. L. Gonse a fait remonter jusqu'au
'milieu du xvᵉ siècle,' cet ouvrage 'qu'on pourrait
comparer à certains portraits de Jean van Eyck.'
Mais la physionomie vivante, les yeux qui regardent . . .
le beau modelé du double menton . . . nous ramenent
avec vraisemblance, sans certitude absolue toutefois,
à Hubert.   La date d'exécution de ce portrait d'un
moine est difficile à établir, faute de renseignements
fournis par le costume.   Mettons-la, très provisoire-
ment, vers 1410–15."

LI. Christ in the Act of Blessing

Berlin : Kaiser Friedrich Museum (No. 528A).   Oak.   7¼ in. ×
5¼ in. (0.18 × 0.13).

Apparently a fragment of a larger picture.
Purchased in London in 1888.

In profile to the right, the right hand raised in
the act of blessing, is only partly seen.   To the left
are the cruciform rays on a gold ground and the
edge of the Gothic frame.

1908. Weale, 210, where it is reproduced.   This appears to
the writer to date from the end of the fifteenth century.

LII. Portrait of Bonne of Artois

Berlin : Kaiser Friedrich Museum (in the Store-room).   Oak.
8½ in. ×6½ in. (0.21 ×0.16).

The duchess is represented at half-length,
turned to the right, her face seen in three-quarters ;
her arms and hands resting on a parapet.   She
wears a full-sleeved fur-trimmed dress open in
front, and a crespine head-dress, over which is
spread a linen kerchief.   A ring adorns the fourth
finger of her right hand.   On the front of the

parapet is the legend : " Dame Bonne Dartois la Duchesse de Bourgongne."

Bonne, daughter of Philip of Artois, Count of Eu, and of Mary, daughter of John, Duke of Berry, the second wife of Duke Philip (married November 30, 1424, died September 17, 1425).

It most probably reflects the work of Hubert before the Duchess's marriage in 1424, but may show to us her features as seen by John van Eyck between May and September of the following year.

1904. HULIN, in *Bulletin de la Société d'Histoire de Gand*, XII, 172.
1908. WEALE, 179. This, if I am not mistaken, was formerly in the collection of Simon Peter van Overloope, at whose sale at Bruges, May 7, 1770, it fetched 32fr. 65c.

LIII. PORTRAIT OF JACQUELINE OF BAVARIA

Copenhagen : Royal Gallery (No. 195).   Oak.   2 ft. 5½ in. × 1 ft. 4¼ in. (0.75 × 0.41).

A sixteenth-century copy of a portrait said to have been painted by John van Eyck.

Dollmayr[1] and Glück[2] attribute this copy to John Mostaert of Haarlem.

In this half-length portrait the countess, turned to the left, her face seen in three-quarters, wears a loose robe of cloth of gold lined with ermine, the wide sleeves of which, turned over at the wrists, let those of a close-fitting heraldic dress be seen ; these show the colours of the Wittelsbach dynasty : Fusilly in bend *argent* and *azure*.   Her arms rest on a

[1] *Jahrbuch der kunsthistorischen Sammlungen*, XIX, 398. Wien.
[2] Beiträge zur Kunstgeschichte, 68-69, Wien, 1903 ; and in *Mitteilungen des Gesellschaft für vervielfältigen Kunst*, I, 1. Wien, 1905.

parapet. In her right hand, laid on the left in an affected position, she holds a pink ; a ring adorns the little finger. Her hair, brushed back off the forehead, is confined in two cauls of silken material blazoned with the arms of Hainault : Quarterly, 1 and 2 *or* a lion rampant *sable*, 2 and 3 *or* a lion rampant *gules*, and bordered with a triple row of pearls and precious stones ; and over this is laid a cambric veil dependent behind.[1]

LIV. PORTRAIT OF BONNE OF ARTOIS

Cadiz : Museum.

This painting is a copy,[2] later than the drawing in the Leboucq Collection at Arras (Town Library M.S. 266) of the painting in the store-room at the Kaiser Friedrich Muséum, Berlin.[3]

LV. PORTRAIT OF MICHAEL OF FRANCE

Munich : Baron de Bissing.

A portrait that passes as representing *Michael of France* was lent by the late George Salting to the New Gallery's Exhibition of Pictures by Masters of the Flemish and British Schools, 1899–1900, and was catalogued (No. 34) as a portrait of *Michelle de France*, by an unknown painter of the early Flemish School. The lady is seen at half length and almost in profile to the right, and wears a light brown and

[1] Kaemmerer (1898, p. 47) thinks the original of this portrait may have been painted by John van Eyck at the Hague, in 1422 or 1423 ; but Jacqueline would certainly not have gone near that town after 1418, for fear of falling into the clutches of her pitiless uncle. Moreover, this portrait represents a woman of at least twenty to twenty-five years of age.

[2] See A. L. Mayer : " Un Ritrato de Jan van Eyck in el Museo de Cadiz" in *Boletin de la Comision provincial de Monumentos de Cadiz*, II, 221–223, photo-type, Cadiz, 1909.

[3] See p. 188.

gold brocaded robe.   The frame is inscribed :
"Michelle de France fille de Charles VI. roy
de France et d'Isabeau de Baviere.   Mariee en
juin 1409 a Philippe le Bon duc de Bourgogne."
Mr. Hermann Nasse, writing on this picture, which
has lately been cleaned and has passed into the
collection of Baron de Bissing at Munich, claims
that it emanates from the studio of Henri Bellechose,
but was painted under the influence of the Flemish
School.[1] Friedländer, however, did not hold so
exalted a view of it before it was cleaned.   Writing
of it in 1900, he described it as "Eine unerhebliche
Copistenarbeit vom Ende des xv Jahrhunderts."[2]

LVI. Our Lady and Child, and a Lady protected by Saint Mary Magdalene

Liége: Episcopal Museum.   21 in. × 18½ in. (0.55 × 0.48).

Formerly in the possession of the Abbé Beeckmans
in Bruges, from whom it passed to M. Steyaert of
the same town, previous to passing into the collection of M. J. P. Weyer, of Cologne.   At the sale of
that collection on August 25, 1862 (No. 244) it
was bought by W. H. James Weale for 93 thalers.
    The Virgin is enthroned, and with her right hand
holds one of the legs of the Infant Saviour, who
grasps with both hands the lady's chaplet.   The
latter, who wears a black dress trimmed with white
fur, a red corsage, and a *hennin*, kneels on the left
before a small desk on which is a book.   Behind
and more to the left stands Saint Mary Magdalene,
holding a vase in her right hand.   The scene takes
place in a gallery which is paved with coloured tiles
and is enclosed by three rounded arches.   It leads

[1] *Revue Archéologique*, May–June, 1912, pp. 406–412.
[2] See *Repertorium für Kunstwissenschaft*, 1900, p. 251.

out on to a garden, on the far side of which is a crenelated wall, over which a man and a woman are leaning as they regard a river with shipping and a fortified town on the bank. To their left stands a man wearing a red conical hat, the lappet of which passes over his right shoulder.

The sash of the Virgin bears an inscription, read by some as—

Margareta E Eyc.

The background bears some resemblance to that seen in the Rolin picture (see p. 89).

1862. *Messager des Sciences et des Arts*, 475.

LOST PAINTINGS

LOST PAINTINGS

THERE can be no doubt that the Van Eycks painted many more pictures than those described in the present volume.[1] Mention of works attributed to them have come down to us ; some of these they certainly executed. Drawings are also preserved of portraits, some of which at least must have been painted by Hubert or John. Moreover, hypothetical deductions as to lost authentic paintings may be made from a certain number of pictures which can, with varying degrees of probability, and even certainty, be regarded as preserving for us the main elements of such originals.

§ 1. Alphonsus V of Aragon, King of Naples, had, as we are told by Facio [2] in his " Liber de Viris illustribus," written in 1454–55, a triptych by John, representing *The Annunciation, Saint John the Baptist, and Saint Jerome*. On the shutters were painted John Baptist Lomellini

---

[1] DURAND-GRÉVILLE, 1910, p. 29, points out that no single Van Eyck picture in any public gallery is now officially assigned to Hubert, but that "c'est Jean qui règne sans partage sur les cartouches et dans les catalogues . . Supposons qu'au moment de la mort de Jean, il ait existé trente tableaux de chacun des deux frères ; combien y a-t-il de chances pour que les trente ouvrages d'Hubert aient tous disparu, tandis que ceux de Jean se seraient tous conservés ? " He goes on to calculate that the chances against the thirty pictures that he thinks fit to place to Hubert's credit in the past centuries having been destroyed and a like number by John preserved may be calculated as "quatre milliards de milliards de chances contre une ! " Unwise inferences based on unsafe assumptions and worked out with the aid of mathematical, but in this instance purely unscientific formulae, could hardly go farther. Several pictures now assigned to John were formerly given to Hubert.

[2] See Bibliography, p. 281.

("Baptista Lomellinus[1] cuius fuit ipsa tabula") and his wife Jeronima ("mulier, quam amabat praestanti forma").

§ 2. Facio[2] also tells us that John painted for Duke Philip a curious representation of *The World* ("mundi comprehensio, orbiculari forma") in its spherical shape—a work unsurpassed by any other executed in his time, as it not only showed the various countries and localities, but figured them at the correct distances from each other, as might be tested by measuring.

A picture that may be mentioned in this connection was in the collection of Jonkheer Victor de Stuers, Minister of Fine Arts at the Hague. It was a late fifteenth-century panel of a "Representation of the World." The idea was, no doubt, taken from Van Eyck.

§ 3. Ottaviano, a member of the Florentine family of the Ottaviani, created a cardinal by Gregory XII in 1408,[3] had in his possession some remarkable paintings by John.[4] Facio describes in general terms one of these pictures. It represented *Women of noble form coming out of a Warm Bath*, slightly veiled with fine linen drapery ; of one only the face and breast were seen, but a mirror reflected the back of her head and body. In the same picture a light was shown as if really burning ; also, an old woman perspiring, a dog lapping water, and in a landscape, horses and men, mountains, groves, villages, and castles, so skilfully painted that they appeared to be far distant from each other. Nothing

---

[1] The Lomellini were a Genoese family, whose arms were: Per fesse *gules* and *or*. The only member of the family of whom we have found mention in contemporary documents, is one Jerome Lomellini, a merchant living at Bruges in 1392.

[2] *Op. cit.* p. 46.

[3] See CHACON, *Vitae et res gestae Pontificum Summorum*, II, 771. Romae, 1677.

[4] "Sunt item picturae eius nobiles apud Octavianum cardinalem," is Facio's statement.

in this picture was more wonderful than the mirror in which every detail was reflected accurately as in a real mirror.[1]

§ 4. A similar subject was in the collection of works of art formed by Cornelius Van der Geest of Antwerp, in the beginning of the seventeenth century.[2] A copy of this picture of a *Lady at her Toilet* [3] is seen in a painting by William van Haecht, dated 1628, representing the visit of the Archdukes Albert and Isabella to the Gallery on the 15th of August, 1615, in the company of Rubens and other notabilities.[4] It shows the nude figure of a maiden at her toilet, standing near a window. At her left an attendant stands holding a water-bottle. She is clad in a red dress with long white under-sleeves, and a crespine head-dress, over which a linen kerchief is spread. A Bolognese dog lies on a mat in the foreground, and close by are a couple of pattens of white wood with black leather latchets.

§ 5. Another lost painting would appear to be the "*Testa de Donna Vecchia*," by John van Eyck, which is entered in the Inventory of Paintings belonging to the Countess of Arundel at Amsterdam at the time of her death in 1655.[5]

§ 6. The Town Museum at Leipzig contains a beautifully executed picture (Oak. H. 0.21; B. 0.16) of the middle of the fifteenth century, which

[1] This picture afterwards belonged to Frederick I, Duke of Urbino. See MUNTZ: Raphael, p. 5, note 1.

[2] A portrait of this art patron by Van Dyck is in the National Gallery (No. 52). It seems to have been painted about 1619 during Van Dyck's first Flemish period.

[3] Reproduced in Weale, 1908, p. 176.

[4] This picture, now in the collection of Lord Huntingfield at Heveningham, measures 3 ft. 3½ in. × 4 ft. 3¼ in. (1.00 × 1.30). It was exhibited at Burlington House in 1906 (No. 52), and at Bruges in 1907 (No. 172). See Weale, 1908, p. 175; *Athenæum*, Jan. 26 and Feb. 2 and 9, 1907; and *Repertorium*, XXX, 381. Although signed and dated, it was in August 1865 said to be by Gonzales Coques, and held to represent one of the rooms in the Old Palace at Brussels, and to depict Albert and Isabella with the Marquis de Moncada and other Spanish nobles!

[5] See *The Burlington Magazine*, XVII, p. 177.

may possibly be a free copy of a lost original by John. It has been entitled "Le Sortilège d'Amour." In the middle of a room a maiden is seen standing near a fireplace, nude save for a long thin scarf which falls from her right arm and encircles her lower limbs. With a steel in her left hand she strikes a flint held in her right, and at the same time squeezes a sponge ; the sparks and the drops of water fall on a wax heart that lies in an open coffer placed on a three-legged stool at her side. Five scrolls float in the air or lie about the floor of the chamber, which is strewn with flowers ; a Bolognese dog lies on a mat in the foreground. To the right, an aumbry, on which are a salver with comfits, a glass goblet, and a long fringed cloth ; and on a shelf beneath, a beaker in a dish ; above, two windows, the upper part alone glazed. On the wall between them hangs a mirror, with a feather dusting-brush beneath it ; a parakeet is perched on the window-sill. In the background to the left a youth, pushing the door open, is entering the room ; to the right is a cupboard, in which are a hanap and a flagon ; on a shelf above are a book, and a number of pots and other articles.[1]

§ 7. Alphonsus V of Aragon had, besides the Lomellini triptych referred to above (§ 1), a painting representing *Saint George*, for which, on June 25, 1445, he paid 2000 sueldos.[2] It will be remembered (see p. 10), that John van Eyck was sent, in company with Duke Philip III's ambassadors, on an embassy, to Alphonsus V in the summer of 1427. Was it then that John was commissioned, soon after the death of Hubert, to paint the *Saint George*, or was it procured for the King by Louis Dalmau ? Can

---

[1] See H. LÜCKE, "Liebeszauber Flandrische Gemälde," in *Zeitschrift für bildende Kunst*, XVIII, 379-383, 1882.

[2] See the important document ordering the payment of this sum, published by CASELLAS, "La Novela den Sanpere," IX, in the *Veu de Catalunya*. Barcelona, 1906.

the small picture of that subject have any connection with that now in the collection of General Plaoutine at St. Petersburg (see p. 161)?

§ 8. Among the paintings in the Duke of Uceda's palace, at the commencement of the eighteenth century, there was a small panel of *Our Lady and Child* by John van Eyck, which Palomino describes as a work of supreme excellence and exquisite finish.[1]

§ 9. Don Diego de Guevara possessed a *Portrait of a Portuguese Lady* painted on cloth in tempera by John van Eyck, which he, before 1516, presented to Margaret of Austria, Governess of the Netherlands. This Portuguese lady was clad in a red dress trimmed with fur, holding in her right hand a roll with a miniature of Saint Nicholas at the head.[2] What is reputed to be a copy of this portrait is said to be in the collection of M. Abbegg, at Mannheim.[3]

§ 10. The *Portrait of a Moorish Prince*, by John van Eyck, is recorded in the Inventory of Paintings " qui formaient le fonds de commerce d'un grand marchand de tableaux de la fin du XVII siècle, Diego de Duarte. Cet inventaire a été dressé en 1682 et se trouve à la Bibliothèque Royale de Bruxelles.[4] Au verso du folio 23 :—

---

[1] "Una pintura de una imagen de Nuestra Señora, con el Niño Jesus, en una tabla pequeña, de mano del referido Juan de Brujas, de una tercia de alto, y quarto de ancho, hecha con estremado primor y sutilega." A. A. PALOMINO DE CÂSTRO Y VALASCO, *El Museo pictorico*, 1, 47. Madrid, 1715.

[2] "Ung moien tableau de la face d'une Portugaloise que Madame a eu de Don Diego. Fait de la main de Iohannes, et est fait sans huelle et sur toille, sans couverte ne feullet." Inventaire des Peintures, etc., de Marguerite d'Autriche, dressé en 1516. Lille : Archives of the Department of the North, B3507. "Ung aultre tableau de une jeusne dame, accoustrée à la mode de Portugal, son habit rouge fouré de martre, tenant en sa main dextre ung rolet avec ung petit sainct Nicolas en hault, nommée La belle Portugaloise." Inventaire des Peintures, etc., de Marguerite d'Autriche, dressé en son palais de Malines, le 9 Juillet, 1523." Paris : Bibliothèque Nationale, Collection Colbert.

[3] Don Diego also acquired after 1490 the "Portrait of John Arnolfini and his Wife," now in the National Gallery (No. 186), see p. 114.

[4] See Hulin in *Bulletin d' Histoire et d Archéologie de Gand*, 1907, XV, 91–92.

"*Een mooren koninck ofte prins van Ioan van Eyck, eersten schilder in olyverf, geschildert*, 1414 ... gl. 5."

Hulin, commenting on the above, says that the mention of the artist's name, at a time when the Van Eycks' pictures were held to have little more than archæological interest, must have been due to the pictures having been signed and dated. He adds, however, that the figures 4 and 8 being often confused by critics, the date may have been 1418.

§ 11. Serrure informs us that a member of the family of De Visch-Van der Capelle, by a will dated in 1413, bequeathed to his daughter Mary, a nun in the Benedictine convent of Bourbourg, near Gravelines, " une œuvre de [maître] Hubert." [1]

§ 12. Margaret of Austria had also a painting of *Our Lady* by John, which had belonged to Duke Philip.[2]

§ 13. The "Anonimo" of Morelli records that in the house of Messer Camillo Lampagnano, or of his father, Messer Niccolò Lampagnano at Milan was: " A little picture with half-length figures representing a patron making up accounts with his agent." Its owner seems to have attributed it to Van Eyck, but the Anonimo appears to have regarded it

---

[1] This is referred to by Hulin, *op. cit.* p. 91. The fact here mentioned was communicated to Weale by the late M. Serrure in 1870, but Weale attached no particular importance to it until in 1902 he was shown by Count Durrieu the photographs of the miniatures in the Turin Hours. So far as we know, Hubert van Eyck is the only painter of that time bearing this Christian name.

It is interesting to recall that the donor in Gerard David's " Marriage of Saint Katherine " in the National Gallery (No. 1432), painted some sixty years after John van Eyck's death, is Richard De Visch-Van der Capelle.

[2] " Ung tableaul de Nostre Dame, du duc Philippe, qui est venu de Maillardet, couvert de satin brouché gris et ayant fermaulx d'argent doré et bordé de velours vert. Faict de la main de Iohannes." See " Inventaire des Peintures, etc., de Marguerite d'Autriche, dressé en 1516." Lille, Archives of the Department of the North, B3507.

as the work of Memlinc ("*de man de Zuan Heic credo Memelino Ponentino* ").[1]

The "Anonimo" here clearly confuses the names of two distinct painters, John van Eyck and Hans Memlinc.

§ 14. Early in the sixteenth century there was at Padua, in the house of Messer Leonico Tomeo, in the street of San Francesco, a painting on canvas, one foot high, representing an *Otter-Hunt*, with various figures in a landscape, attributed to John (Gianes de Brugia).[2] Such a scene is depicted in a contemporary "Hunting Tapestry" at Hardwick.[3]

§ 15. In the church of Our Lady of the Servites at Venice, there were, in 1580, a *Nativity* and an *Adoration of the Magi* by John.[4]

§ 16. The inventory of Lorenzo de' Medici, drawn up in 1492, and now preserved among the State Archives at Florence includes a *St. Jerome*. It is described as " Una tavoletta di Fiandra suvi uno San Girolamo a studio, chon uno armarietto de piu libri de prospettiva e uno lione a piede, opera di maestro Giovanni di Bruggia, cholorita a olio, in una guaina, f. 30." [5] It was priced at 30 francs. The composition clearly recalls the picture of *St. Jerome in his Study* now assigned to Antonello da Messina in the National Gallery Catalogue (No. 1418). It was in the Baring sale in 1848, and at

[1] See Frizzoni: "Notizia d'Opere di disegno da Morelli." See also G. C. Williamson, "The Anonimo of Morelli " 1903, p. 65.

[2] Frizzoni: "Notizia d'Opere del disegno da Morelli," 1884, p. 32. See also The "Anonimo" of Morelli, edited by G. C. Williamson, 1903, p. 18.

[3] Reproduced in the *Art Workers' Quarterly*, I, 77. London, July, 1902. The large Flemish tapestry of the second quarter of the fifteenth century representing the "Otter Hunt and the Bear Hunt" is now lent by the Duke and Duchess of Devonshire to the Victoria and Albert Museum (Room 43).

[4] Sansovino: Descrizione di Venezia, Venezia, 1580.

[5] See Muntz : *Les Collections des Medicis au xvᵉ Siècle.* Paris, 1888, p. 78.

the Coningham sale in the following year was acquired by the Earl of Northbrook, from whom it was bought by the nation in 1894. It is a remarkable fact that it was exhibited at the British Institution in 1845 as being by Van Eyck, and at Burlington House in 1871, as the work of John van Eyck.[1]

§ 17. Known to us only by the old copy, preserved in the Prado Gallery (No. 1511), under the title of "The Triumph of the Church over the Synagogue" (see p. 175); is the lost original called "*The Fountain of Living Water.*" It adorned the chapel of Saint Jerome in the *cathedral of Palencia*, where it still hung in 1783. It is recorded by Ponz, who describes it in the following terms : " Una pintura muy singular, como lo es su conservacion, y trabajo de infinita prolixidad, qual parece imposible ver cosa igual en el estilo antiguo, ó digase Aleman, al modo del de Durero ; pero en la inteligencia de que poco hay de este artifice tan acabado. Su composicion y lo que esta significa es dificil de comprehender á primera vista. Parece el complemento de las Profecías, destruccion de la Sinagoga, y establecimiento de la ley de Gracia. A un lado se ve un Sacerdote de la Ley Antigua con estandarte roto, y algunos Doctores, ó Rabinos con muy tristes semblantes. Al otro estan los Doctores de la Iglesia Griega y Latina. Encima, la Santisima Trinidad, y á los lados nuestra Señora, S. Juan Bautista; Apòstoles, y otras figuras : desciende un arroyo con muchas hostias sobre el agua, que caen en una taza, con otras alegorías, que seria largo referir. Ello es, que en su termino es pintura muy rara, y estimable, de la qual he visto algunas copias en Castilla, pero infinitamente distantes de la exácta execucion de esta."—*Viage de España*, XI, 155, Madrid, 1783.

[1] Weale and Richter: *Catalogue of Lord Northbrook's Collection*, 1889, pp. 105–108.

The original disappeared at some period before 1815.

For the bibliography and the remarks of critics in regard to this lost original, see pp. 177–179.

1869. BÜRGER, in *Gazette des Beaux Arts*, 2 P., I, 10. After a careful study of this picture on several occasions, he expresses his absolute conviction that it was painted by John. He informs us that he saw at Paris, in the hands of the dealer Haro, an old copy, the signature of which he reproduces.

§ 18. A small panel *Portrait of Bonne d'Artois* (0.22 × 0.165) was in the collection of M. Antoine J. Essingh (1787–1864) of Cologne. It was in the sale catalogue of that collection, sold on September 18, 1865 (No. 52), held to be of the School of Van Eyck, and to represent her as "jeune, regardant du côté gauche. Au dessus de son bonnet brodé de perles, elle porte un voile blanc a riches plis ; sa robe rouge est bordée de pelleterie. Sur le tableau se lit cette inscription : DAME BOÑE D'ARTOIS, DUCHESSE DE BORGOGNE. Fond de couleur foncée. Dans un cadre doré. Tableau très délicatement peint, remarquable au point de vue historique."

The description as well as the inscription clearly recall the portrait in the store-room of the Kaiser Friedrich Museum, Berlin (see p. 188).

1843. PUTTMANN, in *Kunstschatze am Rheine*. Maintz.
1865. SIRET, A. "Collections Essingh à Cologne." In *Revue de l'Art chrétien*, t. IX, p. 526, where it is reproduced.
1865. HEBERLE, J. M. (Lempertz, H.). Catalogue illustré de la Collection de Mr. Antoine Jos. Essingh.
1911. *Revue Archéologique*, XVII, 172, where it is suggested that this picture was in the collection of A. J. Essingh, sold at Köln in 1865.

§ 19. A portrait that now passes as representing *Isabella of Portugal* is the *Portrait of a Lady* in the Louvre (No. 997C *or* No. 1052), which was formerly held officially to represent Isabella of Bavaria. It is, doubtless, a contemporary copy of a lost original, of about 1430–1440, of Isabella of Portugal. At that date Isabella of Bavaria was sixty years of age, as Hulin has pointed out.[1]

§ 20. In the Louvre also is preserved, and classed as being by a nameless fifteenth-century painter of the school of Burgundy, a *Portrait de Philippe le Bon, Duc de Bourgogne* (No. 997B or No. 1003). He is clean shaven, and wears a black dress, a white undershirt, edged with black, and a black chaperon. Round his neck is the order of the Golden Fleece. His hands rest on a balustrade ; he wears a ring on his right hand, and holds a roll of paper. This bust-length, less than life-size portrait painted on a greenish blue ground measures 0.32 × 0.23. It was formerly in the Julienne (No. 218) and Sauvageot collections.[2] Here we have, doubtless, an old copy of a lost original.

§ 21. Another portrait in the Louvre, described as being by an unknown fifteenth-century artist of the Burgundian school, is held to represent *Jean sans Peur, Duc de Bourgogne* (No. 997A or No. 1002). He is seen in profile to the left, and has a ruddy complexion. He wears a black dress trimmed with a fur collar, a red hood, and a black cap adorned with a pearl. His left hand rests on a table, and a coat of arms is embroidered on his left shoulder. This small picture measures only 0.19 × 0.20, and represents him less than life size. It was formerly in the Sauvageot collection, and is in all probability but an echo of a lost portrait painted from life.[3]

[1] Hulin, *Bulletin de la Société d'Histoire et d'Archéologie de Gand*, 1903, XI, 241–243. See also P. Mantz, *La Peinture Française*, 1897, pp. 180–181.

[2] See Sauzay, *Catalogue du Musée Sauvageot*, 1861, No. 986, as of the Ancienne Ecole Flamande.

[3] See Hulin, *Bulletin de la Société d'Histoire et d'Archéologie de Gand*, 1904, XII, 172; and Lafenestre and Richtenberger, *Le Musée National du Louvre*, 1908, p. 148.

On the back, in writing of the sixteenth century,[1] is said to be the inscription :—

" IOAN · INTREPID · DVX BURG.   COMES FLAND · OBIIT 1419 · VAN EYCK PINXIT."

§ 22. The Museum at Ghent possesses, and catalogues as works of the fifteenth-century Flemish school, three small panel pictures that are officially held to represent *Jean sans Peur and Marguerite de Bavière, Philippe le Bon and Ysabeau de Portugal, Charles le Temeraire and Ysabeau de Bourbon*. They measure 0.215 × 0.29, 0.217 × 0.285, and 0.22 × 0.29 respectively. It is claimed that they are old copies of a lost series of portraits of the Counts of Flanders of the house of Burgundy.[2]

§ 23. In the Department of Engravings at the Victoria and Albert Museum is a line engraving inscribed " L. Garreau, sculp., 1791," and entitled *"Le Portrait d'un Peintre du tems par Hubert et Jean van Eyck,* gravé d'après le tableau sur bois de 14 pouces de hauteur sur 10 pouces de largeur.   Tiré du Cabinet du C<u>en</u> Le Brun, Peintre et M<u>d</u>."

§ 24. We do not know the present whereabouts of the centre panel, said to have represented the *Adoration of the Magi,* of the triptych, of which the St. Petersburg "Calvary," and "Last Judgment" were at one time the shutters (see p. 153).

§ 25. It is recorded that two portraits of *A Man* and *A Woman* by John van Eyck were included in the *Catalogue Mortuaire* (Nos. 179, 180) of Rubens in 1640.[3]   Noel Sainsbury says they were classed among "Pieces of the Old Masters." [4]   Michel thought

---

[1] See *Catalogue du Musée des Beaux Arts de Gand,* 1909, p. 81.
[2] See Sauzay, *Catalogue du Musée Sauvageot,* 1861, No. 985, under Ecole de Van Eyck.
[3] *Catalogue des Tableaux, etc., trouvés à la Mortuaire de M. le Chevalier P. P. Rubens l'an* 1640 ; 1794.
[4] *Original Papers relating to Rubens,* 1859, p. 179.

fit to describe them as the *Portraits de Jean van Eyck et sa Femme*.[1]

§ 26. The catalogue of the collections formed by Jerome van Winghe, who became canon of the cathedral of Tournay on April 19, 1591, includes a portrait of a *Burgomaster of Köln* stated to be either an original by Van Eyck or a copy by Quentin Metsys after Van Eyck.[2] The picture was given to the canon by his aunt in August 1616.

§ 27. No importance attaches to the Triptych attributed to the brothers Van Eyck, which was dealt with at some length, and accompanied by an engraving, by Louis Hacault, of a very unconvincing signature, by Jules Bosmans.[3]

§ 28. In the inventory of Rembrandt's effects drawn up on July 25–26, 1656, on the occasion of his bankruptcy, there was stated to be " Een oude tronie " (old man's head) by Van Eyck. It hung " In de Caemer agter de sydelcaemer " (in the room behind the side room).[4]

§ 29. The *King James III of Scotland with his Queen*, referred to in an inventory of 1624 as being by Joan Vanek are, of course, the panels by Hugo van der Goes at Holyrood.[5]

§ 30. If there be any truth in Mark van Vaernewyck's statement that the Ghent polyptych had a predella down to 1550, it may be briefly mentioned here. The subject, however, must have been Purgatory, and not Hell, as he affirms (see pp. 38 and 61).

§ 31. It may be useful under this head to refer briefly

---

[1] J. F. M. Michel: *Histoire de la Vie de P. P. Rubens*, Bruxelles, 1771, p. 282.
[2] W. H. J. Weale in *Burlington Magazine*, 1908, XIV, 43–44.
[3] Bosmans in *Annales du Cercle Archéologique d'Enghien*, Louvain, 1882.
[4] Bode : *Complete Work of Rembrandt*, Paris, 1906, viii. 237.
[5] See Fry and Brockwell : *Catalogue of an Exhibition of Old Masters held at the Grafton Galleries*, 1911, Nos. 218–221, pp. 120–122.

to a certain number of pictures, still preserved, which appear to be copies of lost originals. Those pictures have been already dealt with at some length in section H. Such works include the three pictures now at Berlin, representing the *Madonna in a Church* (pp. 167–169); the *Madonna, Saint Barbara, and a Carthusian* (pp. 169–172), the *Madonna by a Fountain* (pp. 172–174); and various renderings of *The Holy Face* (pp. 179–183). It would be idle to claim that the Metropolitan Museum's "Madonna" (p. 174), which appears to be a mere imitation, can in any real sense suggest the former existence of a lost original.

Note. For other lost paintings, from which Drawings were made and have been preserved, see p. 211.

DRAWINGS

AND DRAWINGS MADE FROM PAINTINGS

o

PORTRAIT OF A GOLDSMITH

SILVER-POINT DRAWING. BERLIN: ROYAL PRINT COLLECTION

Plate XXXIII

DRAWINGS

AND DRAWINGS MADE FROM PAINTINGS

§ 1. DRAWINGS

WE have already dealt with those drawings,[1] bearing directly on Eyckian paintings, that have come down to us :—

(I.) The silver-point drawing by John at Dresden, from which the " Nicholas Albergati " in the Vienna Gallery was painted (p. 106). This is the only known authenticated drawing by either of the Van Eycks.

(II.) The two silver-point drawings, now in the Louvre, which Crowe considered to be the original designs for " Adam " and " Eve " on the outermost panels of the Ghent polyptych (p. 48). They may perhaps be feeble copies of lost drawings by Hubert.

(III.) The pen drawing of " Nicholas Rolin " in the Town Library at Arras (p. 90).

(IV.) The silver-point drawing of a " Goldsmith," (Plate XXXIII), at Berlin, which may be studied in connexion with the " Léal Souvenir " painting in the National Gallery (p. 109).

(V.) The drawings at Nürnberg and Vienna after John van Eyck's " Madonna " (p. 140) in the collection of M. Helleputte. The former was at one time ascribed to Roger Van der Weyden, and the latter to John van Eyck, and later to Peter Christus.

---

[1] Several of these are reproduced in Weale, 1908.

(VI.) The pencil drawing after the portrait of Sir Baldwin de Lannoy in the Town Library at Arras (p. 149).

(VII.) The pen drawing of " Our Lady in a Church," which was formerly in the collection of Count Ludwig Paar at Vienna and recalls the pictures of that subject (p. 167).

(VIII.) The drawing of a " Falconer," at the Staedel Institute at Frankfort-on-Main, which may be conjectured to reveal the appearance of Henry van Eyck (see p. 23).

§ 2. DRAWINGS MADE FROM PAINTINGS

Among the portraits of contemporaries of the Van Eycks, of which one or more copies have been preserved, there are some which may with great probability be traced to one or other of the brothers.

(I.) The earliest is that of " *Michael of France*," first wife of Duke Philip III (married June 1409, died July 1422). She is represented seen in three-quarters, turned to the left, clad in a plain dress, within the wide sleeves of which her hands are laid one upon the other.[1] This portrait was in the possession of Denis de Villers,[2] chancellor of the cathedral of Tournay, in whose house it was copied by Anthony de Succa[3] on the 5th of December

[1] This, like several with which we are about to deal, is reproduced in Weale, 1908, p. 178.

[2] Denis de Villers, born at Tournay in 1546, doctor of laws of the University of Louvain and protonotary apostolic, was in 1586, after the death of Bishop Morillon, elected chancellor by the chapter. He was a distinguished scholar, and had a remarkable collection of paintings, medals, and Greek and Roman antiquities, which he bequeathed, together with his manuscripts and printed books, to the cathedral—now the town—library, founded by himself and Canon Jerome de Winghe, abbot of Liessies. Catalogues of the books of each of these benefactors are preserved.

[3] Anthony de Succa, inscribed in 1598 as free-master in the register of the Antwerp gild of Saint Luke, was, by letters patent dated October

ISABELLA OF PORTUGAL, DUCHESS OF BURGUNDY

Plate XXXIV

1601.[1] At the head of the sheet of paper on which it is drawn is the following inscription : " Dame Michiele de France, fille du Roy Charles V de France, et première femme de monseigneur le duc Phelipe de Bourgonde, comte de Flandres, dict le bon, fils du ducq Jehan. Laquelle ala de vie à trespas le . . . Levé ceste effigie au logis de Monsieur le chanchellier Villers du chapitre de l'église de Nostre Dame à Tournay le 5ᵉ jour de Décembre 1601, par moy Anthoine de Succa." Succa, evidently not quite satisfied with his copy of this remarkable figure, added a more carefully finished copy of the head at the side.

(II.) A drawing of *Bonne of Artois* in the Leboucq Collection at Arras [2] is a copy either of the painting in the store-room at Berlin or of the original picture.

(III.) In the possession of Denis de Villers there were a number of other portraits besides that of Michael of France described above. Of these the most interesting is that of *Isabella of Portugal* (Plate XXXIV), third wife of Duke Philip (d. 1473),[3] as it at once suggests the surmise that it may have been one of the two portraits painted by John at the palace of Aviz, in 1429. Succa's copy is now in the Royal Library at Brussels. The duchess is clad in a widesleeved robe, confined at the waist by a broad sash, and has a crespine head-dress, over which is spread a large kerchief ; her face, seen in three-quarters

---

11, 1600, commissioned by the Archdukes Albert and Isabella to visit churches, convents, etc., and copy portraits, statues, tombs, etc., of sovereigns of the Netherlands and members of their families. Succa died September 8, 1620.

[1] See Hulin, *Bulletin de la Société d'Histoire de Gand*, 1904, XII, 172.

[2] Arras, Town Library, MS. 266. (See pp. 188 and 203).

[3] In the margin : " Isabel de Portugal, 3 espeuse du duc Phelipe de Bourgonde." That in the Louvre, first identified by M. G. Hulin, in 1902, and the original from which that in the Museum of Ghent is a copy, are certainly of later date.

turned to the right, has suffered from rubbing. It is certainly an early portrait, with a pleasing expression.

(IV.) On the same sheet of paper as this is a portrait of *Jacqueline of Bavaria*, the face seen in three-quarters turned to the right, her hands joined in prayer ; she wears a full-sleeved dress trimmed with fur, open in front, and confined at the waist by a plain sash. A crespine head-dress completes her costume. This is, with the exception of the miniature in the Turin Hours, the earliest representation of that unfortunate princess, dating in all probability from about the time of her second marriage, April 4, 1418.[1]

(V.) De Villers also possessed a portrait of her second husband, *John IV, Duke of Brabant* (d. 1427), a half-length figure turned to the right, the face seen in three-quarters.[2]

(VI.) De Villers also owned another of *Philip, Duke of Brabant*, brother of John IV (d. 1430), the face seen in three-quarters turned to the left.[3]

(VII.) The Print-room of the Städel Institute at Frankfort contains a silver-point drawing on paper of *A Lady*, formerly ascribed to Roger De la Pasture, and said to be the portrait of his wife. This Glück considers to be an original study from life

[1] In the margin : " Dame Jacoba de Baviere fille Comte de Haynaut, Hollande, Zeelande et de Frise, dame de diceulx pays, espeuse a Jehan duc de Lothric, Brabant, Lembourg, aisné fils du duc Anthoine de Brabant." At the foot is the following certificate in the chancellor's hand : " L'an 1601, le 5 Décembre, passant par Tournay, le S^re Antoine de Succa tira de mon logis copies de figures designées en ceste feuille de papier, tesmoing mon nom, Denis de Villers." SUCCA, Mémoriaux, fol. 7.

[2] The original, or more probably a copy of the original, of this portrait, was formerly at Louvain. See DE RAM, Note sur un portrait du Duc de Brabant, Jean IV, ayant appartenu à la gilde des arbaletriers de Louvain, in *Bulletins de la Commission royale d'Histoire*, 3 S., 1, 295, with a chromolithograph, Brussels, 1860 ; also E. VAN EVEN, Louvain dans le passé et dans le présent, 549–550. Louvain, 1895.

[3] Signed : " Levé ces figures en Tonray à la maison de Mons. de Vilers chancelier." SUCCA, Mémoriaux, fol. 7.

of dame Jacqueline, but it appears to us to be a copy.[1]

(VIII.) A drawing in the Leboucq Collection in the Town Library at Arras represents the same *Lady* at about the same age, turned to the right, the face seen in three-quarters, her hands laid one upon the other.

(IX.) The portrait of *John of Bavaria*, the Pitiless, Count of Holland and Zeeland, in the Leboucq Collection of the Town Library at Arras, is believed to be the only one of him.[2] Can the painting, now lost, from which it was copied, have been an early work of John van Eyck ?

(X.) There is in the Louvre a silver-point drawing (0.12 × 0.09) which has been much retouched.[3] It is the *Portrait of a Man*, turned to the right, wearing a headkerchief, the long lappet of which hangs down over his right shoulder. It may possibly be a copy of a work by John.

(XI.) In the collection of Baron Adalbert von Lanna there was a silver-point drawing of a man which has been described as " almost good enough to have been drawn by John van Eyck, under whose name it is catalogued." [4] It measures 9 in. × 6½ in., and was included in the Von Lanna sale held at Prague, May 1910 (No. 244), when it was described as " Kopf eines Mannes mit breit krämpigem Hut."

(XII.) In the collection of John Malcolm of Poltalloch there was a silver-point drawing, on a dark slate-coloured ground. It was a *Portrait of an*

[1] E. W. MOES, *Iconographia Batava*, I, 480, Amsterdam, 1897, mentions several other portraits of the countess. In the most interesting of these, painted after her marriage to Frank van Borsselen, 1433, now in the Amsterdam Museum, she wears the collar of the Order of Saint Anthony.

[2] Reproduced in Weale, 1908, p. 196.

[3] Reproduced in Weale, 1908, p. 206.

H. W. S. in *The Burlington Magazine*, XVII, 60, 1910.

aged Monk (?), and represented him at half-length and turned three-quarters to the left, his hands being joined in prayer. The drawing, which had formerly been in the collection of Sir Charles J. Robinson, was lent to the Grosvenor Gallery in 1878–79 (No. 629).

(XIII.) There is at Dresden a sheet of drawings that may be described as *Seven Studies of Female Costume.*

Further pursuit of this subject would be both unprofitable and hazardous.

OBSERVATIONS

OBSERVATIONS

IT is remarkable how widely the critics differ in their views as to which of the pictures were painted by Hubert and which by John, or by the two in collaboration. Moreover, the wide range of the dates assigned by various writers to these pictures is no less noteworthy.

In the *Catalogue raisonné* which we have drawn up in the preceding pages we have thought it well to classify twenty-four of the pictures as authentic, and that without unduly emphasising the fact that certain works must be accepted as genuine, although some of them lack documentary authentication. Of this number the Ghent polyptych (I.) was begun by Hubert and completed by John, while in our view the elder brother left uncompleted the Copenhagen picture (II.) and the "Three Marys" (III.) at Richmond.

One or other of the brothers, or possibly both, painted, as we claim, seven others. These are now at Hermannstadt (IV.), in the Rothschild Collection at Paris (V.), at Berlin ("Esquire of the Order of St. Anthony," popularly known as "The Man with the Pinks ") (VI.), at Dresden (VII.), in the Louvre ("The Rolin Madonna ") (VIII.), The "Saint Francis" at Philadelphia (IX.), and the St. Petersburg "Annunciation" (X.).

The fourteen authentic works that remain to complete our total of twenty-four must, as we hold, be assigned to John, and of this number three are in the National Gallery.

The nine that are placed in the category of works of doubtful authenticity (XXV-XXXIII) show varying degrees of quality. This remark applies also, but in a different sense, to the twenty-three achievements of lesser importance (XXXIV-LVI); which we have grouped together under the heading of " Copies, Variants, Derivatives, and Imitations."

In conclusion, we have attempted to state the essential and ascertainable facts in regard to thirty lost paintings, eight drawings, and thirteen drawings made from paintings, as known to us by authentic or unauthentic material, and by records of various kinds.

As to the internal evidence which the works of art offer, what are the features which can help us, in support of such documents as exist, to form a correct opinion as to their probable authorship and date ? We may deal with the following points in detail :—

    (I.) Architecture.
    (II.) Perspective.
    (III.) Lighting.
    (IV.) Composition.
    (V.) Landscape.
    (VI.) Snow-capped mountains.
    (VII.) Flocks of wild geese or cranes in the air.
   (VIII.) Exotic Plants and Flora.
    (IX.) Costume.
    (X.) Arms and Armour.
    (XI.) Portraiture.
   (XII.) Alleged portraits of the Van Eycks.

   (I.) *Architecture*—The architecture in the Bruges altar-piece (p. 120) is late Romanesque ; in the *Saint Barbara* (p. 129), third-pointed ; and in the Ypres triptych (p. 135), late Romanesque with third-pointed vaulting. Kern is of opinion that the first of these represents a circular Romanesque church. The Antwerp pa..el (p. 129) shows an octagonal third-pointed tower, there introduced as the emblem characterising Saint Barbara. This admirable drawing can hardly be an original design of John's, and as no such building is known, it may possibly have been copied from some master-mason's design. The columns in the Bruges altar-piece (p. 120) and in the Ypres triptych (p. 135) have capitals adorned with interlaced foliage and animals, whilst those of the piers in the former are storied. This system has been carried out in all the other paintings here described which present architectural interiors. The capitals of the columns offer a considerable variety of design. He, doubtless, made drawings of certain columns and capitals where he chanced to see them, and his facility of draughtsmanship and his sense of composition enabled him later on to introduce them, either from memory or with the aid of such sketches, into his pictures with telling effect.

Of the architecture in other paintings, that of the Berlin Virgin and Child (p. 167) is alone real, based on a three-aisled cruciform apsidal church, having a crypt beneath the choir—the cathedral of Ghent, according to M. Hulin ; [1] Saint Denis, according to Dr. Voll ; [2] in the writer's opinion it is impossible to say which, if either, suggested the design.

In the St. Petersburg Annunciation (p. 98) and the Dresden triptych (p. 82) the architecture is quasi-real, the details, taken separately, being correctly given ; but the very stilted arches of the chief arcade in the former have been apparently drawn from those of an apse and straightened out, while the square - headed triforium is an adap-

[1] See *Congrès de Bruges*, 1902, *Compte rendu*, p. 21.
[2] *Altniederländische Malerei*, p. 39.

tation of that in the transept of the cathedral of Tournay.[1]

In the Dresden triptych the bases are of a much later date than the capitals of the columns which they support.

The cloisters or porticos in the Rothschild panel (p. 76), the Rolin altar-piece (p. 87), and the Berlin Madonna with Saint Barbara and a Carthusian (p. 169), are not real but scenic pasteboard architecture. The quaint introduction of rabbits at the angles of the base of one of the columns in the Louvre picture giving an appearance of strength, may have been suggested by examples in the church of Saint Ambrose at Milan. Saint Barbara's emblematic tower in the Rothschild panel (p. 76) reproduces Italian-Gothic forms, and the image of Mars is certainly copied from an antique bronze. The throne of Our Lady in the Rolin panel (p. 87) is adorned with mosaic. The pavement in the earlier pictures is composed of tiles, generally blue and white, apparently Valencia tiles ;[2] in the later, it consists of slabs of rich and varied marbles in geometric patterns, quite in Roman style.[3] In one picture—the Saint Petersburg Annunciation—we find a splendid specimen of a storied pavement, reminding one of that at Rheims ; surely this and the mural paintings of scenes in the life of Moses must have been sketched in some French church.[4] The red sandstone or tufa

[1] John van Eyck was at Tournay in October 1427. It is, however, possible that he may have taken this detail from the baptistery at Parma. See DEHIO and BEZOLD, II, pl. 203.

[2] In the two panels of the polyptych occupied by the Choirs of Angels (pp. 42–43), the upper zone of the Madrid panel (p. 176), the Van der Paele altar-piece (p. 120), the Rothschild panel (p. 76), and the Frankfort Madonna (p. 145).

[3] In the lower zone of the Madrid panel (p. 176), the Rolin altarpiece (p. 88), the Berlin Madonna with Saint Barbara and a Carthusian (p. 170), and the centre panel of the Ypres triptych (p. 136).

[4] The windows of both ecclesiastical and domestic interiors are generally filled with roundels ; in the Ince Hall panel (p. 109), the Saint Petersburg Annunciation (p. 100), and the Berlin panels (pp. 167 and 169), lôzenge glazing occurs.

buildings of the town in the background of the Saint Petersburg and Berlin Calvary pictures (p. 153) and of the Three Marys (p. 69) was no doubt intended to convey the idea of the East ; the Temple of Jerusalem in the last is the most correct early representation of that building known.

One peculiarity remains to be noted. In the Virgin's room (p. 51) on the exterior of the polyptych, and in the Madrid panel (p. 175), the bases and capitals of the columns are identical, a peculiarity which the writers have met with in some churches in the Mosan region.

(II.) *Perspective.*—In all the Eyckian paintings the figures in the foreground are too tall relatively to the architecture, and often occupy too great a space ; as, for instance, Our Lady in the centre of the Dresden triptych (p. 82).[1]

In the half-distance and the background the figures are relatively more correct ; as, for instance, the two men in the garden of the Rolin panel (p. 88), and the workmen at the foot of the tower in the Antwerp picture of Saint Barbara (p. 130). It seems pretty evident that neither of the Van Eycks had a full, that is to say a mathematical, knowledge of the laws of perspective, and, consequently, there is no room for astonishment if the perspective in a later painting is less perfect—supposing such to be the case—than in earlier works. It seems quite likely that the Van Eycks did not attach any great importance to the point, any more than to the representation of trees and plants in exact relative height.

The doubts expressed as to the authorship of the Berlin panel of Our Lady and Child with Saint Barbara and the Carthusian (p. 169) are in part founded on the linear perspective, and on the windows being glazed with lozenges instead of

---

[1] For Kern's remarks on perspective and for plans, see Weale, 1908, pp. 188–189.

with roundels. (Lozenges, of course, appear in authentic pictures by the Van Eycks.) The occurrence of a statue outside the porch in that picture (which at Berlin is officially catalogued as the work of Peter Christus) as in the " Portrait of a Man," by Peter Christus, bequeathed to the National Gallery (No. 2593) in 1910 by Mr. George Salting, together with the metallic look of the hair, are given as reasons for assigning to him the panel formerly in the collection of the Marquis of Exeter.

(III.) *Lighting.*—The lighting of the Virgin's room in one of the exterior panels (p. 51) of the Ghent polyptych ; of the Ince Hall " Madonna " (p. 109), the " Arnolfini " picture in the National Gallery (p. 114), the Bruges altar-piece (p. 120), the St. Petersburg " Annunciation " (p. 98), the " Madonna in a Church " at Berlin (p. 167), the " Lucca Madonna " at Frankfort (p. 145), and the centre and dexter panels of the Dresden triptych (p. 82) is excellent. However, in the sinister shutter of the last, the light falls on Saint Katherine's face, although she is standing with her back to the window. Again, in the picture of the " Three Marys " (p. 69) the background is lighted from the right, the foreground from the left. We should not conclude with Mr. Marks that these were "painted by the two brothers working in collaboration," but from sketches. Nor can we accept the theory of M. Durand-Gréville, that these deviations are due to the fact that Hubert " était un peu distrait ; qu'il a laissé échapper, dans les *Trois Marie*, une forte inadvertance." Or can this be by moonlight or by sunlight reflected from a white cloud ? Is it not most probably due to the picture having been painted from sketches made by various hands at different times ?

(IV.) *Composition.*—As regards the Ghent polyptych, the only painting on which it is known for certain that both brothers worked, is there in the composition of the different portions anything to

warrant the inference of dual design ? The composition of the entire work is strictly symmetrical ;
this, as far as concerns the exterior, the upper zone,
and the lower central panel, is at first glance seen
to be the case. Laban, however, claims that this
is not so on the inner face of the shutter panels
of the lower zone. He maintains that in these,
although the arrangement is in fact symmetrical,
such symmetry is ingeniously concealed. He points
out that the three younger men in the Knights of
Christ (p. 47) ride in front, and their elders follow ;
while in the Holy Hermits (p. 48) the three eldest
hermits march at the head, their juniors bringing
up the rear. Again, one of the young knights
bends his head, while the other two hold theirs up ;
one of the hermits raises his head, while the other
two bend theirs down. This curious system, it
will be found, extends even to the colouring : when
red has been used on the dexter panels, the corresponding details in the sinister shutters are blue,
and *vice versa.*

(V.) *Landscape.*—The landscape in the Ghent
polyptych, as in all the Eyckian paintings, is arti-
ficial.

The Van Eycks had, by entirely suppressing the
uniform gold backgrounds employed by fourteenth-
century painters, introduced a new feature, a real
ground on which their figures stand, and by means
of which they are, so to say, brought together ;
but although the landscape in no one of their
pictures is reproduced from nature as a whole, they
are so cleverly composed that they convey the impression of representing the view of some particular
place, and this has led many to try and identify the
localities. The town in the background of the Louvre
altar-piece (p. 89) has been declared to be Bruges,
Lyons, Maastricht, and Liége ; the river in this and
in the Rothschild (p. 76) and Berlin Carthusian
(p. 169) panels to be the Rhine, while others say it is

P

the Maas, and Rosen and Voll go so far as to assert that the view is that seen from the citadel of Liége.

These contradictory assertions are all alike easily disproved. In the Rothschild panel the cathedral to the left of the river is unmistakably Old Saint Paul's seen from the south; in the Rolin altarpiece a noble cathedral of a decidedly French type occupies a similar position, and the tower of Saint Martin's at Utrecht, which is also seen in the background of the central panel of the *Adoration of the Lamb* (p. 44), stands near the bridge.[1]

The background of the Turin Saint Francis is said by Hymans to be a view near Assisi; another critic claims it to represent Montserrrat.

(VI.) *Snow-capped Mountains.*—Snow-capped mountains are represented in the distance in eight Eyckian paintings, namely, in the panel of the *Knights of Christ* in the polyptych (p. 46); in the *Three Marys* (p. 70), in the Rothschild panel (p. 78), in the Rolin *Madonna* (p. 89), in the Heytesbury-Johnson *St. Francis* (p. 94), in the left shutter of the Dresden triptych (p. 85), in the *Christ on the Cross* at Berlin (p. 159), and in the St. Petersburg *Calvary* (153).

Gilbert has high praise for these views, and says that Van Eyck evidently appreciated the beauty of mountain-form.[2] Rosen (1903, p. 104) declares the mountains in the Rolin altar-piece to be better painted than those in the polyptych, and says that those in the Berlin Calvary represent the Bernese Alps, the Stockhorn, Niesen, and, high above them, the Blümli Alp. The present writers cannot identify any one, and are convinced that all the Eyckian landscapes are made up from sketches and reminiscences of foreign travel. Fancied identifications are, however, if difficult to disprove, impossible to prove.

---

[1] Reproduced in Weale, 1908, p. 186.
[2] *Landscape in Art*, 1885, pp. 53, 146, 150, 153, and 164

(VII.) *Flocks of Wild Geese or Cranes in the air.*—
In most of the paintings with landscape backgrounds a flock of wild geese or cranes is seen high
up in the air flying in V-like array. We do not
remember the occurrence of this feature in the
paintings of any earlier or contemporary master,
and are inclined to agree with Mr. Marks that it
was used by the Van Eycks as a sort of signature.
Eyck, oak (*Aldeneyck,* old oak), was most probably
by the French pronounced and written *Eck,* angle.[1]
This may have suggested the adoption of the
symbol. Flocks of wild geese or cranes are seen in
the panel of the Holy Hermits (p. 48) of the polyptych ; in the Three Marys (p. 70) ; in the Saint
Barbara at Antwerp (p. 130), in the Rothschild
panel (p. 78), in the Heytesbury-Johnson Saint
Francis (p. 94), and in the Rolin altar-piece (p. 89).
The geese in the last picture are seen through the
arcade on the left, but are not discernible in an
ordinary photograph.

(VIII.) *Exotic Plants and Flora.*—These exotic
plants include the olive, citron, cypress, stone-pine,
date-palm, and palmetto—all southern Mediterranean plants, which, in the polyptych at least, are
generally recognised to be splendidly painted.
Rosen, however, declares the date-palm and the
stone-pine to be incorrectly drawn. Exotic plants
are represented more or less faithfully in the centre
and left-shutter panels of the polyptych (p. 48), in the
Copenhagen panel (p. 67), in the "Saint Francis"
belonging to Mr. Johnson (p. 94), in the Berlin
"Christ on the Cross" (p. 157), and in the "Three
Marys" (p. 70), but are not found in either the
Saint Barbara at Antwerp (p. 129), or in the Helleputte triptych (p. 135).

In the Turin "Saint Francis" (p. 165) the palmettos are poorly painted ; Rosen (1903, pp. 105–109)

---

[1] *See* Documents 13, 14, 15, 16. Maaseyck is situated on a bend of
the river, and the form Mazeck occurs in 36 and in other documents.

says, from dried plants brought to Bruges by a
sailor ! but they were most probably merely copied,
as was the V-shaped flight of geese, or they may
have been painted from drawings.

In the picture in the collection of Sir Frederick
Cook at Richmond (p. 70) not only are palmettos
growing, but the mullen, teasel, white nettle, and
flag-lily also are found among the flowering plants.

Drawings of plants are found in pre-Eyckian
times.

(IX.) *Costume.*—The costume worn by donors
of paintings is an excellent guide to the discovery
of their personality and the dating of their portraits.
Had Kaemmerer attended to this, he would not have
aspersed the character of B. Nicholas Albergati;
neither would he nor Hymans have described De
Leeuw (p. 128) or the Leipzig donor (p. 183) as canons.
Attention should be paid to the signification of
accessories, such as a ring showing the holder to be
a goldsmith, a white wand denoting the bearer to
have held the office of chamberlain. As an example
of the importance of such details as guides to the
identification of persons portrayed, it may be well
to draw attention to the case of the individual first
misnamed "*A Duke of Burgundy*"; then, and still
incorrectly, "*The Man with the Pinks,*" which desig-
nation affords no clue. For these Mr. Weale four
years ago substituted the fitter title of " An Esquire
of the Order of Saint Anthony "; the pinks held in
his hand may be said generally to indicate that he
was a bachelor, a rose usually indicating a man
already married.

(X.) *Arms and Armour.*—The details of armour
worn by knights and soldiers afford also important
evidence as to the date of a painting. Armour is
represented in five of the pictures described in the
present work : the polyptych (p. 47); the Saint-
Petersburg "Last Judgment" (p. 154); the Dresden
triptych (p. 84); the Bruges altar-piece (p. 121); and

the " Three Marys at the Sepulchre " (p. 70). The helmets and upper part of the armour worn by Saint Michael and Saint George, apparently copied from the same suit, are pseudo-classic, and much resemble the suit made for Charles V by Bartholomew Campi, in 1546.[1] The leg-armour of the archangel in the Saint-Petersburg picture is decidedly earlier than that of the other figures. We have commented at some length (p. 74) on the difficulties presented to certain critics by some of the armour in the *Three Marys*.

(XI.) *Portraiture.*—Portrait-painting, so far as we know, was not introduced until the second half of the fourteenth century, although portraiture is found in sculpture and monumental brasses at an earlier period. The earliest known are profile portraits ; towards the end of the century some portraits show the body in three-quarters, with the head in profile, as in those of Philip II, Duke of Burgundy, 1383–1404, and John, Duke of Berry, 1340–1416, authentic copies of which have been preserved,[2] and that of John the Fearless, Duke of Burgundy, 1404–1419, in the Louvre (No. 1002). Another portrait of the last-named, in the Antwerp Museum (No. 540) shows the body and head turned in the same direction ; the painter of that portrait was evidently working tentatively, as the tip of the nose cuts across the contour of the further half of the face.[3] It will be recalled that the *Portrait of John II of France*, now assigned in the Department of Drawings in the National Library of Paris to

---

[1] Exhibited at the Golden Fleece Exhibition at Bruges, 1907. See *The Connoisseur*, XIX, 28–33.

[2] In A. Thevet's *Les vrais pourtraits et vies des hommes illustres*, p. 267, Paris, 1584, there is a woodcut of Philip's portrait, which was then in the Charterhouse of Dijon. A copy of that of John, Duke of Berry, is in the Gaignières collection in the Print-room of the National Library at Paris.

[3] Westendorp (1906, p. 72) thinks this may be the portrait painted by John Malouel in 1415, and sent as a present to John I, King of Portugal.

Girard d'Orléans, is held to have been painted as early as 1359, during the King's captivity in England.[1]

The Van Eycks went a step farther than their predecessors, and succeeded in representing persons seen in three-quarters, the nose foreshortened, with plastic truthfulness. Frequently the addition of hands added to the characterisation of their portraits. Dvořák, as also Westendorp, gives John the credit of having been the first who succeeded in producing satisfactory portraits. But the earliest portrait proved to have been painted by John is that of the *Blessed Nicholas Albergati*, cardinal of Saint-Cross (1431), whilst we have those of *Jodoc Vyt and his Wife* on the shutters of the Ghent polyptych, and presumably that of *Michael Giustiniani* in the Dresden triptych, and a copy of a portrait of *Michael of France*, first wife of Philip III, Duke of Burgundy (died July 8, 1422), which were most probably painted by Hubert.

(XII.) *Alleged Portraits of the Van Eycks.*—In the foreground of the dexter shutter-panel of the Adoration of the Lamb, one of the Just Judges is represented riding on a white horse, and not far from him a much younger man clad in black, with a large headkerchief, and wearing a red coral rosary round his neck, has his head turned towards him, but is not looking in his direction. These two, according to Luke De Heere,[2] are portraits of Hubert and John. Owing to his poem having been affixed to the wall of the Vyts' chapel, this statement was read by those who went to see the picture, was widely circulated, and obtained ready credence, as at that time it was a common practice for painters to introduce their own portraits into the works they executed. De Heere's statement did not repose on any old tradition, or the sacristan who showed

[1] This picture was included in the Exhibition of French Primitives held in Paris in 1904 (No. 1.)

[2] Strophe 9 of the Ode he composed in 1559 ; see pp. 56, 240, and 285.

Münzer the picture in 1495 would certainly not have omitted to relate it ; moreover, at that time it was not known that the polyptych was the work of two painters. De Heere's story, repeated by Vaernewyck, Van Mander, and a host of others, has been, until recently, accepted by all writers.[1] The two portraits have been copied by painters and engravers as portraits of the Van Eycks.

One of the earliest copies, on an oak panel (H. o.228 ; B. o.34), formerly in the Orleans Gallery, and later in the possession of Mr. J. Field,[2] of Dornden, Tunbridge Wells, shows the two men as busts juxtaposed, clad much as in the polyptych, save that John has a red under-dress and no rosary. Beneath the elder is the legend, *Hubertus ab eyck obijt* 1426 ; and beneath the younger, *Ioannes ab eyck.* The following mendacious verses are added :—

"Wij hebben aldereerst met olie verw gheschildert
die anghenaemigh' is de werelt door verwiedert
't jaer 1410 was eerst dies const gesien."

Catalogues of the eighteenth and the early part of the nineteenth centuries mention the sale of portraits said to be those of the two brothers. The highest price that the writers have noted as having been paid for a pair is twenty-two guineas, by Sir H. P., at the Earl of Bessborough's sale on February 7, 1801. (See Appendix B.)

Crowe and Cavalcaselle (in 1857, p. 98) were, the writers believe, the first who recognised, as portraits

---

[1] Laban (1898) remarks that the figure assumed to be a portrait of John by himself, is looking down at the elder man, as if saying, "I am following you," while in the corresponding panel of the Holy Pilgrims, Saint Christopher (p. 48) seems to be calling to his older companion to follow him. We may add here that the black funeral palls were in mediæval times charged with a red cross in memory of the Redeemer's death. Our readers must judge for themselves whether the red rosary worn over the black dress was intended to convey a special meaning. The writers are of opinion that it was simply used as an effective contrast of colour.

[2] It was purchased by him at the Samuel Rogers' sale, May 3, 1856 (No. 651), p. 63, where it was catalogued as being by Albert Dürer.

of the brothers, two figures on the right of the Madrid *Fountain of Living Water*—one wearing a red mantle trimmed with grey fur, with an order (?) [1] hanging over his shoulder, as Hubert ; the other, standing behind him on the extreme right, as John. Mr. Marks, however (1903, p. 7), though agreeing as to the former, thinks the young man to the left of the elder is John. The photographic reproductions of the five figures will enable our readers to judge for themselves. Hotho (1858, 11, 169) says that in the Calvary picture at Saint-Petersburg, the two brothers are represented standing at the foot of the cross—an astounding statement, as these two men are evidently mocking the dying Saviour. De Smet (1902, p. 243) suggests that Hubert is represented in the Adoration of the Lamb, on the left behind SS. Stephen and Livin. Durand (1905, pp. 23–25) considers the portrait of a man in the National Gallery (No. 222), dated 1433, to be the portrait of John painted by himself (p. 113).

A picture on panel entitled "The Painter's Head," and assigned to Van Eyck, is in the collection of the Marquess of Exeter at Burghley, near Stamford. It measures 18½ in. × 13 in. The man wears a red dress, open at the neck, and a black biretta. The right hand is raised and holds a paint brush. In the background are buildings and two small figures. It is a bust length portrait. It is included in Blore's *Guide to Burghley House* of 1815, p. 53.

In point of fact, the portraits of B. Nicholas Albergati, of the Man with the red headkerchief, of John De Leeuw, have all been described as portraits of John Van Eyck.

---

[1] Can it be meant for the bough of an oak (*eyck*)? Attached to it is a square-based jewel, rising in pyramid form to a point, as Marks has pointed out in a letter to Weale.

APPENDICES

APPENDIX A

THE (SO-CALLED) CONSECRATION OF SAINT THOMAS OF CANTERBURY

THIS picture, in the collection of the Duke of Devonshire at Chatsworth, having been long held to be an exceedingly early work by John van Eyck, and even to be his earliest dated picture, it is necessary to refer to it at some length in these pages, if only for the purpose of easy reference.

It was shown at the Burlington Fine Arts Club in 1902 (No. 7).

The picture was exhibited at Bruges, 1902 (No. 8), as the work of John van Eyck, and stated, on the basis of the inscription which was then generally accepted to be genuine, to have been painted by him in 1421. It was, however, added that the panel had "unfortunately been entirely repainted towards the end of the fifteenth century." It was catalogued as "The Consecration of Saint Thomas of Canterbury."

When shown at the Guildhall in 1906 (No. 5) as "The Enthronement of Thomas à Becket as Archbishop of Canterbury," by John van Eyck, the "pedigree" which had for so many years passed muster was again accepted. It was described in the catalogue as :—

"In a church of the latest Norman style, Thomas à Becket is seen standing in the foreground under a scarlet canopy, with the Holy Ghost hovering near, and above is a splendid crown, in which the figure of the risen Christ is introduced ; above the crown is a circle with the Virgin and Child. Three bishops are engaged in placing upon the head of the saint the archiepiscopal mitre, while a priest, kneeling, holds an open book before him. On the right are the clergy, and on the left the laity, with King Henry II at their head. . . . On the border is the inscription . . . which is important, not only as authenticating the painting, but because 1421 is still the earliest known date on a picture by Van Eyck."

1901. STRONG, S. Arthur.   Masterpieces in the Duke of Devonshire's Collection of Pictures, p. 15. "The importance of the picture lies in the signature. . . . Unfortunately, in its present state it shows no sign of the hand of Van Eyck."

1906. In criticising the exhibition, Sir Claude PHILLIPS wrote in the *Daily Telegraph*, May 3 : "Still more strongly do we repudiate the famous—we might say the notorious—'Enthronement of Thomas à Becket as Archbishop of Canterbury,' which, notwithstanding all the ink that has been spilt in connection with it by critics, British and foreign—especially during and since the Bruges Exhibition—is again put forward as a Jan van Eyck of the year 1421. . . . We must record our opinion that the picture in its origin—that is, before it was disfigured by additions and afterwards by repaints—was a work painted little, if any, before 1500, and by some artist affiliated to the school of Gerard David."

1906. The critic of *The Times*, May 4, pointed out that "the catalogue professes to trace its pedigree back to the time of Henry V, but we believe that the evidence of its history before the days of the famous collector, the Earl of Arundel, is very doubtful. There may possibly be Van Eyck's work at the bottom of it, but it has been so mercilessly overpainted, perhaps in Lord Arundel's time, that in its present state it is of little interest. A scientific restorer might well be allowed to try his hand upon a portion of it."

1907. A. MARKS, on "A Picture at Chatsworth ascribed to John van Eyck," in the *Burlington Magazine*, x, 383–384, writes : "Walpole, who, I believe, first published

the story, says : 'The tradition is that it was a present to Henry V from his uncle, the Duke of Bedford,
Regent of France ; but tradition is no proof.' In our
days the tradition, doubtfully quoted, is replaced by
a positive assertion. Assertion and tradition are
destitute of foundation. The Duke of Bedford died
in 1435. No connoisseur would to-day be found to
contend that the picture, as we now see it, was painted
before 1435. It is generally ascribed to John Gossart,
whose birth-year is supposed to be 1470. This dis-
poses of the tradition and of the date, 1421, as relating
to the existing picture. . . . It is contended that
underneath the visible picture is one actually painted
or drawn by John van Eyck, to which the description,
with the date 1421, belongs. There is, however,
nothing in the picture, as we see it, at all suggestive,
either in composition or treatment, of John van Eyck.
Clearly, then, we are in presence of a forgery of one
kind or another. Either the inscription is forged, or
a genuine inscription belonging to an obliterated work
has been allowed to remain, to give false testimony as
to the over-painting. . . . The probability is, therefore,
that the forgery is of the more direct kind : that a false
inscription has been attached to the work of a later
master. The date is remarkable, not to say open to
grave suspicion. It is separated by eleven years from
the earliest uncontested date on John's signed pictures.
. . . There is a close agreement between that of the
Chatsworth picture and that on a portrait in the National
Gallery (No. 222), 'A Man's Portrait. In a cloak
and fur collar, with a red chaperon twisted round the
head like a turban.' . . . The two inscriptions are,
then, identical (in the circumstances), except as to
date. And here we shall find that there has been a
mere transposition of figures. . . . The fraud has been
completed with great economy of effort ; no more has
been done than to shuffle the figures, and to substitute
'o' for '3.' The time at which the fraud was committed
is not beyond the limit of reasonable conjecture. Both

pictures were at one time in the possession of the Earl
of Arundel, the greatest collector of his day, who
employed an agent to collect for him in the Low Countries. But the Earl of Arundel had also in his collection a head, said to be of Becket, ascribed to John
van Eyck. This work is now known only by Hollar's
engraving. [See p. 184] The circumstances all point
in the direction of a fraud perpetrated with the object
of foisting a picture on the great collector."

1907. WEALE, in the *Burlington Magazine*, XI, 45, says :
"Mr. Marks has, I think, cleared up the mystery. . . .
Who can have painted the two pictures which were
either in Lord Arundel's possession or in that of the
person from whom he acquired them ? I can only
think of one person by whom they may possibly have
been executed—Dirk Barentz, *alias* Theodore Bernardi,
of Amsterdam, who came to England in 1519, and
seems to have remained here. He worked for churches
in Sussex and Hampshire. There is a series of panel
pictures by him at Amberley Castle, and other works
at Boxgrove Priory Church, and in the palace and
cathedral at Chichester, these last the most ambitious."

1908. WEALE, 210.

1912. WEALE AND BROCKWELL. The view as to the
authorship of the paintings at Amberley Castle, Boxgrove, and Chichester, as being similar to that of
the Chatsworth picture, is largely conjectural. The
paintings in the Queen's Room at Amberley Castle
are now in a very bad state of repair. They have
been variously held to represent a "Series of Female
Portraits," "Sybils," "Impersonations of certain Foreign
Towns," and "Nine Worthies of the World."
    The ceiling of the dining-room of the Bishop's Palace
at Chichester is painted with coats of arms and initials
of distinguished families ; they appear to be in a good
state of preservation.
    The vaulting of Boxgrove Priory Church is covered
with paintings representing foliage and fruit in traceries

of a peculiar blue-green colour ; similar tracery painting is found on the vaulting of the Lady Chapel in Chichester Cathedral.

See *Sussex Archæological Society*, 1856, VIII, 318–319, and 1865, XVII, 200–215 ; and Weale on " Dirk Barendsz " (Theodoricus Bernardi ") in *Allgemeines Lexikon der Bildenden Künstler*, 1908, II, 492.

Note.—In the collection at Chatsworth there is another picture by the same hand. It represents an " Episode in the Life of a Benedictine Saint " ; it was exhibited at Bruges in 1902 (No. 147), and at the Guildhall in 1906 (No. 24), as " Departure of a Saint," by G. David.

APPENDIX B

List of Pictures (and some Drawings) sold at Public Auction under the name of the Van Eycks

Date.	No.	Attributed.	Subject.	Owner.	Where Sold.	Price.	Measurement.	Purchaser.	Remarks.
1662, April 17	153	Jan v. Eyck	Een L. Vrouw met een Cathuyser geschildert	John Chrysostom De Backer, choordeecken of Eindhoven	Hague	...	...	...	Reprinted by Bredius in Archief voor Nederlandsche Kunstgeschiedenis, Rotterdam, 1883. Mireur III, 121
1708, Mar. 6		John	Une Femme Couchée	...	Amsterdam	82 francs	...	...	Mireur III, 121
1740, Sept. 13	82	Hubert	Een Heilige Familie zeer uitvoerig, zynde geweest de eerste Schilder in olyverwe	Commis Guerin	Hague	15g. 15s.	...	...	Weale [1]
1761, Oct. 26	45	Hubert	De Aanbidding der drie Wysen	Gaspar d'Heyne, Heere van Leeuwerghem	Ghent (?)	£11 3 6	...	...	Weale Duplessis
1761[2], Nov. 14		Hubert	Enfant Endormi sur une tête de mort.	Collin de Vermont	...	120 francs	...	...	Mireur III, 122[2]
1761, Nov. 14		Hubert	Une tête de Vieillard	Collin de Vermont	...	121 francs	...	...	Mireur III, 122
1766, May 14	11	...	The Nativity	L. F. Rotsaert d'Hertaing	Bruges	56l. 10s.	1 ft. × 1 ft. 7 in. panel	...	Weale
1766, May 14	27	...	Death of the Blessed Virgin	L. F. Rotsaert d'Hertaing	...	4l. 10s.	3 ft. × 2 ft. 3 in.	...	Weale

Date		Attribution	Title	Owner	Place	Price	Dimensions	Buyer	Source
1770, Mar. 24	26	John	Holy Family in a Landscape	Count Bruhl, Prime Minister, of late King of Poland	...	£4 4 0	...	...	Weale
1770, May 7	67	...	Portrait of Bonne d'Artois, Duchess of Burgundy	Simon Pierre van Overloope	Bruges	32 francs, 65 cents.	Panel 8 in. × 6 in. = 0.21 × 0.16	...	Weale (Now at Berlin)
1770, May 4	68	...	Les Trois Marie	Jacques Winckelman, Seigneur de ᵗ Metersche	...	...	...	...	Weale (Now at Richmond)
1772, Mar. 7	16	John	Woman's Head	...	Christie's	£2 17 6	...	Dr. Bray	Weale
1773, April 7	25	Hubert	Holy Family: The St. Joseph represents John van Eyck	...	...	£11 0 6	1 ft. 5⅝ in. × 1 ft. 2 in.	Duntze	Weale
1773, April 7	36	Van Eyck	Blessed Virgin presenting a flower to the Child	...	...	£4 14 6	13 in. by 10 in.	Stephens	Weale
1774, April 25	103	J. van Eyck	Des Joueurs de cartes, hommes et femmes autour d'une table sur laquelle un nombre de pièces d'or Tableau d'une grande verité	M. C. D. (? M. Caulet-d'Hauteville)	Paris	...	1 pᵈ × 1 pᵈ 5 pouces	...	Weale Duplessis
1776, Mar. 29	53	...	Adoration of the Magi	Baron J. Got. de Grote de Hannover	Christie's	£6 6 0	...	...	Weale

[1] See Weale: "Notes on Sales of Paintings attributed to the Van Eycks" MS. in National Art Library, Victoria and Albert Museum.

[2] The date, 1761, given by Mireur must be wrong, as according to Duplessis, *Ventes aux xvii. et xviii. Siècles*, 1874, p. 20, § 414, the Sale of the Cabinet de M. Hyacinthe Collin de Vermont took place on November 14, 1761. Duplessis goes back as far as 1611.

APPENDIX B

Date.	No.	Attributed.	Subject.	Owner.	Where Sold.	Price.	Measurement.	Purchaser.	Remarks.
1778, Feb. 21	10	Van Eyck	Riposo	John Blackwood	Christie's	£16 5 6	7¼ in. × 6¼ in.	Birch	Weale
1781, Mar. 23	70	Van Eyck	Baptism of Christ	Imported	Christie's	£9 19 6	...	Hampden	Weale
1781, June 1	91	Van Eyck	Curious and undoubted picture of this Master	...	Christie's	£1 1 0	...	Lord Bagot	Weale
1782, April 20	37	Van Eyck	Blessed Virgin and Child, very highly finished	...	Christie's	£7 17 6	...	Van der Gucht	...
1784, Mar. 12	98	John v. Eyck	Emblematical Subject	...	Christie's	£3 3 0	...	Simmonds	Weale
1787, May 8	44	Jan van Eyck	The Wise Men's Offering . . . For its antiquity is perfect and well preserved	Imported by Mr. Bertels from Brussels	Christie's	...	...	...	...
1787, Nov. 12	48	John v. Eyck	Bacchanales dans un paysage, qui paroissent faire allusion à un Espagnol que l'on voit assis et vers lequel les acteurs de tous les groupes se dirigent	Le Comte de ...	Le Brun	...	2 p^d 1 po × 2 p^d 8 po Toile	...	Weale
1793, Feb. 28	71	Van Eyck	Holy Family with Angels; a very curious and antique performance	...	Sale at Cumberland House	£7 17 6	...	Nixon	Weale

Date	Artist	No.	Subject	Former owner	Sale	Price	Dimensions	Buyer	Reference
1793, May 23	J. van Eyck	59	Christ among Doctors in Temple	...	Amsterdam	...	...	Hodges (? for Woodburn)	Weale
1793, May 23	J. van Eyck	60	Adoration of Magi	...	Amsterdam	35 gulden	32 d. × 28 d.		Weale
1796, April 7	Van Eyck	52	Flight into Egypt; highly finished	Mr. Noble	Christie's	£11 0 6	...	Bought in	Now N. G. 1082 and 1084. Weale
1796, April 7	Van Eyck	53	Visitation, companion to 52	Mr. Noble	Christie's	£4 14 6	...	Bought in	Weale
1796, May 7	Van Eyck	34	Vision of a Pope	Lord Besborough	Christie's	£12 1 6	...	Bought in	Weale
1797, Dec. 9	Van Eyck	71	Holy Family, a very curious Gothic picture, highly finished	...	Christie's	£10 0 0	...	Woodin	Weale
1798, May 25 or 26	Van Eyck		Fathers of Church	Duke of Argyle	Phillips	£31 5 0 (Weale) £3 0 0 (Redford)	Panel 39 × 36 in.	...	Weale Redford, I. 67
1799, May 10	Van Eyck	92	Adoration of Magi	Mr. Parr	Christie's	£6 16 6	...	Bought in	Weale
1799, May 31	Van Eyck	104	St John the Baptist	Lord Hampden	Christie's	£12 1 6	...	Wood	Weale
1799, Dec. 2	Van Eyck	20	Landscape with a Riposo		39 Conduit St.	£2 13 0	...	Bought in	Weale
1800, Mar 1	Van Eyck	45	Holy Family	Mr. Jeffrey	Christie's	£5 5 0	2½ in. × 1½ in.	Bought in	Weale
1800, Mar. 5	Van Eyck	17	Een fraai Buurtje	Corneille Ploos van Amstel	Amsterdam	...	...	...	Duplessis Weale
1800, Mar. 5	John	54	St. Barbara, 1437. Engraved on copper by C. van Noorden, and published, with a description, by C. Ploos van Amstel, 1769	Corneille Ploos van Amstel	Amsterdam	35g. 10st.	13 in. × 8 in.	Oyen	Now in Museum at Antwerp Duplessis
1800	John	47	Een staen Vrouwenbeeld met couleuren	...	...	...	...	...	Weale

APPENDIX B

Date.	No.	Attributed.	Subject.	Owner.	Where Sold.	Price.	Measurement.	Purchaser.	Remarks.
1800	48	Hubert	Een staend mans en vrouwen beeld met couleuren gewasschen	...	...	10 gulden	...	...	Weale
1800	BBB	John	Een Vrouwen Pourtrait met de pen en roet	...	...	...	...	...	Weale
1800		John	Portraits of Hubert and John	...	Burrell & Foster	10½ guineas	...	...	Weale
1800		John	Portraits of the Brothers van Eyck	Duc d'Orléans	London	275 francs	...	...	Mireur III. 121 (apparently same as preceding one)
1801, Feb. 7	12	Van Eyck	Portraits of Hubert and John van Eyck	Earl of Bessborough	Christie's	£23 2 0	...	Sir H. P.	Weale, and see p. 285.
1801, Feb. 7	73	Van Eyck	Entombment of a Cardinal. The figures are all undoubtedly genuine portraits from life; one of them is visibly a king of France. An invaluable curiosity, it being extremely rare to find an Original Picture of this master, the FIRST INVENTOR OF OIL PAINTING, in such high preservation	Earl of Bessborough	Christie's	£89 5 0	...	Foxhall	Weale. (Now in National Gallery, No. 783). See also Oct. 8, 1822

Date	No.	Artist	Subject	Owner	Place	Price	Dimensions	Bought in / Huddleston	Authority
1801, April 4	55	John Van Eyck	Nativity	Mr. Abbott	Christie's	£4 14 6	...	...	Weale
1801, May 8	35	Van Eyck	Adoration of Magi	Mr. Gwennap	Christie's	£4 0 0	...	...	Weale
1802, May 16	41	John	Wise Men's Offering; a rare, curious, and covetable specimen of the art	...	Coxe	...	...	...	...
1803, Feb. 12	37	John	Blessed Virgin and Child with Saints, on a gold ground	Mr. Grant	Christie's	£5 0 0	...	Champemon	Weale
1803, Mar. 4	70	John	St. Hubert, in a small highly finished landscape	Mr. Abbott	Christie's	£2 15 0	..	Bought in	Weale
1803, May 21	37	John	The Pharisee and the Publican	Count de Hagen of Dresden	Christie's	£5 5 0	...	...	Weale
1804, Feb. 18	28	Van Eyck	Portraits of Hubert and John van Eyck	...	Christie's	£5 15 6	...	...	Weale
1805, June 21	24	John	Triptych: The History of Christ	...	Christie's	£21 offered by Newton	...	Bought in	Weale
1806, Feb. 8	128	John	Triptych: The History of Christ	...	Christie's	£19 8 6	...	...	Weale. (Same as preceding one)
1806, Mar. 19	43	John	Wise Men's Offering. A curious specimen of this early time	Marquis of Lansdowne	Coxe, at Lansdowne House, Berkeley Sq.	£14 14 0	...	...	Weale (see May 15, 1813)
1807, Feb. 20	11	Van Eyck	Portraits of Hubert and John van Eyck	Mr. Morland	...	£6 0 0	...	Bought in	Weale
1807, Dec. 1	52	Van Eyck	La Chaste Susanne aux Bains	François de Marenzi	Bruges	31 francs	...	...	Weale
1808, June 6	36	Hubert and John	In eenen Gottischen tempel vertoont zich een op het Oude en Nie uwe Verbond zinspelend tafereel, rijk van ordinantie, ongemeen uitvoerig en fraai geschilderd	Gerrit van der Pot, heer van Groeneveld	Rotterdam	210 gulden	51¾ in. × 40 in.	...	Weale (Now in Amsterdam Museum, No. 485)

Date.	No.	Attributed.	Subject.	Owner.	Where Sold.	Price.	Measurement.	Purchaser.	Remarks.
1808, July 4	87	John	Destruction of Sodom and Gomorrah	...	Christie's	£7 0 0	...	...	Weale
1808, Dec. 31	23	John	Christ bound	Mr. Bartie	Christie's	£1 12 0	...	...	Weale
1809, May 30	80	John	Three Crosses ; the Blessed Virgin and St. John. Highly finished	Mr. Hill	Christie's	£17 5 0	...	Edmunds	Weale
1810, May 26	11	Van Eyck	Original portraits of Hubert and John van Eyck	Marquis of Lansdowne	Christie's	£7 17 6	...	Bought in	Weale
1811, Mar. 16	26	Van Eyck	Blessed Virgin and Child attended by Angels. An elaborate picture	...	Christie's	£15 4 6	...	Lord Gray	Weale
1811, Nov. 25	7	John	Portrait de Maximilien d'Autriche, debout, vu à mi-corps, les mains gantées, tenant un rouleau de papier. D'un fini rare	M. D. P., conseiller d'Etat du Grand Duché de Berg	Paris	...	0.311×0.216 panel	...	Weale Soullié
1811, Nov. 25	6	John	La Sainte Vierge tenant l'Enfant Jesus. Elle est assise sur un trône, entouré par S. Katherine. S. George, et le donateur. Ce petit chef-d'œuvre d'un fini parfait est aussi remarquable pour l'admirable richesse du coloris	M. D. P., conseiller d'Etat du Grand Duché de Berg	Paris	...	0.25×0.169	...	Weale Soullié

246

Date	No.	Painter	Subject	Vendor	Sold at	Price		Buyer	Authority
1813, Feb. 29	39	Jan van Eyck	Adoration of the Magi, with compartment on each side containing a Norman Warrior in armour, and St. James of Compostella with the Habiliments of his Pilgrimage. Painted with all the care and finish of enamel	...	Coxe	...	...	...	...
1813, Feb. 26	55	John v. Eyck	Portrait	Mr. Farr	Christie's	£0 15 0	...	Linnell	Weale
1813, May 15	57	Van Eyck	Adoration of Magi. An undoubted specimen; from the Lansdowne Collection	Mr. De Jonghe	Christie's	£15 4 6	...	...	Weale (see Mar. 19, 1806)
1813, June 26	25	Van Eyck	Moses before the Burning Bush. Highly finished	From abroad	Christie's	£7 0 0	...	Woodburn	Weale
1814, June 2	27	Van Eyck	Martyrdom of St. Katherine	Delahante	Phillips	£87 3 0	:	...	By or after Dirk Bouts
		Van Eyck	St. Louis bestowing Alms	...	...			Atkinson	Weale
1814, July 9	4	John	Divinity and Medicine; interior with figures, well coloured and highly finished; a curious specimen, bought in Spain	Rose Campbell of Cadiz	Christie's	£4 6 0	...	Pinney	Weale
1817, April 25	37	Van Eyck	The taking of Our Saviour in the Garden; tooled and illumined with gold	From St. Petersburg	Christie's	£12 1 6	...	Bought in	Weale

APPENDIX B

Date.	No.	Attributed.	Subject.	Owner.	Where Sold.	Price.	Measurement.	Purchaser.	Remarks.
1817, May 12	20	Hubert	Portrait of a Female; in a rich landscape, with buildings; highly finished	Wm. Beckford, Fonthill. (Mr. Pittar's property)	...	£16 5 6	...	Bryan	Weale
1818, May 26	142	Van Eyck	Christ Betrayed; partly illumined with gold	Mr. Danis (? Davis)	Christie's	£10 0 0	...	Gilbert	Weale
1821, May 12	7	John	Portrait of a Lady; small	Mr. Woodburn	Christie's	£2 2 0	...	Taylor	Weale
1821, Dec. 7	120	Van Eyck	Crucifixion	Mr. Tremenheere	Christie's	£5 5 0	...	Bought in	Weale
1822, Feb. 8	48	Van Eyck	Crucifixion	Mr. Tremenheere	Christie's	£4 16 0	...	Bought in	Weale
1822, Mar. 15	15	Van Eyck	Descent from the Cross	Mr. Bullock	Christie's	£5 5 0	...	Bought in	Weale
1822, June 15	45	Van Eyck	Crucifixion	...	Christie's	£2 2 0	...	Adams	Weale
1822, Oct. 8	80	Van Eyck	The Entombment of a Cardinal, with many portraits; an elaborate and very curious specimen. From the collection of the late Earl of Bessborough, at Roehampton	W. Beckford, Fonthill	By Christie at Fonthill	£47 0 0	...	Bentley	Weale. (See Feb. 7, 1801) (Now National Gallery, 783)
1823, May 15	46	Van Eyck	Crucifixion, with many Saints, and the Passion of Our Saviour represented in 4 small compartments, and underneath. Very curious and highly finished	Mr. Goodwin	Christie's	£7 10 0	...	Bartie	Weale

Date	No.	Artist	Description	Seller	Place of sale	Price		Buyer	Reference
1823, June 23	14	Van Eyck	Crucifixion; highly finished	David Garrick, Esq.	Christie's	£10 10 0	...	Ruttley	Weale
1823, Oct.	412	Van Eyck	The Virgin in rich crimson drapery holding the infant Jesus on her lap—an Angel presenting an Apple, and a Saint kneeling, with uplifted hands at prayer. A landscape and fortified town in the distance—a curious and rare production of this master, in fine preservation	Fonthill: 27th day of sale	Phillips at Fonthill	£75 12 0	...	Thane	Weale Redford
1824, Jan. 20	47	Van Eyck	St. Veronica exhibiting the Sudarium	Edward Eyre, Esq., 5 Lansdowne Crescent, Bath	? at Bath	£2 2 0	...	Dr. Gillum	Weale
1824, May 29	4	John	Our Saviour; small, delicately finished	R. Reinagle	Christie's	£4 18 0	...	Bought in	Weale
1825, Apr. 16	31	Memlinc	Adoration of the Magi	M. Urbino Pizzetta	Christie's	£21 10 6	...	Sevestre	Weale Sold as Margharita van Eyck on June 16, 1866, No. 287. Exhibited at Bruges 1902, No. 327

APPENDIX B

Date.	No.	Attributed.	Subject.	Owner.	Where Sold.	Price.	Measurement.	Purchaser.	Remarks.
1825, May 7	38	...	Blessed Virgin and Child, and near them a cross with roses and a spring of water. A highly finished early specimen, partly on a gold ground	Simon M'Gillivray, Esq.	Christie's	£4 15 0	...	Adams	Weale
1825, June 14	84	John	The Blessed Virgin and Child	...	...	£5 5 0	...	Pinney	Weale
1826, May 5	29	John	Purification in the Temple: a group of many highly finished figures; parts of the picture are illumined with gold	Mr. Pinney	Christie's	£30 9 0	...	Bought in	Weale
1826, May 29	148	Van Eyck	The Blessed Virgin seated with the Infant at the foot of an apple tree, in which are cherubs employed in gathering fruit; the middle distance presents the story of Herod's cruelty. A highly interesting and elaborate specimen	Mr. Wright	...	£11 0 6	...	Noseda	Weale

Date	No.	Painter	Description	From	Where sold	Price		Bought in	Authority
1826, Aug. 8	90	Dans le genre de Memling	Le Resurrection ; sur le premier plan la Sepulture entourée des soldats profondement endormis ; plus loin les vierges ; la lointain orné de beaux bâtiments	M. Bernard Bauwens	Bruges	...	...	...	Weale (Now at Richmond)
1826, Nov. 20	9	Van Eyck	Flagellation ; on a gold ground	...	...	£2 12 6	...	Bought in	Weale
1828, Feb. 16	79	Van Eyck	The taking down from the Cross, with many figures ; with the monogram of the painter on St. Mary Magdalen's vase. An elaborate and curious picture	Mr. Vansittart	Christie's	£0 0 0	...	Bought in	Weale. (See Jan. 16, 1829)
1828, June 6	10	Van Eyck	The Crucifixion, on panel ; The Blessed Virgin and Child ; and the Adoration of the Magi	Mr. Mayo, bankrupt	Christie's	£3 0 0	...	...	Weale
1828, Ap. 12	48	Van Eyck	Virgin and Child, and a Family in Devotion ; a pair with arched tops	Mr. Flight	Christie's	...	...	...	Weale

APPENDIX B

Date.	No.	Attributed.	Subject.	Owner.	Where Sold.	Price.	Measurement.	Purchaser.	Remarks.
1829, Jan. 10	17	Van Eyck	The Virgin and Child, and a Family at Devotion; a pair with arched tops: Christ bearing his Cross, circular, Early German, and a Head of Christ on panel	— Flight, Esq.	Christie's	£5 10 0	...	Bought in	Weale
1829, Jan. 16	76	Van Eyck	The taking down from the Cross; numerous figures; elaborate	Rev. Dr. Vansittart	Christie's	£7 0 0	...	Bought in	Weale. (See Feb. 16, 1828)
1829, Feb. 14	96	Van Eyck	Dead Christ and St. Mary Magdalene; with the Crucifixion and St. Mary Magdalene, with the Crucifixion in the background	Mr. Wiggans	Christie's	...	...	...	Weale
1830, Dec. 4	1	Van Eyck	St. Jerome and another Father	Mr. Baumgärtner	Christie's	£0 13 0	...	Wasse	Weale
1830, Dec. 4	69	Van Eyck	Adoration of Magi	Mr. Baumgärtner	Christie's	£1 4 0	...	Adams	Weale
1831, Feb. 26	33	Van Eyck	Altar-piece: The Nativity, Adoration, and Circumcision	Mr. Serrell	Christie's	£2 10 0	...	Bought in	Weale. (Said to have been bought in again on Mar. 19, 1860, for £4.)

Date	No.	Artist	Subject	Seller	Place	Price	Panel	Bought in	Reference
1831, June 25	8	Van Eyck	Crucifixion with Saints	Mr. Stachsmidt	Christie's	£0 18 0	Panel, upright Bois (27–18)	Bought in	Weale
1832		Hubert	La Salutation Angélique et l'adoration des Bergers. Tableau à volets	Chevalier Erard (au Château de la Muette)	Paris	1600 francs		...	Mireur, III. 123 Soullié
1833, Feb. 27	51	Van Eyck	La Sainte Vierge, assise sous un arbre chargé de pommes, tient l'Enfant Jésus nu sur ses genoux. D'une grande finesse. Conservation parfaite.	...	Salle Vivienne. Paris	...	Bois, 35 po × 24 po	...	Weale
1833, Aug. 26	140	Van Eyck	Philip, Duke of Burgundy	Hon. Percy Wyndham	Christie's	£3 3 0 / 2	...	Fuller	Weale
1833, Oct. 8		Jean v. Eyck	Nymphe et Diane: Deux Pendants	Verbelen, Marchand de Tableaux	Bruxelles	250 francs	...	...	Mireur Soullié
1833, Oct. 8		Jean v. Eyck	Couronnement de la Vierge	Verbelen, Marchand de Tableaux	Bruxelles	175 francs	Estampe	...	Mireur Soullié
1834, Mar. 22	79	Van Eyck	Adoration of Magi	Mr. L. Mark	Christie's	£1 5 0	...	Adams	Weale
1835, Nov. 14	23	Van Eyck	A Martyrdom; and Abram and the Angels	Mr. Foster	Christie's	£1 9 0	...	Sherratt	Weale
1836, May 6	123	Van Eyck	Adoration of Magi	Professor von Rotterdam	Christie's	£267 15 0	...	Bought in. Valued at £420	Weale Now in Museum at Brussels Probably by Gerard David
1836, Aug. 25	80	...	Annunciation; rich decoration and architecture	J. J. van Hal, Antwerp	Antwerp (?)	...	Panel 78 × 64	...	Weale

Date.	No.	Attributed.	Subject.	Owner.	Where Sold.	Price.	Measurement.	Purchaser.	Remarks.
1836, Oct. 13	83	Van Eyck	Veronica between SS. Peter and Paul; on right of St. Peter is St. Eligius; by St. Paul, a monk praying. Rome in the background	F. X. de Burck, Courtrai	Courtrai	...	Panel 0.98 × 1.68	...	Weale Soullié
1837, May 1	175	...	Christ with hand on the Orb, and the Virgin with hands joined	Count F. de Robiano	Brussels	...	Panel 0.37 × 0.25	...	Weale
1837, May 1	176	...	Virgin and Child and St. Joseph	Count F. de Robiano	Brussels	...	Panel Diam. 0.33	...	Weale
1837, June 3	1	Van Eyck	Adoration of Magi; richly coloured and highly finished	Sir G. Warrender	Christie's	£12 1 6	...	Holford	Weale
1838, Mar. 9	31	Van Eyck	Crucifixion	Mr. Greenhill	Christie's	£1 11 6	...	Bought in	Weale
1838, Mar. 24	61	John van Eyck	Virgin and Child Enthroned, an Angel presenting an apple and a Bishop in adoration; a beautiful landscape is seen through the opening of an arch, the ornaments of which are richly sculptured and festoons of fruits are suspended from the figures; exquisite specimen	William Esdaile of Clapham Common	Christie's	£28 7 0	...	Norton	Weale. (See also Oct. 1823, under Sale at Fonthill.)

Date	No.	Artist	Description			Price	Size	Buyer	Notes
1838, Mai 15	112	Jean van Eyck	Sainte Vierge accroupie sur un gazon émaillé de fleurs. . . . Ste. Anne caresse l'Enfant . . . Dieu le Père apparaît au ciel. Au fond, un Jardin	...	...	250 francs	10p. × 8p.	...	Weale
1838, Mai 15	113	Jean van Eyck	S. Katherine et S. Agnès assises	...	...	350 francs	21½p. × 8½p.	Steyaert	Weale
1838, Mai 15	114	Jean van Eyck	S. Katherine (?), un anneau à la main droite, une fléche à la gauche, et une autre Sainte, derrière un personnage tenant un sceptre accompagné de deux autres.	...	...	255 francs	12½p. × 8½p.	...	Weale
1838, May 24	57	Hubert and John van Eyck	Adoration of Magi. Philip, Duke of Burgundy, is represented as the principal of the Magi. . . . The portraits of the two brothers, Hubert and Jean, are seen through the opening of a window casement. . . .	Lord Northwick	Christie's	£115 10 0	...	Bought in	Weale. (See also Northwick Sale, July 27, 1859, No. 172
1838, May 26	117	Van Eyck	Virgin and Child. Circular, on a very old panel, which forms a frame to the painting. . . .	Lord Northwick	Christie's	£3 15 0	...	Greenland	...

Date.	No.	Attributed.	Subject.	Owner.	Where Sold.	Price.	Measurement.	Purchaser.	Remarks.
1839, Jan. 12	35	Van Eyck	Virgin and Child	Mr. Pittar	Christie's	£0 18 0	...	Marchant	Weale
1839, Ap. 26	16	Hubert van Eyck	Head of St. John in a Charger, over which angels are lamenting; a frieze of small figures beneath: treated with admirable truth and delicacy	Mr. Robinson	Christie's	£3 15 0	...	Green	Weale (Nat. Gall., No. 1080)
1839, Ap. 26	51	Hubert van Eyck	Blessed Virgin and Child, and St. Elizabeth, in a landscape	Mr. Robinson	Christie's	£9 19 6	...	Green	Weale
1839, Ap. 26	59	Margaret van Eyck and John van Eyck	Holy Family attended by Angels . . . St. John Evangelist blessing the Chalice; on R. wing St. John Baptist. . . . From the windows of a church in background emanates, between the deep shades of the trees, a miraculous light. The landscape and architecture by John van Eyck	Mr. Robinson	Christie's	£42 0 0	...	Green	Weale

Date	No.	Artist	Subject	Mr. Robinson	Christie's	Price	12 ft × 15 ft	Lemme	Weale
1839, Ap. 26	60	Hubert and John van Eyck	Adoration of Lamb, in 12 divisions, on canvas. Originally in the Chapel of the Town House at Ghent. Sold on approach of the French army under Pichegru to Mr. Charles Hisette, of whose widow Mr. Aders bought it in 1819.			£99 15 0		Lemme	Weale (Now at Antwerp Museum). (See p. 59)
1839, May 25	59	Van Eyck	Crucifixion	David Baillie, Esq.	...	£39 18 0	...	Bought in	Weale
1839, June 29	50	...	Christ carrying the Cross, attended by the Marys	...	...	£3 10 0	...	Bought in	Weale
1839, July 8	1064	...	Holy Family, an angel presenting grapes. St. Catherine and St. Barbara	Duke of Hamilton	...	£178 10 0	...	Agnew	Weale
1840, Feb.	64	...	Triptych, the Crucifixion	Lord Teignmouth	...	£5 0 0	...	...	Weale
1840, Feb. 29	25	...	Adoration of Magi	Heilbronn	...	£3 13 6	...	Guy	Weale
1840, Ap. 10	97	...	Holy Family, with the Flight into Egypt in the background	Lieut.-Gen. Sir Herbert Taylor	...	£3 7 0	...	Emmanuel	Weale
1842, May 19		John van Eyck	A Marriage	Horace Walpole, Earl of Orford	...	£24 3 0	...	Earl of Derby	Weale

APPENDIX B

Date.	No.	Attributed.	Subject.	Owner.	Where Sold.	Price.	Measurement.	Purchaser.	Remarks.
1844, Oct. 21	46	Jean van Eyck	2 volets d'un triptyque dont on a fait un tableau. Ils représentent les donateurs accompagnés de S. André et de S. Katherine...	Joseph van Huerne	Bruges	400 francs	0.57 × 0.44	Verhelst Gand	Weale
1844		Hubert van Eyck	Portrait d'homme en fourrure et casquette rouge	Middleton	Londres	7870 francs	...	...	Mireur, III, 122? Incorrect. (See below, under 1851) Weale
1845, Mar.	260	Hubert van Eyck	Virgin and Child; Mary seated, hands joined; the Child has turned away from the breast and is smiling; Mary has a dark blue dress bordered with pearls and precious stones on a gold lace, white veil, red mantle	Cardinal Fesch	Rome	73 francs	Panel 1 ft. 7 in. × 1 ft. Split in the middle	...	Weale
1845, Mar.	261	École des van Eyck	Virgin and Child	Cardinal Fesch	Rome	...	10 in. × 7 in.	...	...
1847, Ap. 19	22	Jan van Eyck	Virgin and Child seated in a Chapel, with a landscape background	...	...	90 g.	1 el. 17 in. × 82 in.	L. de Vries	Weale

Date	No.	Artist	Subject	Seller	Place	Price	Support & size	Buyer	Notes
1847, Nov. 16	45	Van Eyck	St. Jerome seated in his Study, a peacock in the foreground	Sir Thomas Baring	Christie's	£139 13 0	...	...	Weale. Now Antonello da Messina, in National Gallery, No. 1418
1848, June 3	66	...						Coningham	N. G., No. 1418
1849, June 9	2	...	St. Jerome seated in his Study	Coningham	Christie's	£162 15 0	...	...	N. G., No. 1418
1850, Ap. 10	10	...	Portrait de Saint Liévin	Schwelling of Aix-la-Chapelle	Bruxelles	400 francs	Bois (44—33)	...	Mireur Soullié
1850, Ap. 10	10	...	St. Christophe portant l'Enfant Jésus	Schwelling of Aix-la-Chapelle	Bruxelles	400 francs	Bois (46—33)	...	Mireur Soullié
1850, Ap. 10	10	...	Portrait d'homme, le donataire et ses Enfants	Schwelling of Aix-la-Chapelle	Bruxelles	370 francs	Bois (46—33)	...	Mireur Soullié
1850, Aug. 12	1	Jean van Eyck	Annonciation de la Vierge	William II of Holland	Hague	5375 florins	0.89 × 0.33	Bruni, for Emperor of Russia	Now at St. Petersburg. See p. 98.
1850, Aug. 12	2	Jean van Eyck	Vierge de Lucques	William II of Holland	Hague	3000 florins	0.64 × 0.47 Toile	Städels Museum	Now at Frankfort. See p. 145.
1850, Aug. 12	3	Jean van Eyck	Vierge et Enfant	William II of Holland	Hague	600 florins	Bois 0.56 × 0.59	Nieuwenhuys	Now in Metropolitan Museum, New York. See p. 174.
1850 Aug. 12	57 58 59 60 61 62	D'après van Eyck, par Michiel Coxcie. Six copies made for Philip II	S. Cecilie / Chœur d'Anges / Eremites en pélérinage / Même Sujet / Milices du Christ / Même Sujet	William II of Holland	Hague	2400 florins	...	...	...

APPENDIX B

Date.	No.	Attributed.	Subject.	Owner.	Where Sold.	Price.	Measurement.	Purchaser.	Remarks.
1850	...	...	A Pope kneeling in a Vision, Angel, Two Monks and Cardinal	Lord Besborough	...	£112 7 0	...	Webb	Redford
1851, Sept. 9	35	École des van Eyck	Présentation au Temple	Second part of Gallery of William II of Holland	Hague	...	0.32 × 0.22 Bois	...	...
1851, Sept. 9	36	École de ran Eyck	Portrait d'Érasme. École antique	Second part of Gallery of William II of Holland	Hague	...	...	...	...
1851, Sept. 9	38–43	Michiel Coxcie, d'après van Eyck	Six copies as in previous sale of this collection	Second part of Gallery of William II of Holland	Hague	...	...	...	...
1851, July 31		Van Eyck	Portrait	Viscount Midleton	...	£315 0 0	Farrer	...	Now in National Gallery, No. 222. See p. 112. Acquired by the Gallery from Farrer in 1851 for £365.
1852, Mar.		Van Eyck	Présentation au Temple	De Quédeville	...	1490 francs	...	...	Mireur
1852, June 19	10	Van Eyck	Virgin and Child, small	...	...	£12 12 0	...	Smith	Soullié Weale

260

Date	No.	Artist	Description	Seller	Where sold	Price £ s d	Dimensions	Buyer	Reference
1854, June 5	49	Van Eyck	Virgin in green dress and red mantle, with Child in her arms. She is placing her hands in an earthen dish on a table before her. St. Joseph is cutting a lemon. Landscape background	Lord Delawarr	Christie's	£14 3 6	...	...	Weale
1854, June 12	29	Van Eyck	Virgin and Child: the Virgin's long hair on shoulders: the child in her arms playing with a parrot	E. J. de Bammeville	Christie's	£64 1 0	...	Nieuwenhuys	Weale. Sold by N. in 1857 to T. Baring for £120. Later in Northbrook Collection. See p. 159
1854. May 27	63	Van Eyck	St. Giles seated in a landscape, with landscape, extracting an arrow from the back of a fawn	Thomas Emmerson	...	£51 9 0	...	Webb	Weale Now in National Gallery, No. 1419
1855, Mar. 13	923	School of Van Eyck	A Female Saint, in a rich dress, with a turban, holding a model of a tower	R. Bernal	Christie's	...	10¾ in. × 6½ in.; arched top	...	Sale Catalogue
1855. Mar. 13	930	School of Van Eyck	A Lady, as the Magdalen; she is in a rich dress ornamented with jewels, and blue and gold turban, her long, light hair falling behind; she holds a green marble vase of ointment	R. Bernal	Christie's	£11 11 0	...	Morant	Sale Catalogue Redford

APPENDIX B

Date.	No.	Attributed.	Subject.	Owner.	Where Sold.	Price.	Measurement.	Purchaser.	Remarks.
1855		Jean van Eyck	Sujet religieux	Banque de Cassel	...	800 francs	...	...	Mireur Weale
1855, June 14	73	Van Eyck	Diptych. The Annunciation; the Virgin kneeling; the Angel, richly clad, holds a sceptre. On exterior, the donors	James Dennistoun. (From the Weyer Collection at Cologne.)	Christie's	£39 18 0	...	Farrer	Weale. (See Aug. 25, 1862
1855, May 14	15	Van Eyck	Head of Christ	...	Christie's	£5 5 0	...	...	Weale
1856, April 5	73	Van Eyck	Triptych, with figures lamenting over the dead body of Christ.	P. Hinds	Christie's	£25 14 6	...	...	Weale
1856, May 2	585	Van Eyck	Virgin with the Child in her lap in a Gothic niche	Samuel Rogers. (From the Aders Collection.)	Christie's	£267 15 0	...	Bentley, for Thomas Baring	Weale. (Now in Lord Northbrook's Collection, No. 1)
1856, May 3	651	A. Dürer	John and Hubert van Eyck	Samuel Rogers	Christie's	...	...	...	Weale. See p. 227
1856, May 21	71	Van Eyck	The Virgin, with the Infant in her arms	Thomas Emmerson	Christie's	£6 10 0	...	Waters	Weale
1857, July 6	76	J. van Eyck	Portrait of the Great Artist, in a brown dress edged with fur, holding a letter in his hand, in a head-dress of brilliant crimson.	Earl of Shrewsbury, at Alton Towers	Sold by Christie at Alton Towers	£37 16 0	...	Nieuwenhuys	Weale. (Now at Berlin.) See p. 146. Museum No. 523A

Date	No.		Subject	Collection	Sold by	Price		Nieuwenhuys or Collett	Redford (D. 1472)(?); and Sale Catalogue
1857, July 9	347	J. van Eyck	Interior, with a Monk introducing a gentleman to the Virgin and Child. Dated 1572 (?)	Earl of Shrewsbury, at Alton Towers	Sold by Christie at Alton Towers	£87 3 0	...	...	
1859, Sep. 31(?)	...	...	Sujet Religieux	From the Collection of Count A. de Stolberg (?) de Hanovre, Brabeck	...	...	...	...	Mireur ("Stolberg") Soullié ("Stobberg")
1859, April 28 –29	...	...	Présentation au Temple	Moret. Pictures from the Fesch Collection	...	635 francs	...	...	Mireur Soullié
1859, July 27	172	Van Eyck	Adoration of the Magi; the principal figure is the portrait of Philip, Duke of Burgundy, who wears the Order of the Golden Fleece. John and Hubert are seen through the opening of a window casement. A capital work in most perfect preservation	Lord Northwick	Sold by Phillips at Thirlestane House, Cheltenham	£519 15 0	...	J. W. Brett	Weale. (See May 24, 1838) and Redford

Date.	No.	Attributed.	Subject.	Owner.	Where Sold.	Price.	Measurement.	Purchaser.	Remarks.
1859, Aug. 3	593	John van Eyck	Head of the Saviour. Painted natural size. A picture of extraordinary brilliancy, and in fine preservation	Lord Northwick	Sold by Phillips at Thirlestane House, Cheltenham	£17 17 0	...	Moses (Bristol)	Redford
1859, Aug. 23	1727	Van Eyck School	Portrait of a Man in a black cap and a crimson dress	Lord Northwick	Sold by Phillips at Thirlestane House, Cheltenham	£22 1 0	...	Colnaghi & Co.	Sale Catalogue
1861, Feb. 21–22		John van Eyck	Le Père Eternel	Leroy d'Etiolles	Paris	690 francs	...	...	Mireur Soullié
1862, Aug. 25		John van Eyck	Vierge et Enfant	J. P. Weyer, Cologne	Cologne	1189 francs	...	...	Mireur Soullié
1862, Aug. 25	206	Hubert van Eyck	Vierge et Enfant Jésus sur un trône	J. P. Weyer, Cologne	Cologne	3690 francs 900 thalers	...	...	Mireur Now in the Brussels Gallery, Quentin Metsys
1862, Aug. 25	213	John van Eyck	Portrait du Duc de Bourgogne	J. P. Weyer, Cologne	Cologne	731 francs	0.34×0.25	...	Mireur Soullié
1862, Aug. 25	205	John van Eyck	L'Image du Sauveur	J. P. Weyer, Cologne	Cologne	820 francs	...	...	Mireur Soullié
1862, Aug. 25		John van Eyck		J. P. Weyer, Cologne	Cologne	451 francs	...	...	Mireur Soullié

1862, Aug. 25	211	John van Eyck	L'Enfant Jésus endormi sur le sein de Marie	J. P. Weyer, Cologne	Cologne	172 francs	0.33 × 0.24	...	Mireur Soullié
1862, Aug. 25	215 216	John van Eyck	Vierge et Enfant Jésus, St. Luc fait le portrait de la Vierge	J. P. Weyer, Cologne	Cologne	2156 francs	Bois 0.33 × 0.21 arrondi du haut	...	Mireur Soullié From Bettendorf Collection
1862, Aug. 25	217 218	John van Eyck	La Vierge reçoit l'Annonciation de l'Ange Gabriel	J. P. Weyer, Cologne	Cologne	3825 francs	0.91 × 0.73	...	Mireur Soullié Gerard David, Sigmaringen Museum
1862, Aug. 25	219	John van Eyck	Adoration des Mages	J. P. Weyer, Cologne	Cologne	2362 francs	0.79 × 0.63	...	Mireur Soullié Jerome Bosch
1862, Aug. 25	221	John van Eyck	Ange assis faisant de la musique	J. P. Weyer, Cologne	Cologne	217 francs	Bois 0.22 × 0.16	...	Mireur Soullié
1862, Aug. 25		Margaret van Eyck	Vierge et Enfant Jésus	J. P. Weyer, Cologne	Cologne	1087 francs	Bois 0.39 × 0.24	...	Mireur Soullié
1865, June		Jean v. Eyck	Vierge de douleurs soutenue par St. Jean	Desperet	Paris	67 francs	Pen drawing	...	Mireur
1865		École des van Eyck	Tableau en deux parties: Solomon and Queen of Sheba, &c.	Comte de Pourtalès	...	630 francs	0.54 × 0.52	...	(Later ascribed to H. met de Bles. Exhibited, Bruges, 1902, No. 277)
1865, Sept. 18	51	Jean v. Eyck	L'Annonciation	Ant. Joseph Essingh	Cologne	341 francs	0.38 × 0.295	...	Mireur Soullié
1865, Sept. 18	52	École de van Eyck	Portrait de Bonne d'Artois	A. J. Essingh	Cologne	...	0.22 × 0.165	...	See p. 203

APPENDIX B

Date.	No.	Attributed.	Subject.	Owner.	Where Sold.	Price.	Measurement.	Purchaser.	Remarks.
1866, Feb. 10	113 G	Van Eyck	Virgin and Child; circular	William Goldsmith	Christie's	£8 5 0 (with 2 others)	...	Noseda	Weale
1866, June 16	271	Van Eyck	Portraits of the Duke and Duchess of Burgundy—a pair	Henry Farrer	...	£12 12 0	...	Webb	Weale
1866, June 16	287	Margharita van Eyck	Adoration of the Magi, with four subjects from the life of Christ at the sides. An exquisite work, finely preserved. Described in Stanley's Synopsis, p. 366	Henry Farrer	...	£127 1 0	...	Lloyd	In sale of M. Urbino Pizzetta on April 16, 1825, No. 31, was sold as a Memlinc. Lent to Bruges Exhibition, 1902, No. 327, by Sir G. Donaldson
1867, April 5	371	Van Eyck	Annunciation	...	Christie's	£11 0 0	...	Ayerst	Weale
1867, April 22	22	Van Eyck	Coronation of Virgin	Peleguer	Paris	1000 francs	...	...	Soulié
1867, June 8	25	John van Eyck	Virgin and Child, with an architectural background	...	Christie's	£8 18 6	...	Brisco	Weale
1867, June 8	136	Van Eyck	Annunciation (exhibited at Manchester)	...	Christie's	£39 18 0	...	De Cosson	Weale

Date					Christie's	£15 0 0		Underdown	Weale
1867, Nov. 30	104	Margaret van Eyck	Diptych: The Annunciation; and on reverse of one panel a portrait of person for whom it was painted	...	...	£15 0 0	...	...	Weale
1868, Jan. 13		Jean van Eyck	Répétition de la petite Madone du Musée d'Anvers	Comte X.	...	3050 francs	0.32 × 0.15	...	Mireur
1868, May		Jean van Eyck	Vierge assise, tenant son Fils, est couronnée par deux Anges	Germeau	...	700 francs	1.17 × 0.66	...	Mireur
1868, April 6		Jean van Eyck	Episode de controverse religieuse du xvi Siècle (!)	Marquis Du Blaisel	...	1300 francs	...	...	Mireur Soullié
1868		Van Eyck School	Deux Femmes à genoux, vêtues de riches costumes flamands du temps	Robinson	...	...	0.26 × 0.19	...	Mireur(?)
1869, Jan. 22	1492	Van Eyck	Three parts of a Triptych: the Presentation of the Virgin; and St. Sebastian	Peter Norton, of Soho Square	...	£5 5 0	...	Henry	Weale
1870, Ap. 26–27 or May 7		John van Eyck	Annunciation	Saint Remy	Febvre	800 francs	...	...	Mireur Soullié Weale
1871, Feb. 11	538	Van Eyck	Virgin and Child appearing to a Saint	W. Anthony	Christie's	£5 5 0	...	Pearce	
1871, Feb. 11	539	Van Eyck	A pair of Miniatures of German Emperors in ormolu frames (!)	W. Anthony	Christie's	£2 2 0	...	Grindlay	...

APPENDIX B

Date.	No.	Attributed.	Subject.	Owner.	Where Sold.	Price.	Measurement.	Purchaser.	Remarks.
1871, Mar. 11	14	Van Eyck	Adoration of the Magi	Rev. Geo. Chetwode	Christie's	£9 9 0	...	Addy	Weale
1871, July 1	50	Van Eyck	St. Jerome	Hon. F. Byng	Christie's	£9 9 6	...	Myres	Weale
1872, Jan. 26	140	Van Eyck	The Three Marys at the Sepulchre	William Middleton. (Received from Brussels)	Christie's	£335 0 0	...	Johnson	Weale. Now in Cook Collection. See p. 69
1873, Mar. 26		Jean van Eyck	Christ en Croix	Poncelet, d'Auxerre	...	400 francs	...	...	Mireur Soulié
1875, Mai. 10 –14		Jean van Eyck	Portrait de Philippe le Bon. Le duc est représenté de face avec le manteau de la Toison d'Or ouvert sur l'épaule droite. Une ombre formant auréole couvre le front	Emile Galichon	...	6000 francs	Pencil drawing	...	Mireur Soulié
1875, July 19	129	J. van Eyck	Virgin and Child	...	Christie's	£25 4 0	...	Waters	Weale
1876, May 15	18	Hubert van Eyck	Virgin and Child in a landscape. Mary seated giving the breast to the babe. Landscape with buildings on left	C. R. Ruhl No. 18	Köln	...	Panel 0.84 × 0.62	...	Weale
1876, May 15	19	John van Eyck	Our Lady standing in a semi-circular apse, kissing Child, whom she holds on her left arm. He stretches out his	C. R. Ruhl No. 19	Köln	...	Panel 0.54 × 0.40	...	Weale "Photogr. by A. Schmitz. Probably painted for or in Spain."

Date	No.	Attribution	Description	Place	Price	Dimensions	Buyer	Authority
1876, May 27	27	Van Eyck	hand for a fruit which she holds up	Christie's	£22 1 0	...	Boynton	Weale
1876, May 27	28	Van Eyck	Annunciation	Christie's	£14 3 6	...	Waters	Weale
1876, May 27	29	Van Eyck	Virgin and Child, adored by a priest, attended by St. George	Christie's	£31 10 0	...	Johnson	Weale
1879, May 23	57	Van Eyck	Madonna and Child enthroned, a monk kneeling before them, and two saints behind	Christie's	£116 11 0	...	Waters	Weale
1880, Mar. 12		...	Virgin and Child	Harley Place	£18 0 0	...	...	Weale
1881, May	279	Van Eyck	Vierge et Enfant. (Engraved by C. Vion as a work by Memlinc)	Paris	20,100 frs.	Bois 1.0 × 0.55	...	Weale / From Collection of Queen of Spain
1881, May	280	École des Van Eyck	Deposition de la Croix: Triptych	Paris	2020 francs	0.75 × 0.60 and 0.75 × 0.27 Bois	...	Mireur
1881, May	281	École des Van Eyck	Vierge et Quatre Saints personnages	Paris	6000 francs	0.75 × 0.96 Panel	...	Mireur
1881, May	282	École des Van Eyck	Vierge et l'Enfant Jésus	Paris	920 francs	0.29 × 0.21 Panel	...	Mireur
1881, May	283	École des Van Eyck	Vierge allaitant l'Enfant Jésus	Paris	420 francs	0.36 × 0.27 Panel	...	Mireur
1881, June 27	65	Van Eyck	Triptych, with Virgin and Child, St. John Baptist, and St. John; on the reverse of the wings is the Annunciation	Christie's	£42 0 0	...	Escozura	Weale

APPENDIX B

Date.	No.	Attributed.	Subject.	Owner.	Where Sold.	Price.	Measurement.	Purchaser.	Remarks.
1882, July 8	1064	Van Eyck	Triptych, with the Holy Family in the centre, with an Angel presenting grapes, St. Catherine and St. Barbara, on the wings	Duke of Hamilton	Christie's	£178 10 0	...	Agnew	Weale
1882, Mar. 20 –23		Hubert van Eyck	Adoration des Mages	Jean Gigoux	Paris	50 francs	Pen Drawing	...	Mireur Soullié
1883, May 4		John v. Eyck	Portrait d'une femme de Philippe le Bon	Nieuwenhuys	Brussels	20,000 frs.	...	...	Weale
1883, Mai 21 –22		Jean van Eyck	Vierge et Enfant	Baron de Beurnonville	Paris	12,000 frs.	...	...	Mireur Soullié
1883, Mai 21 –22		Frères van Eyck	Vierge et Enfant	Baron de Beurnonville	Paris	12,600 frs.	1.00 × 0.55	...	Mireur Soullié
1885, Mar. 21	487	Hubert and John van Eyck	Two Female Saints seated in a landscape under architectural canopies. On the reverse of the panel are two Saints, painted in grisaille	Henry G. Bohn	Christie's From the Collection of Lady Stirling-Maxwell	£14 14 0	32 in. × 11 in.	A. D. Clark	Weale
1885, Mar. 21	488	Hubert and John van Eyck	Two Females in Prayer	Henry G. Bohn	Christie's From the Baron de Laage's Collection	£63 0 0	22 in. × 15 in.	Shepherd	Weale

Date	No.	Artist	Description	Vendor	Sale	Price	Dimensions	Purchaser	Authority
1885, Mar. 21	489	Hubert and John van Eyck	The Deity and the Virgin, enthroned, with attendant Angels	Henry G. Bohn	Christie's	£5 5 0	6 in. × 4½ in. on gold ground	Brocklebank	Weale
1885, Mar. 21	490	Hubert and John van Eyck	The Vision of St, Gregory	...	Christie's	£21 0 0	20 in. × 14½ in.	Barton	Weale
1885, May 9	224	Van Eyck	A Diptych, with the Annunciation, a portrait of the donor on the reverse	S. Herman de Zoete	Christie's From the Weyer of Cologne and Dennistoun Collections	£52 0 0	16½ in. × 12½ in.	Colnaghi & Co.	Weale (See June 14, 1855, and Aug. 25, 1862)
1886, May 15	30	J. van Eyck	Madonna and Child in a sculptured Gothic niche, with figures of Saints	A. J. B. Beresford-Hope	Christie's From King of Holland's Collection	£315 0 0	...	Lesser	Weale Now in Metropolitan Museum, N.Y.
1886, July 17	67	J. van Eyck	Portrait of the Great Artist, in a robe trimmed with fur, and crimson head-dress, holding a letter in his right hand	C. J. Nieuwenhuys	Christie's From Alton Towers	£399 0 0	11 in. × 8 in.	Sedelmeyer	Weale The Arnolfini Portrait in Berlin. See p. 146.
1886, Dec. 4	29	Van Eyck	Holy Family Triptych, with the Crucifixion in the centre, with saints and nuns on the doors, St. James and St. Anthony outside	General Bell	Christie's	£10 10 0	...	Hughes	Weale
1887, July 2	63	Hubert van Eyck			Christie's	£31 10 0	...	Davis	Weale

APPENDIX B

Date.	No.	Attributed.	Subject.	Owner.	Where Sold.	Price.	Measurement.	Purchaser.	Remarks.
1887, Oct. 28		Hubert	Salvator Mundi: arched panel and frame	Mrs. J. P. Weyer. (Exhibited at Köln: Historical Art Exhibition, 1876, No. 10)	Köln	...	One piece of oak 0.33 × 0.21	...	Weale. (See 25, August 1862)
1888, June 9	288	John	The Virgin holding the Infant Saviour in her arms ... an abbot in monastic dress kneeling before them, and presented by St. Margaret ... a city with numerous buildings and distant landscape	Marquis of Exeter	Christie's	£2625 0 0	8½ in. × 6 in.	Murray	Weale Now in Berlin Gallery (see p. 169, where it is fully described
1888, June 30	74	John v. Eyck	Moses and Burning Bush	...	Christie's	£199 10 0	17½ in. × 14 in.	M. Colnaghi	Weale. Belonged to M. Colnaghi, H. Willett, and Kann
1888, July 28	134	John v. Eyck	Prince Antiochus, the Queen Stratonice, and the Physician Erosistratus	A baronet	Christie's	£58 16 0	...	Buller	Weale

272

1888, Dec. 1	72	Van Eyck	Marriage of the Virgin, with scenes from her life	...	Christie's	£262 10 0	...	Shaw	Weale
1889		Jean v. Eyck	Vierge et Enfant	Sellar		2000 francs	0.56 × 0.31	...	Mireur This cannot be proved. D. P. Sellar, of 68 Princes Gate, sold pictures at Christie's on March 17, 1894, but the pictures sold July 8, 1897, were nearly all withdrawn.
1890, Feb. 3		J. van Eyck	Adoration of Magi	Prince Pierre de Bourbon Duc de Durcal	Paris	17,000 frs.		...	Weale Soullié
1892, June 11	81	Van Eyck	The Wings of a Diptych (sic); painted with portraits of donors, attended by a Saint and a Bishop, with an Angel and female Saint in grisaille on the back	José Guedes de Queiroz. From the Collection of the Marquis de Foz	Christie's	£210 0 0	On high carved oak stand of Gothic design	Duveen	Weale On exterior, the "Annunciation"
1892, June 11	82	John van Eyck	A Diptych. The Annunciation	José Guedes de Queiroz. From the Collection of the Marquis de Foz	Christie's	£141 15 0	Signed	Millns	Weale

APPENDIX B

Date.	No.	Attributed.	Subject.	Owner.	Where Sold.	Price.	Measurement.	Purchaser.	Remarks.
1892, June 25	29	Early Netherlandish School, formerly attributed to John van Eyck	The Shutter of a Triptych, representing an Angel with a scroll appearing to St. Giles while saying mass	Earl of Dudley	Christie's Exhibited at Burlington House, 1871 & 1892	£3570 0 0	24¼ in. × 18¼ in.	Vokins	Now in the Collection of Colonel Stuart Mackenzie. The companion wing is now in National Gallery, No. 1419
1893, Jan. 19	147	Hubert van Eyck	Interior of a Cathedral, with the Baptism of Antoine, son of Philip Le Bon, Duke of Burgundy, and Isabelle of Portugal, with their portraits as donors, also portraits of the nephew of the Emperor Frederic, the Bishop of Cambrai, Duchess of Cleves, and the Comtesse de Namur	...	Christie's (Formerly the property of the town of Dijon)	£9 9 0	...	Cousens	Weale This picture represents the Circumcision, with a donor and his wife
1893, Feb. 23	111	Van Eyck	Marriage of Virgin	G. Barker & Co.	Robinson & Fisher	£540 0 0	...	Schaffer	Roberts

Date		Attribution	Description	Seller	Sale	Price	Dimensions	Buyer	Authority
1893, April 8	61	Van Eyck	St. Luke painting the Virgin	Henry Graves	Christie's	£9 19 6	...	Ward	Weale
1893, April 8	62	Van Eyck	The Fountain of Life: a Triptych	Henry Graves	Christie's	£6 16 6	...	Strelletski	Weale
1894, May 11	50	Van Eyck	Two Donors in Prayer	M. R. Blane	Christie's	£42 0 0	Bois	Alexander	Weale, Mireur, Soullié
1894, Nov. 14 –24		Jean v. Eyck	Ecce Homo	Henri Baudot	Dijon	36 francs	0.33×0.22 Bois	...	Mireur, Soullié
1894, Nov. 14 –24		Jean v. Eyck	Le Christ et la Vierge: Diptych	Henri Baudot	Dijon	115 francs	0.20×0.15		Weale
1895, April 6	98	Van Eyck	Portraits of Two Donors; wings of a Triptych	Wm. Angerstein	Christie's	£25 4 0	...	Buttery	Weale
1896, Feb. 29	28	School of Van Eyck	A Gentleman in black dress and crimson cape, with gold chain; a missal on a ledge before him	Perkins, of Chipstead	Christie's	£12 12 0	17½ in. × 12 in.	Butler	Weale
1896, Feb. 29	100	Van Eyck	Portrait of the Artist's sister	Perkins, of Chipstead	Christie's	£330 15 0	On panel, circle	Wertheimer	Weale
1898, Feb. 12	73	Margaret Eyck v.	Annunciation of the Virgin	John D. Chambers	Christie's	£6 6 0	On panel	Farr	Weale
1898, May 21	71	Hubert v. Eyck	Mary Magdalen, in yellow and red dress, yellow head-dress and veil, jewelled ornaments, holding a vase of unguent in her left hand, stands by a female donor, in deep red dress, with black	Joseph Rushton	Christie's. From the Martinengo Collection; and Baron de Laage and Bohn Collections	£199 10 0	Panel 20¼ in. × 14¾ in.	Heyman	...

APPENDIX B

Date.	No.	Attributed.	Subject.	Owner.	Where Sold.	Price.	Measurement.	Purchaser.	Remarks.
1898, Nov. 12	84	Van Eyck	Virgin Mary supporting the Dead Saviour, coif and jewelled chain, who kneels in the act of prayer	...	Christie's	£3 3 0	Panel	Wetherby	Weale
1899, Nov. 20 –21		Les Frères van Eyck	Sainte Famille	Piérard de Valenciennes	Paris	920 francs	0.74 × 0.55	...	Mireur
1899, Mar. 25	103	School of Van Eyck	Triptych representing the Adoration of the Magi, with St. James of Compostella and St. Hubert on the wings	Sir Richard Westmacott	Christie's	£462 0 0	Panel 10½ in. × 14 in.	Colnaghi & Co.	Roberts
1901, April 27	87	J. van Eyck	Portrait of the Artist, in brown dress with fur	...	Christie's	£267 15 0	Panel 16 in. × 12 in.	Gribble	Weale
1902, May 31	138	J. van Eyck	Marie d'Anjou, wife of Charles VII	General A. W. H. Meyrick	Christie's	£99 15 0	Panel 8 in. × 5 in.	Dowdeswell	Weale
1902, May 31	139	J. van Eyck	A Lady, in red dress, with white head-dress	...	Christie's	£126 0 0	Panel 6½ in. × 5 in.	Noseda	Weale
1904, Ap.		...	Two volets, Orientaux discutant	...	Brussels	...	...	...	Weale Hulin says "near to Hubert"
1904, Ap. 28		Hubert van Eyck	Triptych and Saints	M. Green	Silo of New York	460 dollars	...	...	Roberts

276

Date	No.	Jan v. Eyck	Head of Christ	Hugo Helbing	Munich				Auction prices	sale
1906, Dec. 6		Jan v. Eyck	Head of Christ	Hugo Helbing	Munich	£322 0 0	...	...	...	...
1907, May 24	15	Van Eyck	Madonna, Infant Saviour, and angels	Señor Don Alberto Gonzalez-Abreu, of Seville	Christie's	£147 0 0	Panel 52½ in. × 44 in.	Wood	...	
1907, June 7	38	Van Eyck	Head of an Old Lady, with white coif	Duke of Fife	Christie's	£10 10 0	Panel 10 in. × 8 in.	Samuelson	...	
1907, Nov. 23	103	Van Eyck	Adam and Eve in the Garden of Eden	...	Christie's	£60 18 0	23 in. × 17½ in.	Temple	...	
1907, Nov. 23	108	Van Eyck	Two Saints	...	Christie's	£15 15 0	Panel 18 × 10½ in.	Robinson	...	
1908, Mar. 14	85	School of Van Eyck	Triptych: Descent from the Cross, St. Joseph of Arimathaea and Magdalen on the wings	William Connal	Christie's	£60 18 0	Panel mounted as a screen	Mahlmann	...	
1908, Mar. 16	23	M. van Eyck	Madonna and Child	Sir Charles A. Turner	Christie's	£11 0 6	Panel 12½ × 9½ in.	Lewis	...	
1910, Feb. 7	106	Van Eyck	Adoration of Magi	...	Christie's	£241 10 0	Panel 32 × 21½ in.	Glen	...	
1912, Ap. 19	95	School of Van Eyck	Triptych: Madonna and Child, angels and saints	...	Christie's	£304 10 0	Panel 18½ × 13 in.	Schnell	...	

BIBLIOGRAPHY

BIBLIOGRAPHY

NOTE.—It will perhaps be conceded that the following Bibliography is extensive, and even adequate. However, it is not considered by the joint-authors to be exhaustive, unless supplemented by that published in Weale, 1908, pp. lv-cxiv. A certain proportion of the standard authorities cited by Weale four years ago have for convenience been retained here. The details given below will be found to include the most recent publications. The two bibliographies combined will be found, doubtless, to contain all that the student is likely to need.

An asterisk is prefixed to those books and articles which indicate the progress made in clearing up the biography of the Van Eycks or the history of their works.

I

MANUSCRIPTS AND EARLY PRINTED BOOKS

c. 1430. CONTEMPORARY narrative of the journey of the embassy which was sent by Philip III, Duke of Burgundy, to John, King of Portugal, and to which John van Eyck was attached as the Duke's painter. The facts given in this narrative are summarised in our biography of John (p. 8).

c. 1450. PIZZICOLLI, Cyriacus, of Ancona, 1391–1457, is the earliest known author who makes mention of John van Eyck as " insignis pictor."

1454. FACIO, Bartolomeo, " Liber de Viris illustribus," written 1454–55, first printed at Florence in 1745, contains a long and interesting notice, p. 46, of John van Eyck, whom he looks on as a Frenchman : " Ioannes Gallicus nostri saeculi pictorum princeps iudicatus est, litterarum nonnihil doctus, geometriae praesertim et earum artium quae ad picturae ornamentum accederent."

1458. Kronyk van Vlaenderen. On the occasion of the solemn entry of Philip III into Ghent on Saint George's day, April 23, 1458, after the battle of Gavere, there were great rejoicings ; the house fronts were decorated with unusual magnificence, and where space permitted scenic representations were erected in the streets,

The most remarkable of these was on the Poul—Marsh Square—where the Rhetoricians of the town got up a *pageant* in imitation of the Ghent polyptych. The scaffold erected for this purpose, 50 feet high and 28 feet broad, was completely covered with blue cloth and shut in with white curtains. It was divided into three zones ; the uppermost portioned off into five compartments, the figures in which represented those in the five central panels of the upper zone of the polyptych. In the lower portion Hubert's design was not adhered to, for although the Adoration of the Lamb was represented in the centre, the sides were each divided into five compartments in two zones ; four of these occupied by the Knights, the Judges, the Hermits, and the Pilgrims ; the other six by groups ; these and the centre illustrated the Beatitudes, the second being omitted.

1464. AVERULINO, Antonio, surnamed Filarete, wrote a treatise on Architecture, the original manuscript of which, dedicated to Peter de' Medici, is preserved in the Biblioteca Magliabechiana of the National Library at Florence. He mentions (p. 182) master John (van Eyck) of Bruges and master Roger (De la Pasture) as the two painters who had made use of oil colours with the greatest skill.

c. 1485. SANTI, Giovanni, in his Chronicle of the Dukes of Urbino, the manuscript of which is preserved in the Library of the Vatican, wrote as follows in praise of the same two masters :—

> " A Brugia fu tra gli altri piu lodato
> il gran Ioannes, el discepol Ruggero,
> con tanti d'alto merto dotati."

1495. MUENZER, a physician and humanist, travelling through the Low Countries, visited Ghent in the course of this year, and has left an interesting notice of the polyptych, preserved in the Royal Library at Munich (MS. Lat. 631), first published by Dr. Voll, in the Supplement of the *Allgemeine Zeitung* of September 7, 1899.

" De nobilissima tabula picta ad Ioannem, cuius simile vix credo esse in mundo.

" Ecclesia S. Ioannis inter illas tres principales est pulcrior, maior et longior de 156 passibus. Et inter cetera habet unam tabulam depictam supra unum altare magnam et preciosissimam de pictura."

1504. LEMAIRE de Belges, Jean, in "La Couronne Margaritique," a poem commenced by him in 1504 and finished in 1511, first printed at Lyons in 1549, has three lines in praise of John van Eyck.

"Hugues de Gand, qui tant eut les tretz netz,
y fut aussi, et Dieric de Louvain
avec le roy des peintres Iohannes
du quel les faits parfaits et mignonnetz
ne tomberont jamais en oubly vain."

1521. DÜRER, Albrecht. A few days after Easter of this year, Dürer visited Bruges. He was taken about to see various buildings and works of art. After mentioning a visit to the church of Our Lady, he goes on to say : "Darnach führeten sie mich in viel Kirchen, und liessen mich alle gute Gemähl sehen, dessen ein Ueberschwahl do ist, und do ich Iohannes und der andern Ding alles gesehen hab ; do kamen wir zuletz in die Mahler Capelln, do ist gut Ding innen." "Iohannes" in this passage is generally supposed to refer to John van Eyck ; to us it seems far more probable that Saint John's Hospital is here indicated. From Bruges Dürer went to Ghent, and there he says : "Sah ich des Iohannes tafel ; das ist eine überköstliche, hochverständige Malerei und insbesondere die Eva, Maria, und Gott Vater sind sehr gut."

By "des Iohannnes tafel" Dürer most probably meant, not the painting of John van Eyck, nor the painting in St. John's church, but the painting representing Saint John's vision.

T. Sturge Moore, however, in his *Albert Dürer* (London, 1905), pp. 154–155, under the heading of "Dürer's Journey to the Netherlands," under date of April 6–11, 1521, at Bruges and Ghent, translates :—

"After that they took me to many more churches and showed me all the good pictures, of which there is an abundance there ; and when I had seen the Jan van Eyck [1] and all the other works, we came at last to the

---

[1] Among such "good pictures" referred to would have been the "Madonna and Child with Saints Donatian and George and the Canon G. Van der Paele," now in the Bruges Town Gallery. See p. 120.

painter's chapel, in which there are good things. Then they prepared a banquet for me, and I went with them from it to their guildhall, where many honourable men were gathered together, both goldsmiths, painters, and merchants, and they made me sup with them. They gave me presents, sought to make my acquaintance, and did me great honour. . . . On my arrival at Ghent the Dean of the Painters came to me and brought with him the first masters in painting ; they showed me great honour. . . . Then I saw Jan van Eyck's picture ; it is a most precious painting, full of thought, and the Eve, Mary, and God the Father are especially good."

1550. VASARI, in the first edition of his "Vite," mentions Van Eyck in two passages. The first occurs in chapter XXI, in which, treating of painting with oil, he says : "Fu una bellissima invenzione ed una gran commodita all' arte della pittura, il trovare il colorito à olio ; di che fu primo inventore in Fiandria Giovanni da Bruggia." The second mention, in the Life of Antonello of Messina, is the well-known passage in which he gives his account of the invention of oil painting. *See* G. Milanesi, "Le Opere di Giorgio Vasari" (ed. Sansoni), 1878.

1562. VAERNEWYCK, Marcus van. "Nieu Tractaet ende curte bescryvinghe van dat edel graefscap van Vlaenderen.

In this work he makes no mention of Hubert, but attributes all to John. Apparently he derived his information from Vasari's "Vite."

1565. DE HEERE, Lucas, the painter, published this year a volume of poems entitled, "Den Hof en Boomgaerd der Poësien," the only known copy of which is preserved in the Library of the University of Ghent. It contains (pp. 35–38) an enthusiastic Ode in praise of the "Adoration of the Lamb," composed on the occasion of the holding of the twenty-third Chapter of the Order of the Golden Fleece in Saint John's church, July 23–25, 1559.[1] It contains the first mention of Hubert, and of his having had a sister.

This poem was affixed to the wall of the chapel, and was, doubtless, read by those who went to see the altar-piece. Here, no doubt, is the source of the

[1] Given at length by Weale, 1908, pp. LXXVII-LXXXI.

apocryphal legend of the Van Eycks. The discovery of the inscription on the exterior of the frame had revealed the fact that the altar-piece had not been entirely painted by the master (Hubert) buried beneath the chapel, as had been believed up to that time, but that it had been commenced by him and completed by John.

De Heere, fancying that the early painters must have introduced their own portraits into the picture, as was the general habit of painters in his day, fixed on two of the Just Judges as being the portraits of Hubert and John (strophe 9). For comments on the absurdity of the selection, see p. 230. De Heere is also responsible for the statement that Hubert had a sister (nameless), who lived with him, painted great works, and was buried by his side !

1565, April 27. LOMBARD, Lambert, of Liége. In a letter bearing this date, written to Vasari, preserved in the Gallery of the Uffizi at Florence, and printed by Gaye (" Carteggio," III, 176, Firenze, 1540), he mentions Joan di Bruggia.

1567. GUICCIARDINI, Ludovico, a native of Florence, born in 1521, who settled in Antwerp in 1550, undertook a description of the Low Countries, and set about collecting information from every available source in order to produce a standard work. The manuscript, completed in 1561, was printed and published at Antwerp in 1567. In the chapter on Antwerp, writing of the Gild of Saint Luke, he mentions a number of painters : " I principali e più nominati di quelli . . . sono stati Giovanni d'Eick quello il quale . . . fu inventore all'anno MCCCCX del colorito a olio. . . ."

Guicciardini quotes his fellow-countryman Vasari as his authority for all the first portion of his statement, adding thereto the information, derived directly or indirectly from Luke De Heere, here for the first time printed, that John and Hubert lived together, and that they collaborated in painting the Ghent, Bruges, and Ypres altar-pieces. We now know positively that they did not dwell together after 1422 ; and that the Bruges and Ypres altar-pieces were not even ordered until many years after Hubert's death. Guicciardini is the first author who names the year 1410 as the date of the invention of oil-painting by John.

1568. VASARI during this year published the second edition of his "Vite." Since the issue of the first he had received a few notes from Lambert Lombard, Dominic Lampson of Bruges, and Guicciardini ; from them he learned the name of the eldest brother, and by them he was told that the invention of painting with oil colours was made in 1410. The altered passage reads like a paraphrase of Guicciardini. Vasari evidently knew nothing of the Eyckian process, and to conceal his ignorance made out a plausible story as to how it came to be invented. It must be borne in mind that he was a gossip who sought to amuse rather than to instruct his readers.

1568. VAERNEWYCK, Marcus van. "Den Spieghel der Nederlandscher Audtheyt." Ghendt. In this work the author devotes several pages to the Van Eycks, and notes all the gossiping stories he heard from Luke De Heere and others. He gives the epitaphs of both John and Hubert, the latter copied by himself, letter by letter, from the brass tablet, and mentions the preservation of Hubert's arm-bone, which he had himself seen. He says that Hubert's sister's name was Margaret, that she remained a spinster, devoted herself to painting, lived with Hubert, and was buried by his side. He tells us that John was the younger brother but the chief master, that it was he who painted his own and his brother's portraits, and that he died young. The altar-piece is stated by him to have had a predella on which there was a representation of Hell painted in tempera by John, which was effaced by a painter who washed it.

1569. VAERNEWYCK, Marcus van. "Van die Beroerlicke Tijden in die Nederlanden, 1566-1568." In this his last work, Vaernewyck, who died November 20, 1569, gives an account of all that happened in Flanders down to the middle of November 1568. He tells us that in August 1566 the Calvinists sacked the church of Saint Martin at Ypres, but that he did not know whether the painting by John van Eyck, an artistic work surpassing all other works, had been injured. In his account of the wrecking of the cathedral of Ghent, he informs us that on August 19, 1566, two days before the irruption of the iconoclasts, the altar-piece was wisely taken down from the chapel and removed for safety into the tower. In this account occurs for the first time a description—not, however, quite exact—of the exterior of its shutters. We are told that at the foot were represented, kneeling before their name-saints, the persons who had the picture painted, a man and a woman, opposite each other, ugly figures dressed in the old fashion, who, nevertheless, must have been very fine and intelligent, for they had not spared their money when they entrusted the work to such a master whose equal would not be found in a thousand years. He adds that Hubert and Margaret were both great painters, but inferior to John, and refers the reader for a fuller account of them to the twentieth chapter of his *Leecken Philosophie*, a manuscript which is unfortunately lost.

1584. LOMAZZO, Giovanni Paolo. "Trattato dell' Arte della Pittura." Milano. Another edition, 3 vols., Roma, 1844. English translation by R[ichard] H[aydocke], Oxford, 1598, under the title of "A Tracte containing the artes of curious Paintinge."

1604. MANDER, Carel van. "Het Leven der doorluchtighe Nederlandtsche en Hooghduytsche Schilders." Alckmaer, 1604. (Second edition, Amsterdam, 1618.)

He probably did not commence collecting materials for this work until after he had settled at Haarlem in 1583. He was at Bruges in 1574 before going to Italy, and again after his return in 1582, yet on neither occasion does he seem to have looked at a single early picture—his own paintings show that he did not appreciate them—or to have made the acquaintance of any of the painters then living there, such as Pourbus and the Claeissins. His statements as to the Van Eycks are derived from the works of Van Vaernewyck and Vasari ; from the latter he took several paragraphs, translated, and amplified them. So far as the Van Eycks are concerned, no reliance whatever can be placed on this work.

II

BIOGRAPHY AND ART OF THE VAN EYCKS

1694. MEYSSENS. True Effigies, 1.

1695. BULLART. Académie des Sciences et des Arts, II, 377. Bruxelles.

1715. DE PILES, Roger (obiit 1709). Abrégé de la Vie des Peintres, 2e éd., 334–336. Paris.

1729. WEYERMAN, Jacob Campo. De Levens Beschryvingen der Nederlandsche Konst - Schilders. . . . 's Gravenhage.

1739. MEYSSENS. Portraits of Eminent Painters, plate I.

1771. MICHEL, J. F. X. Histoire de la Vie de P. P. Rubens, 282. Bruxelles.

1822. WAAGEN, Gustav F. Ueber Hubert und Johann van Eyck, VIII, and 271 pp. Breslau.

1823. DE BAST, Liévin A. M. Sur le mérite d'Hubert van Eyck comme peintre. In *Messager des Sciences*, I, 89, 155, 257. Gand.
    De Bast has the merit of being the first Belgian who endeavoured to interest his fellow-countrymen in the early painters and their works.

1825. DE BAST, L. A. M. Notice sur le chef d'œuvre des frères Van Eyck, traduite de l'Allemand, augmentée de notes inédites sur la vie et sur les ouvrages de ces célèbres peintres. 90 pp., 4 plates, and 1 cut. Gand.

1830. REIFFENBERG, Baron Frédéric A. F. T. de. Histoire de la Toison d'Or.

1848. WAAGEN, " Anciennes Écoles Flamandes de Peinture," in *La Renaissance*, x, 115–118. Bruxelles.

1849., LABORDE, Léon E. S. J. de. Les Ducs de Bourgogne. Études sur les lettres, les arts et l'industrie pendant le xve siècle, 2e partie, I et II. Paris, 1849–1851.

1850. KERVYN DE LETTENHOVE. Histoire de Flandre, v, 41–46. Bruxelles.

1854. WAAGEN, G. F. Treasures of Art in Great Britain. 3 vols. London.

1857. CROWE, Joseph A., and CAVALCASELLE, Giovanni Baptista. The early Flemish Painters ; notices of their lives and works, 26–115, and 337–346 ; 5 engr. London.
    The first serious English work on the subject. The documents, etc., quoted, carelessly transcribed.
    Traduction par O. DELEPIERRE, I, 27–114, et II, 119–129. Bruxelles.

1858. LE BLANC, C. Trésor de la Curiosité, II, 473.

1859. SAINSBURY, W. Noel. Original Papers relating to Rubens, 179.

1860. VITET, Louis. Les Van Eyck et Hemling. In *Revue des Deux Mondes*, XXIX, 934–959. Paris.

1860. WAAGEN, G. F. Handbook of Painting. The German, Flemish, and Dutch Schools. Based on the handbook of Kugler ; enlarged and for the most part rewritten, I, 50–64 ; cuts. London. *See* under 1874.

1861. BURGER, W. (Thoré). Le Musée d'Anvers. In *Gazette des Beaux Arts*, XI, 25–30.

1861. LECLERCQ, Emile. Van Eyck et Stuerbout au Musée de Bruxelles. In *Gazette des Beaux Arts*, X, 283–288.

1861. WEALE, W. H. James. Catalogue du Musée de l'Académie de Bruges, 1–20 ; 2 lithographs. Bruges.

1861. WEALE, W. H. James. Notes sur Jean van Eyck. Réfutation des erreurs de M. l'abbé Carton et des théories de M. le comte de Laborde, suivie de nouveaux documents découverts dans les Archives de Bruges. IV and 32 pp. ; I lithograph. Bruxelles. See under 1904.

1862. LOFTIE, W. J. Weale's Notes on John van Eyck. In *The Saturday Review*, 134, February I, pp. 134–135.

1862. WEALE, W. H. James. Bruges et ses Environs.

1863. *RUELENS, Charles. Annotations aux " Anciens Peintres Flamands " de Crowe et Cavalcaselle. CLXXIII pp. Bruxelles.

1864. WORNUM, R. N. The Epochs of Painting : a biographical and critical essay on Painting and Painters, 137–144. 3rd edition. London.

1864. LE JEUNE, Théodore. Amateur de Tableaux, II, 300–301.

1865. *PINCHART, A. Annotations aux " Anciens Peintres Flamands " de Crowe et Cavalcaselle. 162 pp. Bruxelles.
    Valuable and generally reliable.

1865. PAOLI, Betty. Wiene Gemälde Gallerie in ihres Kunsthistorischen Bedeutung. Wien.

1870. SEGUIER, F. P. A Critical and Commercial Dictionary of the Works of Painters, p. 66. London.

1870. WORNUM, R. N. The Pictures by the Old Masters in the National Gallery, photographed by Signor L. Caldesi, with letterpress descriptions, historical, biographical, and critical, 270–275. London.

1872. *CROWE J. A., and CAVALCASELLE, G. B. The Early Flemish Painters. Notices of their lives and works. 2nd edition, 30–134 ; 5 engr. London.
    Many errors in the first edition are rectified in this,

T

and subsequent discoveries made by Pinchart and others added.

Deutsche Ausgabe bearbeitet von Anton SPRINGER, 30–149. Leipzig, 1875.

Italian translation, 32–157. Firenze, 1899.

1873. CROWE, in *Im Neuen Reich*. Leipzig.

1873. HELBIG, Jules. Histoire de la Peinture au pays de Liége, 53–62. Liége. (2nd edition, 50–58. Liége, 1903.)

1874. WAAGEN, G. F. Handbook of Painting. Thoroughly revised and in part rewritten by J. A. CROWE, I, 49–74.

1874. WEALE, W. H. James. The date on which John van Eyck moved his abode from Bruges to Lille. In *The Academy*, July 11, p. 43.

1876. *FROMENTIN, E. Les Maîtres d'autrefois : Belgique, 420–438. Paris. Remarkable from a literary point of view, and as an excellent example of art criticism. Worthless as biography.

1878. *Harper's Magazine*, LVI, 698–704. Hubert and Jean van Eyck.

1882. WOLTMANN, Alfred, and WOERMANN, Karl. Ge-schichte der Malerei, II, 8–22 ; 16 cuts. Leipzig.

1883. WEALE, W. H. James. Les Trésors de l'Art Chrétien en Angleterre. 8 pp. ; 4 facsimiles. In *Revue de l'Art Chrétien*, 3 S., I, 62–66, and 193–195. Bruges.

1884. DIDELOT, M. Étude d'un Triptyque attribué aux Van Eyck provenant de Mauves, près Tournon. Valence.

1885. GILBERT, Josiah. Landscape Art before Claude and Salvator, 146–155. London.

1886. MANTZ, Paul, in *Gazette des Beaux Arts*, 2 P., XXXIII, 513.

1887. BODE, W. La Renaissance au Musée de Berlin ; l'ancienne École Flamande. In *Gazette des Beaux Arts*, 2 P., XXXV, 209–215 ; 1 etching and 4 cuts. Paris.

1887. *CONWAY, W. Martin. Early Flemish Artists and their Predecessors on the Lower Rhine, 95–97, 117–159, and 271–275 ; 3 cuts. London.

1888. BODE, Dr. W. Ein neu erworbenes Profilbild des Heilands von Jan van Eyck in der Berliner Gallerie. In *Zeitschrift für Christliche Kunst*, I, 347–352. Düs-seldorf.

1888. HYMANS, H. Le Saint François de Jean van Eyck. In *Gazette des Beaux Arts*, 2 P., XXXVII, 78–83.

1889. WEALE, W. H. J., and RICHTER, J. P. Catalogue of Lord Northbrook's Collection, 105–108.

1890–1900. REBER, Professor F. von, and A. BAYERSDORFER, in Classical Picture Gallery, I, 31; IV, 121; V, 85, 121; VII, 121; VIII, 85, 121–132; X, 79; XI, 92, 121, illustrate various works by the Van Eycks.

1893. SEDELMEYER. Catalogue of 300 Paintings, pp. 43–44. Paris.

1894. SEIDLITZ. Porträt-Werk, I, 9.

1896. EASTLAKE, C. L. Pictures in the National Gallery, II, 107–109.

1897. MANTZ, Paul. La Peinture Française, pp. 180–181.

1898. *LABAN, Ferdinand. Das Gleichgewicht der innenseiten Flügel des Genter Altars. In Zeitschrift für bildende Kunst, X, 33–43. Leipzig.

1898. *KAEMMERER, L. Hubert und Ian van Eyck. 118 pp.; 88 phototypes. Bielefeld.

1899. WEALE, W. H. J. Van Eyck and Memlinc. In the Weekly Register, July 29. London.

1899. FRIEDLAENDER, Max. Austellung von Kunstwerken des Mittelalters und der Renaissance aus Berliner Privatbesetz: Malerei, 5, 6, 7. Berlin.

1899. *VAN DER HAEGHEN, Victor. Mémoire sur des documents faux relatifs aux anciens peintres, 26–27, 78–87, 94–97, 111–114, 122. Bruxelles.

1899. *SEECK, Otto. Die charakteristischen Unterschiede der Brüder Van Eyck. 77 pp.; 1 cut. Berlin. Extract from Abhandlungen der königl. Sächsischen Gesellschaft der Wissenschaftcn, III. Göttingen.

1899. PHILLIPS, C. The Picture Gallery of the Hermitage, St. Petersburg. In The North American Review, CLXIX, October, 454, November, 712.

1900. EASTLAKE, G. L. Pictures in the National Gallery, with descriptive text. Munich.

1900. KUHN, T. Albert. Allgemeines Kunstgeschichte, 288–301. Einsiedeln.

1900. VOLL, Karl. Altes und Neues über die Brüder Van Eyck, in Repertorium für Kunstwissenschaft, XXIII, 92. Berlin.

1900. *SEECK, O. Ein neues Zeugnis über die Brüder Van Eyck. In Kunstchronik, N.F., XI, 66–71 and 80–87. Leipzig.

1900. *VOLL, Karl. Die Werke des Jan Van Eyck, eine kritische Studie. XVI and 136 pp. Strassburg.

1900. WEALE, W. H. James. Les frères van Eyck. 6 pp. ; 2 phototypes. In *Revue de l'Art Chrétien*, 4 S., XI, 281-286. Bruges.

1900. WEALE, W. H. James. Hubert Van Eyck. 5 pp. ; 2 phototypes. In *Zeitschrift für bildende Kunst*, N.F., XI, 251-255. Leipzig.

1900. WEALE, W. H. James. The Van Eycks. 6 pp. In *The Nineteenth Century*, 785-790. London.

1901. SEDELMEYER. One Hundred Masters, p. 16. Paris.

1901. MACCOLL, D. S. The Painting of Flanders. In *The Saturday Review*, XCI, 266.

1901. SEECK, O. Zu dem Werke des Hubert van Eyck. 3 pp. In *Kunstchronik*, N.F., XII, 257-262. Leipzig.

1901. WEALE, W. H. James. Hubert van Eyck. 9 pp. In *Gazette des Beaux Arts*, 3 P., XXV, 474-482. Paris.

1901. *BODE, W. Jan van Eycks Bildnis eines Burgundischen Kammerherrn. In *Jahrbuch der Preussische Kunstsammlungen*, XXII, 115-131; 1 engr. and 2 phototypes. Berlin.

1902. *DURRIEU, Count Paul. Heures de Turin : 45 Feuillets à Peintures provenant des Très Belles Heures de Jean de France, Duc de Berry.

1902. WARBURG, in *Jahrbuch der Königlichen Preussischen Kunstsammlungen*, XXIII, 247-266.

1902. ROOSES, Max. De Teekeningen der Vlaamsche Meesters. In *Onze Kunst*, January 1, 3-8.

1902. LABAN, Ferdinand. Für Hubert und Jan van Eyck. In *Kunstchronik*, N.F., XIV, 297-299, 525.

1902. *WEALE, W. H. J. Catalogue de l'Exposition de Tableaux Anciens à Bruges, xiv-xviii.

1902. *HULIN, Georges. Catalogue critique des tableaux flamands des xive, xve, et xvie siècles exposés à Bruges, Nos. 7-16 et 213, pp. 2-4 et 58. Gand.

1902. *PHILLIPS, Claude. Netherlandish Art at Bruges. In *The Daily Telegraph*, August 23.

1902. The Exhibition of Flemish Art at Bruges, in *The Athenæum*, September 13 and 20, pp. 355-356, 388-389.

1902. PHILLIPS, C. Impressions of the Bruges Exhibition. In the *Fortnightly Review*, October, 588-603.

1902. HYMANS, Henri. L'Exposition des Primitifs Flamands à Bruges, 12-19 ; 1 helioengr., 6 phototypes, 2 engr., and 1 cut. Paris.

1902. *DE SMET, J. L'Adoration de l'Agneau par les frères

Van Eyck. 10 pp.; 9 phototypes and 1 facsimile. In *Inventaire archéologique de Gand*, 241–250. Gand.

1902. SCHOTTMÜLLER, Frida, Eine Verschollene Kreuzigung von Jan van Eyck. In *Jahrbuch der Königlichen Preussischen Kunstsammlungen*, XXIII, pp. 33–35.

1902. *PHILLIPS, Claude. Impressions of the Bruges Exhibition, in *The Fortnightly Review*, October, pp. 588–603.

1902. DE SCHOTTER, Louis. Les Primitifs Flamands. In *L'Epreuve*, 292.

1902. MARKS, Alfred. The Flora of the Van Eycks. In *The Athenæum*, November 1 and December 13.

1902. WEALE, W. H. James. The Flora of the Van Eycks. In *The Athenæum*, December 6, and March 14 and 28, 1903.

1902. *HULIN, Georges. L'Atelier de Hubrecht van Eyck et les Heures de Turin. 6 pp. In *Annuaire de la Société pour le progrès des études philosophiques et historiques*. Gand.

1903. *FRIEDLAENDER, Max J. Meisterwerke der Niederländischen Malerei des xv und xvi Jahrhunderts auf der Ausstellung zu Brügge, 1902. München.

1903. *WEALE, W. H. James. The Early Painters of the Netherlands, illustrated by the Bruges Exhibition of 1902. In *The Burlington Magazine*, I, 48. London.

1903. WITTING, Felix. Von Kunst und Christentum. Strassburg.

1903. Art History in the Netherlands. In the *Edinburgh Review*, April.

1903. WEALE, Frances C. L. M. Hubert and John van Eyck. viii and 32 pp.; 1 photoengr. and 20 phototypes. London.
   See review in *The Athenæum*, 1903, August 22.

1903. *MARKS, A. Hubert and John van Eyck: the question of their collaboration considered. 38 pp.; 3 phototypes. London.
   See WEALE in *The Burlington Magazine*, IV, 98.

1903. *DURRIEU, Paul. Les débuts des Van Eyck. 32 pp., 1 helio-engraving, and 14 phototypes. Paris.

1904. WITT, Mary H. The German and Flemish Masters in the National Gallery, 5–23; 2 phototypes. London.

1904. *WEALE, W. H. James. Popular opinions concerning the Van Eycks examined. 9 pp.; 5 phototypes. In *The Burlington Magazine*, IV, 26–33. London.

1904. *WEALE, W. H. James. The death of John van Eyck: new discovery. In *The Burlington Magazine*, IV, 295.

1904. *HULIN, Georges, de Loo. L'Exposition des primitifs Français au point de vue de l'influence des frères Van Eyck sur la Peinture Française et Provençale.

1904. *SIX, J. A propos d'un repentir de Hubert van Eyck. In *Gazette des Beaux Arts*, 3 P., XXXI, 177–187; 7 phototypes.

1904. *DVOŘÁK, Max. Das Rätsel der Kunst der Brüder Van Eyck. 150 pp. ; 7 plates and 65 illustrations in the text. In *Jahrbuch des Kunsthistorischen Sammlungen des allerhöchsten Kaiserhauses*, XXIV, 162–317. Wien.

1904. *KERN, G. Joseph. Die Grundzüge der linear perspectivischen Darstellung in der Kunst der Gebrüder Van Eyck und ihrer Schule. Die perspectivische Projektion. 14 plates and 3 cuts. Leipzig.
An important contribution to the material for controlling the dates assigned to Eyckian paintings.

1904. WEALE, W. H. James. Paintings . . . formerly in the Arundel Collection. In the *Burlington Magazine*, V, 190–198 ; VI, 249 ; 3 phototypes.

1904. TSCHUDI, H. von. Die Gemälde Galerie zu Berlin, 1–12. Berlin, 1904.

1904. *HULIN. L'Art Français-Flamand au début du XVᵉ siècle et la révolution artistique due aux frères Van Eyck. In *Bulletin de la Société d'Histoire*, XII, 168–205. Gand.

1905. BROCKWELL, M. W., in *The Athenæum*, July 29, pp. 154–155.

1905. *WURZBACH, Alfred von. Niederländisches Künstler-Lexikon, auf Grund archivalischer Forschungen bearbeitet, I, 502–525. Wien.
This account of the Van Eycks and their works is far fuller and more accurate than in any other dictionary.

1905. BODENHAUSEN. Aus der Werkstätte des Hubert van Eyck. In *Jahrbuch der Preussischen Kunstsammlungen*, XXVI, 111–115. Deals with the painting in the collection of Baron Franchetti at Venice.

1905. *DOEHLEMANN, Karl. Die Perspektive der Brüder Van Eyck. In *Zeitschrift für Mathematik*, 419–425. Leipzig.

1906. BOUCHOT. L'Exposition des Van Eyck à Gand. In *L'Art et les Artistes*, March, pp. 176–184.

1906. HEINS, A. La Plus Ancienne vue de Gand . . . representée sur un volet du retable de l'Agneau Mystique. In *Bulletin de la Société d'Histoire et d'Arch. de Gand*, XIV, 115.

1906. FRIEDLAENDER, Max J. Die Leihausstellung in der Guildhall zu London. In *Repertorium*, XXIX, 573.

1906. *VOLL, K. Altniederländische Malerei von Ian van Eyck bis Memling : ein entwickelungsgeschichtlicher Versuch, 7–50 ; 5 phototypes. Leipzig.

1906. GOLDSCHMIDT. Das Rätsel der Kunst der Brüder van Eyck von Max Dvořák. In *Repertorium*, XXIX, 367–369.

1906. PHILLIPS, C. Flemish Art at the Guildhall. In *The Daily Telegraph*, May 3.

1906. WARD, T. Humphry. Flemish Art at the Guildhall. In *The Times*, May 4.

1907. VAN DER HORST, J. J. Hoe Jan van Eyck de oliverf fond. 61 pp. Aelst.

1907. SCHMIDT-DEGENER, F. Les " Sept Vertus " de Jean van Eyck au Musée Néerlandais à Amsterdam. In *L'Art Flamand et Hollandais*, IV, 16–30 and 67–79 ; 16 phototypes. Bruxelles.

1907. SEECK. Die Beweinung mit den Stifter. In *Zeitschrift für bildende Kunst*, N.F., XVIII, 206–210.

1907. P. BERGMANS. Note sur la représentation du retable de l'Agneau mystique des Van Eyck, en tableau vivant à Gand en 1458. 8 pp. Gand.

1907. REINACH, S. Apollo : an illustrated Manual of the History of Art. English translation by F. SIMMONDS, 216–223. London.

1907. *HEINS, Armand. Une vue de Gand peinte par Hubert van Eyck. With illustrations. Gand.
Based on a paper read by the author before the Société d'Histoire et d'Archéologie de Gand on February 11, 1906.

1907. FOURCAUD, L. de. Les frères van Eyck. In André Michel, *Histoire de l'Art*, III, 173–214. 1 collo- and 20 photo-types. Paris.
Carelessly written ; repeats French misstatements long since refuted ; shows very slight acquaintance with recent works on the Van Eycks published outside France. His judgment evidently warped by national

vanity, as displayed in the following passage : "En France et par la France s'est révélé le génie Flamand et s'est éveillée la première gloire Flamande," p. 174.

1907. KONODY, P. G. The Brothers Van Eyck. Bell's Miniature Series of Painters.

1907. BOUCHOT, H. Le paysage chez les primitifs. In *Gazette des Beaux Arts*, XXXVIII, 456–481.

1907. STRANGE, E. F. The Exhibition of the Golden Fleece at Bruges. In *The Connoisseur*, XIX, 28–33.

REVIEWS OF WEALE'S "HUBERT AND JOHN VAN EYCK"

1907. The Brothers Van Eyck. In the *Guardian*, December 4.

The writer of the review says that the original frame, bearing John's signature, of the "Old Man" in the National Gallery, is not painted to imitate marble, but gilded ! !

"The Head of a Man in the Berlin Gallery has no brown beard ; he is clean shaven." Hardly ; the stubble of the beard is brown. We do not consider the figure identical with the alleged Hubert in the Prado "Fountain of Living Water."

1907. ROMMEL, Henri. L'Œuvre des Van Eyck, par James Weale. In *Annales de la Société d'Emulation de Bruges*, LVII, 14.

1907. *The Daily Mail*, December 14, assumes that Hubert and John worked in collaboration, a theory completely disposed of in the present volume. Prefers Jan to John, although the form Jan was, so far as we know, never used by himself or by any of his contemporaries.

1908. BINYON, L. Carpaccio and Van Eyck. In *The Saturday Review*, January 4, CV, 10–11.

1908. Hubert and John van Eyck. In *The Times*, January 16. The dates not of three or four, but of eleven pictures, are positively fixed.

Believes that the Adam and Eve and the paintings on the upper part and reverse of those panels are certainly John's work. We should like to make our view clearer. That the two figures are exclusively John's work, direct from Nature. For the other portions of these panels he probably made use of Hubert's sketches.

1908. *The Nation*, January 18.

1908. *The Connoisseur.* One of his strongest arguments was based on the date of the picture at Chatsworth.

This is misleading. The inscription Weale did believe in, but he has always thought that the entire surface of the picture was covered by later work.

The writer does not seem to realise that many works may be authentic without being documentarily authenticated.

Weale did not anglicise the family names, but has adhered to the practice, formerly universal, of translating the Christian names.

1908. *Revue de l'Art Chrétien,* p. 58.
1908. RINDER, F. A Book of the Day. In *The Daily News,* February 24.

" Mistakenly no translation is given " of the documents and quotations. It would have added to the bulk of the book. The summaries give all the information.

1908. *Morning Post,* January 20. The Masters of Maaseyck.
1908. *BROCKWELL, in the *Athenæum,* April 18, points out several mistakes.
1908. Two Art Books. In *The Westminster Gazette,* July 4.
1908. *MACLAGAN, Eric R. D., in *The Burlington Magazine,* XII, 247–249.
1909. " B." Hubert et Jean van Eyck. In *L'Art flamand et hollandais,* XI, 203. Bruxelles.

1908. FIERENS-GEVAERT. Les Primitifs Flamands, I.
1908. HYMANS, H. Les Van Eyck ; Biographie critique. One of the series " Les Grands Artistes." Paris. 127 pp. ; 24 phototypes.

A facile writer, but negligent. Repeats the Cambrai myth. Pretends to identify localities (Assisi) and persons (Man with the Pinks, as John of Bavaria !)

1908. DE ROME, N. La part d'Hubert van Eyck dans le retable de l'Agneau mystique. In *Le Musée,* v, 56–61.
1908. SAINTENOY, Paul. L'Eglise Saint Jacques de Compostella et le décor architectural de " l'Annonciation " de Jean van Eyck. In *Annales de l'Académie royale d'Archéologie de Belgique,* IX, 238. Anvers.
1908. HULIN, in *Kunstchronik,* N.F., xix, 582–583.
1908. BOUCHOT, H. La condition sociale des Peintres du xiiie au xve siècle. In *Revue des Deux Mondes,* XLIII, 153–177.

1908. MONT, Pol. de. Early Painters of the Netherlands. Translated by Edward G. Hawke, London, p. 1–14.

1908. GRANT, J. Kirby, in *The Connoisseur*, September, p. 4.

1909. WALLENSTEIN, Victor. Die Raumbehandlung in der Oberdeutschen und Niederländischen Tafelmalerei der ersten Hälfte des xv Jahrhunderts, 84–86. Strassburg.

1909. PHILIPPI, A. Die grossen Maler in Wort und Farbe. Leipzig.

1909. WAUTERS, A. J. Le retable de l'Agneau. In *Revue de Belgique*.
Deduces from Münzer that it is entirely by Hubert, with exception of the predella.

1909. CONWAY, Martin. Early Flemish Painters. In *The Quarterly Review*, 156–161.

1909. *RUPP, Fritz. Die angefochtenen Bilder des Jan van Eyck. In *Repertorium für Kunstwissenschaft*, XXXII, 480–496; illustration.

1910. Encyclopædia Britannica, x, 90–91. The article on the two brothers is hopelessly out of date, and is probably the most inaccurate biographical account of them that has appeared in any book published during the last quarter of a century.

1910. DURAND-GRÉVILLE, E. Hubert et Jean van Eyck. Bruxelles.

1910. CUST, L. Hubert et Jean van Eyck, par E. Durand-Gréville. In *The Burlington Magazine*, XVII, 125.

1910. La question des Van Eyck et le retable de Saint Bavon. In *Le Bien Public*, Gand, March 29.

1910. WEALE, W. H. James. John van Eyck painting at Cambrai in 1413 : an apocryphal story refuted. In *The Burlington Magazine*, XVI, 281.

1910. WEALE, W. H. James. Three Portraits attributed to John van Eyck. In the *Burlington Magazine*, XVII, 177.

1910. WAUTERS, A. J. Le Maître du retable de l'Agneau mystique à Saint Bavon de Gand.

1910. CUST, L. Hubert van Eyck. Review of Wauters' "Le maître du retable de l'Agneau mystique." In *The Burlington Magazine*, XVII, 39–40.

1910. DUCLOS, Adolphe. Bruges : histoire et souvenirs, 367–370. Bruges.

1910. STRAATSMANN, Karl. Das Aufnahmen Architekturen, Leipzig, I, 176 ; II, 122, 134, 188.

1910. ROLFS, Wilhelm. Geschichte der Malerei Neapels. Leipzig.

1910. GOEKOOP-DE JONGH, Johanna. In *Elzeviers geillustreerd Maandschrift*, April.

1910 M ONOD, Fr. Exposition Nationale de Maîtres anciens à Londres. In *Gazette des Beaux Arts*, '4 P. IV, March, p. 242.

1910. DURRIEU, P. Quelques portraits historiques du début du XVᵉ siècle. In *Gazette des Beaux Arts*, 4 P. III, 461–469.

1910. DE FIGUEIREDO, José. Arte portugueza primitiva. Lisboa.

1910. REINACH, S. Jean VI. Paléologue et H. van Eyck. In *Revue Archéologique*, 4 S., XVI, 369; illustrations.

1910. *VOLL. Frauenbildnesse von Jan van Eyck und Memling. In *Vergleichende Gemälde-Studien*, N.F. 21–27. München.

1910. *REINACH, THEODORE. L'Inscription du " Retable de l'Agneau " des Frères van Eyck. In *Gazette des Beaux Arts*, 4 P. IV, July, pp. 5–10.

1911. SIX, J. Les portraits de princes sur le polyptique des Van Eyck. In *Revue Archéologique*, II, 401–418. Paris.

1911. MAETERLINCK, L. Un problème Eyckien. In *Chronique des Arts*, p. 205.

1911. HULIN, G. A propos de quelques portraits du commencement du XVᵉ siècle, Gand.

1911. BASCHET, J. La Peinture flamande. Paris.

1911. BODE, W. Great Masters of Dutch and Flemish Painting. Translated by Margaret Clarke.

1911. HEIDRICH, E. Altniederländische Malerei. Jena.

1911. PHILIPPI, A. De grootste Meesters in de Schilderkunst. Leiden.

1911. RAULIN, J. M. La Nativité d'Autun et quelques autres portraits du chevalier de Bourgogne Nicolas Rolin. In *Les Marches de l'Est*. Paris-Nancy, II, 670–686, et III.

1911. VAN DEN GHEYN. L'origine gantoise du retable de l'Agneau mystique. In *Bulletin de la Société d'Histoire de Gand*, XIX, 171–190.

1911. POSSE, Hans. Die Gemäldegalerie des Kaiser Friedrich Museums. Vollständige beschreibende Katalog mit Abbildungen sämtlicher Gemälde. Zweite Abteilung.

1911. REYLANDER, Dr. Curt. Die Entwicklung des characteristischen und Sinnbildnischen in der niederländischen Malerei des xv Jahrhunderts. Tilsit.

1911. VON BEZOLD, Gustav. Beiträge zur Geschichte des Bildnisses : Die Zeit des objectiven Bildnisses ; in *Mitteilungen der Germanisches Museum*, 111–114. To Hubert three central figures and the singing angels. To John, Adam and Eve.

1911. REINACH, S. Portrait de Bonne d'Artois par van Eyck. In *Revue Archéologique*, 4ᵉ S. XVI. January–February, p. 172.

1911. DOEHLEMANN. Die Entwicklung der Perspective in der Altniederländischen Kunst. In *Repertorium für Kunstwissenschaft*, XXXIV, 399–406. 2 illustrations.

1911. PHILLIPS, C. The Adoration of the Lamb. In the *Daily Telegraph*, July 5.

1911. ROBLOT-DELONDRE. Jardin d'Amour de Philippe le Bon. In *Revue Archéologique*, May–June, p. 420–7. Refers to a picture (No. 4021) in the collection at Versailles.

1912. WEALE, J., CYRIL, M. Van Eyck.

1912. NASSE, Hermann. Un Portrait de Michelle de France. In *Revue Archéologique*, May–June, 406–412.

1912. BROCKWELL, M. W., in *The Morning Post*, July 4.

1912. DE PAUW, N. Gand en 1913. Concerns Hubert.

1912. DE PAUW, N. Gand en 1913. In *Bulletin de la Société d'Histoire et d'Archéologie*, § VIII, pp. 12–15.

1912. BERGMANS, Paul. Hommage International aux Frères Hubert et Jean van Eyck. In *Gand Exposition : Organe officiel de l'Exposition Universelle et Internationale de Gand*, 1913, XIII, pp. 157–160, gives a photographic representation of the model of the proposed monument.

III

DISCOVERIES AND TECHNIQUE OF THE VAN EYCKS

1762. WALPOLE, Horace. Anecdotes of Painting in England, I, 24–29. Strawberry Hill, 1762, and four later editions. " If Van Eyck was ever in England, would it not be probable that he learned the secret of using oil here, and took the honour of the invention to himself, as we were then a country little known in the world of arts, nor at leisure enough, from the confusions of the times, to claim the discovery of a secret which soon made such fortune abroad ? " Quite amusing.

1847. EASTLAKE, Charles L. Materials for a history of oil-painting. London.

1878. MILANESI, Gaetano. Commentaria alla Vita di Antonello da Messina. In VASARI, Le Vite, II, 575–589. Firenze.

1891. LAURIE, Arthur. On the durability of pictures painted with oils and varnishes. With observations by W. F. REID, HOLMAN HUNT, &c. In *Journal of the Society of Arts*, XXXIX, 392–399 and 437. London.

1899. HERRINGHAM, Christiana J. The Book of the Art of Cennino Cennini, 1899, p. 225. " Van Eyck and Cennino were contemporaries. Van Eyck's secret must be sought in the preparation and materials of his varnish, and the method by which he conquered the viscousness of varnish, so as to be able to paint in such small touches of such extreme sharpness without impairing its brilliancy and durability."

1901. ALLAN, Hugolin. Van Eyck's Discovery. In the *Architectural Review*, X, 213–217. London.

1902. *HERRINGHAM, Christiana J. Van Eyck's discovery. In the *Architectural Review*, xi. 165–169.

Combats Allan's view that the discovery was merely the purification of oil by washing, and believes that a principal part of his method consisted in the incorporation of a very perfect varnish with the pigments.

1904. DALBON, Charles. Les procédés des Primitifs, les Origines de la Peinture à l'huile. Paris.

1904. NICOLLE, Marcel. Origines de la Peinture à l'huile. In *Bulletin de l'Art Ancien et Moderne*, pp. 237–238.

1905. WURZBACH, Alfred von. Die Erfindung der Oelmalerei. In his " Niederländisches Künstler-Lexikon," I, 515, 516. Wien.

1907. *LAURIE, A. Oils, Varnishes, and Mediums used in the painting of Pictures. In *Journal of the Society of Arts*, LV, 557–567 ; with observations by W. F. REID, etc. London.

1908. Permanence of Colour: Van Eyck. In the *Athenæum*, November 7.

1909. *HOLMES, C. J., "Notes on the Science of Picture-Making."

P. 44 : "To hold the balance evenly needs no little judgment, and few besides John van Eyck, two or three Dutch masters, and Chardin, have done it with complete success."

P. 194 : "The invention of Hubert and John van Eyck was the discovery of a medium that was at once permanent, colourless, and capable of rendering accurately the most minute detail."

P. 196 : "So brilliant, indeed, does the effect sometimes become that one is tempted to wonder whether the medium of the Van Eycks contained any varnish at all, and whether their results were not produced simply with linseed oil and sunshine."

1910. THOMSON, George. The Permanence of Pictures. In *The Athenæum*, January 29, p. 132.

1912. *KERN, G. J. Perspektive and Bildarchitektur bei Jan van Eyck. In *Repertorium für Kunstwissenschaft* XXXV, 27-64.

A COMPARATIVE TABLE

A COMPARATIVE TABLE

Enabling the reader to identify in this book the pictures enumerated by Weale in his *Hubert and John van Eyck: their Life and Work*, published in 1908.

No.	1908.	1908. Pages.	1912. No.	1912. Pages.
	The Polyptych: The Adoration of the Lamb	{ At Ghent, Berlin, and Brussels	29–56	I	35–66
1	Portrait of B. Nicholas Albergati	Vienna	57–63	XI	103–107
2	Portrait of a Man (Léal Souvenir)	National Gallery	63–65	XII	108–109
3	Our Lady and Child	Ince Hall	65–67	XIII	109–111
4	Portrait of a Man	National Gallery	68–69	XIV	112–113
5	Portraits of John Arnolfini and Joan Cenani, his wife	National Gallery	69–75	XV	114–119
6	Our Lady and Child enthroned, Saint Donatian, Saint George, and the Donor	} Bruges	75–85	{ XVI and XXV	120–126, 151–153
7	Portrait of John De Leeuw, Goldsmith	Vienna	86–88	XVII	127–129
8	Saint Barbara	Antwerp	88–90	XVIII	129–131
9	Our Lady and Child by a Fountain	Antwerp	90–92	XIX	131–133
10	Portrait of Margaret van Eyck	Bruges	93–94	XX	133–135
11	Our Lady and Child, and the Donor	Kessel-Loo	95–105	XXI	135–144
12	Portrait of a Goldsmith	Hermannstadt	106–107	IV	75–76

No.	Title	Collection	107–110	II	67–69
13	A Donor protected by Saint Anthony	Copenhagen	107–110		
14	Our Lady and Child, Saint Elisabeth of Hungary, Saint Barbara, and a Carthusian	Baroness G. de Rothschild, Paris	110–114	V	76–80
15	Our Lady and Child and Chancellor Rolin	Louvre	114–119	VIII	87–92
16	The Annunciation	St. Petersburg	119–122	X	98–102
17	Portrait of an Esquire of the Order of Saint Anthony	Berlin	122–124	VI	80–82
18	Our Lady and Child, Saint Katherine, Saint Michael, and the Donor	Dresden	125–130	VII	82–87
19A	The Vision of Saint Francis	Johnson Collection, Philadelphia	131–133	IX	93–97
19B	The Vision of Saint Francis	Turin	133–135	XXXV	165–166
20	Our Lady and Child in a Church	Berlin	135–138	XXXVI	167–169
21	Our Lady and Child	Frankfort	138–139	XXII	145–146
22	Portrait of John Arnolfini	Berlin	140–141	XXIII	146–147
23	Portrait of Sir Baldwin de Lannoy, Lord of Molembaix	Berlin	141–143	XXIV	148–150
24	Our Lady and Child, Saint Barbara, and a Carthusian	Berlin	143–146	XXXVII	169–172
25 / 26	Calvary, and the Last Judgment	St. Petersburg	146–150	XXVI–XXVII	153–157
27	Christ on the Cross, the Blessed Virgin, and Saint John	Berlin	151–152	XXVIII	157–159
28	The Three Marys at the Sepulchre	Cook Collection, Richmond	153–157	III	69–74
29	Our Lady and Child by a Fountain	Berlin	157–158	XXXVIII	172–174
30	Our Lady and Child	Earl of Northbrook	159–160	XXIX	159–160
31	Our Lady and Child	Metropolitan Museum, New York	160–161	XXXIX	174–175
32	The Fountain of Living Water	Madrid	162–165	XL	175–179
33A	The Holy Face	Munich	166	XLI	179–180
33B	The Holy Face	Berlin	167–168	XLII	180–181
33C	The Holy Face	Bruges	168–169	XLIII	181–183
33D	The Holy Face	Oppolzer Collection, Innsbruck	170	XLIV	183
34	Head of a Man	Berlin	170–171	XXXI	162
35	A Donor	Leipzig	171	XLV	183–184
36	Portrait of an Ecclesiastic	Mr. J. P. Morgan, New York	171–172	XLVI	184–185
37	An Old Man	Mr. Alfred Brown	173	XLVII	185–186

INDEX

INDEX

Ouwater, Albert von, xiv
Overloope, Simon Peter van, collection, 189

P., Sir H., collection, 231
Paar, Count Louis, at Vienna, collection, 169, 212
Padua, Museo Civico, Calvary, 186, 187
— collection of Messer Leonico Tomeo at, 201
Paele, Canon G. Van der, his portrait in altar-piece at Bruges, xxvii, 41 note, 120–126, 151–153
Palencia, cathedral of, 177, 202
Palmettos, 70, 94, 97, 166, 227
Paradise, 139
Paris, pictures taken by the French to, 120, 127
— the Louvre: Madonna and Child and the Chancellor Rolin, 80, 87–92, 192, 219, 222–223, 225–227
— — portrait of Isabella of Portugal, 203
— — portrait of John the Fearless, Duke of Burgundy, 204, 229
— — portrait of Philippe III, Duke of Burgundy, 204
— — silver-point drawing of a Man, 215
— — two silver-point drawings in, 60, 211
— National Library, John II of France, 229
Parma, baptistery at, 100, 222
Parral, convent of Our Lady at, 175, 177
Parsons, John M., collection, 183
Patenir, Joachim, xiv, 166, 186
Pattens, 197
Paul IV, Pope, 142
Pavement, 88, 136 ; storied, 99
Peacocks, 88
Perrant, John, painter, 143
Perspective, observations on, 223–224
Peutin, John, goldsmith of Bruges, xxxvi, xxxvii, 17, 19, 148
Pharaoh's daughter, 100
Phillips, Sir Claude, xv., 102, 144, 156–157, 161, 178–179, 236, 292
Pichegru, 59
Pinchart, vii, 289
Plaoutine, General, collection at St. Petersburg, 161–162, 199

Ploos van Amstel collection, 129
Polychromed statue of Saint Anthony, by Hubert van Eyck, 5
Polychromed statues by John van Eyck, xxxviii, 18
Polyptych of the Adoration of the Lamb terminated and placed in the church of St. Bavo, Ghent. See Ghent
Poortier, Hubert van Eyck engaged on a painting for altar erected by Robert, 5, 68
Portejoie, poursuivant, 12
Portraiture, early, 229
— observations on, 229–230
Portraits of the Van Eycks, observations on the alleged, 230–232
Portugal, Isabella of, her portrait painted by John van Eyck, 13 ; her marriage contract, xxvi, 14 ; her portrait at Brussels, 213 ; her portrait at Ghent, 205 ; her portrait in the Louvre, 203–204
— John I, King of, xxvi
— plants in, 96
Portugaloise, la belle, 199
Prague, Von Lanna sale at, 215
Prévost, John, painter, xiv
Private collections. See Collections, private
Prophet Micah, 36, 52
Prophet Zechariah, 36, 52
Purgatory, 206
Put, A. Van de, xv

Quédeville, collection, 164

Rabbits, 222
Ravary, Michael, payment made to him for rent of a house at Lille in which John van Eyck at one time resided, xxxiv
Reade, Charles, his Cloister and the Hearth, xiii
Receivers of Flanders, accounts of the, vii
Reinach, Theodore, 299
Reinhold von Liphart, collection, 163
Rembrandt, inventory of, 206
Renty, poursuivant, 12
Restel, 14
Resurrection, the, 117
Rheims, 55, 222
Rhine, view of the river, 225
Ribadeu, 14
Ritzenberg, Madam Amelia von, collection, 183

THE END

BY W. H. JAMES WEALE

HUBERT AND JOHN VAN EYCK. THEIR LIFE AND WORK. With Forty-one Photogravure Plates and Ninety-nine other Illustrations. Five Guineas net.

SOME PRESS OPINIONS

Times.—" A masterly work, which will long remain the leading authority upon the lives and work of the two brothers who fixed the lines on which northern art was to develop itself during almost two centuries. All students of early Flemish art will unite in congratulating Mr. Weale on the completion of the book. It represents and sums up the labour of fifty years ungrudgingly given."

Daily Chronicle.—" His book is a model to all future scientific art historians : it is a volume indispensable to all who concern themselves with connoisseurship or the history of art. A remarkable book."

Studio.—" This monumental work, with its wealth of fine photogravure plates and other illustrations, the value of which to the student of Flemish painting it is impossible to over-estimate."

Athenæum.—" In the monumental work before us we have one of the most authoritative and scholarly works that have been published in any language for many years. The individuality of the author, his sincerity and his knowledge, are stamped on every page."

Connoisseur.—" Mr. Weale has compiled an astounding biography, a catalogue of all that has been written about the Van Eycks from the fifteenth century to the present day. A monument of original research."

Daily Mail.—" An imposing volume. Mr. Weale has built up, stone by stone, fact by fact, his monumental structure. The volume contains excellent reproductions of all pictures and sketches by and ascribed to the brothers Van Eyck."

Morning Post.—" Practically the research of a lifetime. It is not difficult to account for the fascination exercised by the subject. Undeniably the last word in Eyckian criticism, and should prove invaluable to every student of Netherlandish art."

JOHN LANE THE BODLEY HEAD LIMITED, VIGO ST.,W. 1.

BY W. H. JAMES WEALE

HUBERT AND JOHN VAN EYCK
..THEIR LIFE AND WORK..

PRESS OPINIONS (*continued*)

Outlook.—" This really excellent book is about as valuable as it well can be."

Nation.—" An ample and beautifully illustrated volume. Careful and admirable reproductions of the paintings accompany the text."

Spectator.—" This large book is a monument of learning, and in the future every one who desires to study Van Eyck in detail must consult it."

Daily News.—" Intimate with details of mediæval Flemish life, scrupulously accurate, Mr. Weale has, with untiring zeal, sought, discovered, and sifted original documentary evidence, so that the sum of our positive knowledge should be as complete as may be."

Burlington Magazine.—" The labour of a man who has consecrated the greater part of a long and almost incredibly diligent life to the study of the art and archæology of the Netherlands. It presents in perfect methodical form, and with a restraint and reticence as rare as they are admirable, the sum of positive knowledge on the subject, gradually accumulated by Mr. Weale himself. He has produced a book absolutely indispensable to all students of the early painting of the Netherlands, and one that completely supersedes the majority of its predecessors."

Pall Mall Gazette.—" When such an authority on Flemish Art as Mr. Weale produces a book on one of its greatest artists, we are prepared for something unusually good, and no one will be disappointed in this fine work. The numerous photogravures are reproduced in a style which makes the book a beautiful possession."

Westminster Gazette.—" An exhaustive work. One of the most interesting features of the book is the discussion and analysis of the architectural details which were always so carefully recorded by the Van Eycks."

Academy.—" No one has brought more patience, enthusiasm, and critical acumen to bear upon that difficult subject. We should like to express our congratulations to Mr. Weale in a chorus of praise."

JOHN LANE THE BODLEY HEAD LIMITED, VIGO ST.,W. 1.

BY W. H. JAMES WEALE

HUBERT AND JOHN VAN EYCK
..THEIR LIFE AND WORK..

PRESS OPINIONS (*continued*)

Standard.—"The most complete book ever done on the Van Eycks. When it becomes a question of an authoritative volume on early masters of the Low Countries give us Mr. Weale. He has a genuine student's love of his business. The illustrations have been so chosen that the best work of the pious and gifted brothers is represented in this volume as adequately as black and white can give it."

World.—"The publication of an exhaustive and authoritative book by Mr. Weale on the life and work of Hubert and John Van Eyck is an event of no slight interest."

Quarterly Review.—"Among the hard-working students to whose labours present-day art-lovers owe so much, none has been more meritorious than Mr. W. H. James Weale."

Glasgow Herald.—"A work which cannot fail to be welcome to every student of the fascinating subject which Mr. Weale may almost be said to have made his own, so replete is it with historical learning and critical acumen, for which the author has always been distinguished. It must always be of the utmost value and importance. The arrangement of Mr. Weale's book is excellent."

Birmingham Daily Post.—"The author of this truly sumptuous work has earned the right to be considered the standard authority upon the life and works of the early Netherlandish masters, and he has earned it by patient investigation pursued with untiring energy. The numerous illustrations reach the high-water mark of modern reproduction, and some of them are perfect gems. The book will prove an acquisition to the choicest library."

Scotsman.—"Mr. Weale has devoted an immense amount of time and industry to the elucidation of facts. There is much valuable matter in the volume."

Manchester Guardian.—"It is a scrupulously exact and erudite compilation."

JOHN LANE THE BODLEY HEAD LIMITED, VIGO ST.,W.1.

SOME RECENT ART BOOKS

OLD SHIP PRINTS. By E. KEBLE CHATTERTON. With 15 Illustrations in Colour and 95 in Black and White from old Naval Prints. Demy 4to. £2 2s. *Also a Special Edition on Hand-made Paper with 3 Extra Plates in Photogravure, Hand Printed in Colour, limited to 125 numbered copies.* £5 5s. net.

"The text is full of information, but the illustrations, selected from the wonderful Macpherson collection, are the real glory of the work. Probably no volume has ever held so comprehensive a collection of naval prints."—*Daily Mail.*

PORTRAIT PAINTING: Its Nature and Function. By HERBERT FURST, Author of "The Decorative Art of Frank Brangwyn," "The Modern Woodcut," etc. Illustrated with 166 Reproductions of Portraits. Demy 4to. £1 11s. 6d. net.

"A readable and comprehensive exposition of portrait painting is given by Mr. Herbert Furst, and his pertinent suggestions and opinions are illustrated by 166 reproductions of pictures not well known to the public."—*Morning Post.*

JAN STEEN. Forty Reproductions in Photogravure of the Artist's principal works, with a Critical Study by F. SCHMIDT DEGENER, Director of the Rijksmuseum, Amsterdam, and Notes on the Illustrations by Dr. H. E. VAN GELDER, Director of the Municipal Department of Arts and Sciences, The Hague. Translated by G. J. RENIER. Demy 4to. £2 12s. 6d. net.

This is the first detailed work on this Dutch master to be published in this country. The magnificent reproductions in photogravure are works of art in themselves, and Mr. Schmidt Degener's critical study and Dr. Van Gelder's explanatory notes are of great interest and value.

LINO-CUTS: a Handbook of Linoleum-Cut Colour Printing. By CLAUDE FLIGHT, R.B.A. With 10 Illustrations in Colour and 18 in Black and White by the Author and others. Foolscap 4to. 10s. 6d. net.

"Linoleum cuts have had a considerable vogue in recent years, and in this book Mr. Claude Flight explains their technique and possibilities. Admirable effects have been obtained by this method, which is relatively simple and inexpensive."—*Outlook.*

JOHN LANE THE BODLEY HEAD LIMITED, VIGO ST.,W.1.